D0934750

WINNING BASEBALL Science and Strategies

Cathy A. Shaw
farley Iowa
1977

WINNING
BASEBALL
Science
and
Strategies

Daryl Siedentop
Hope College

Jim Kaat
Minnesota Twins Baseball Team

SCOTT, FORESMAN AND COMPANY   *Glenview, Illinois   London*

For our parents—who have always encouraged
and supported our
interests in baseball.

Acknowledgements

The photographs on pages 90–91 were taken by Don Weiskopf and published in the *Athletic Journal,* Evanston, Illinois, February 1968. Reprinted by permission. The photographs on pages 80–81 were taken by Don Weiskopf and published in the *Athletic Journal,* Evanston, Illinois, March 1968. Reprinted by permission. The photographs on pages 78–79 were taken by Don Weiskopf and published in the *Athletic Journal,* Evanston, Illinois, March 1968. Reprinted by permission. The photographs on pages 76–77 were taken by Don Weiskopf and published in the *Athletic Journal,* Evanston, Illinois, March 1968. Reprinted by permission. The photographs on pages 92–93 were taken by Don Weiskopf and published in the *Athletic Journal,* Evanston, Illinois, February 1968. Reprinted by permission. The photographs on page 33 were taken by Don Weiskopf and published in the *Athletic Journal,* Evanston, Illinois, April 1968. Reprinted by permission.

Library of Congress Catalog Card Number 70-94054
Copyright © 1971 by Scott, Foresman and Company, Glenview, Illinois 60025.
Philippines Copyright 1971 by Scott, Foresman and Company.
All rights reserved. Printed in the United States of America.
Regional offices of Scott, Foresman and Company are located in Dallas,
Palo Alto, Oakland, N.J., and Tucker, Ga.

Preface

Winning Baseball: Science and Strategies is the result of our desire to make a contribution to the technical and professional literature concerning the game of baseball. The book has several unique features which should recommend it to those interested in advancing their knowledge of the skills and strategies of baseball. First, the book is co-authored by a currently active major league player and a college baseball coach who is also a professionally trained physical educator. This combination brings to the book the most up-to-date thinking concerning the development of baseball skills as well as the application of successful game strategies. It also allows for the incorporation of relevant knowledge from cognate areas in professional physical education.

Second, the book outlines ways in which scientific knowledge may be applied to the broad spectrum of baseball skills. Research principles in the area of biomechanics and motor learning are applied whenever relevant. Thus scientific information is translated into the language of baseball. This offers the reader two distinct advantages: It helps him to fully understand the "why" of skill development in baseball; and it insures that the methods and techniques suggested in the book are based on something more substantial than mere opinion.

Third, the book utilizes the principles approach in its presentation of methods and strategies. At the outset of each chapter, principles are presented and then elaborated upon. This approach is useful because it capsulizes the truly important phases of each topic for the reader. After studying the book, he can use those capsulized principles for future reference with a full understanding of their sources and implications.

The structure of the book is developmental in nature. The text follows the sequence that a coach must follow as he begins each new baseball season. Chapters 1–5 contain information relevant to the most basic and fundamental skills of baseball. Many books tend to overlook these fundamentals as being too elementary for most students, but this book takes the position that mastery of these elements is prerequisite to a thorough understanding of advanced theories and techniques. Throughout the book, the reader will be referred to the principles as he begins to study a more advanced aspect of the game.

Chapters 6–10 deal with problems accompanying the development of a baseball team. The requirements, skills, and strategies necessary for successful participation at each position are examined and analyzed. A special section on making the double play is also included. This section will be of interest to coaches at all levels, from little league all the way up to the professional ranks.

Chapters 11 – 14 are concerned with the important topic of winning baseball games. This section covers everything from how to prepare the baseball field to what defensive strategy to utilize when a bunting situation occurs with men on first and second bases and nobody out in an inning. It contains an especially important chapter on pitching strategy.

Chapters 15 – 19 consider the many skills and strategies that must be mastered and properly executed to become a successful baseball coach. The chapter on "How to Teach Baseball Skills" is the only one of its kind in baseball literature. The principles in this chapter are based upon research and theory in the psychology of learning, and they are applied to the special situations which a baseball coach faces. The crucial topic of indoor and outdoor practices is thoroughly treated, but in a generalized manner which makes it applicable to many different facility situations.

The book is structured so that it is both easy to read and easy to learn from. Most coaches and students of the game of baseball are actually involved in teaching baseball skills. This book will enable them to know what the proper skills are and it will help them to find better ways to teach these skills to young baseball players. In this way, each coach will find that his chances of building good players and winning teams have been enhanced.

Throughout this book the reader will note the respect with which we approach the game of baseball. This respect has been built upon the many fine experiences that we have had playing and coaching, and we wish to thank all those with whom we have shared these experiences. We especially wish to pay tribute to Guy Wellman, Dick Kucera, Bob Hoover, and Clare Van Liere who coached us when we played high-school and American Legion baseball. We also wish to acknowledge the important influence that John Sain has had on our approach to baseball, especially to the skills of pitching. In addition, we want to express our appreciation to Coaches John Simmons, Jack Stallings, and Raoul Dedeaux for their critical commentaries on our book. We found their efforts constructive and helpful. We wish further to thank John L. Griffith, publisher of the *Athletic Journal*.

Finally, we would like to thank all the officers and members of the Fellowship of Christian Athletes for developing and continuing a program which allows us to combine our interests and abilities in baseball with our personal commitment.

Daryl Siedentop
Jim Kaat

Contents

Introduction
Baseball:
A National
Pastime

The noted American author John Steinbeck once made the following comment concerning the role of baseball in the life of this nation:

> There is no way to explain that baseball is not a sport or a game or a contest. It is a state of mind, and you can't learn it.

Steinbeck's statement may be psychologically satisfactory, and it seems to echo the feeling that millions of people have about baseball, yet it is almost wholly untrue. The fact is that baseball *is* a sport — and a contest and a game. Steinbeck did not recognize the full cultural implications that a national game carries with it; his statement underestimates both the cultural significance of national games and the role of such games in the lives of boys and girls, men and women. Steinbeck was correct in saying "a state of mind"; however, that characteristic is not an inherent condition of baseball but rather an inherent property of all national games. Just as baseball is a state of mind in the United States, so soccer is a state of mind in Brazil, and bullfighting is a state of mind in Spain.

Steinbeck is most in error, however, when he asserts that this state of mind called baseball cannot be learned. Baseball is very definitely learned. It is learned in a number of ways, including what may be termed "cultural osmosis." For most children, particularly for most boys, growing up in the United States *means* learning baseball, whether they really want to or not. The game is so entrenched in our culture that its lore and language are assimilated by virtually every youngster in the country. If the family or peer group reinforces any spark of interest in baseball, the "cultural osmosis" process is magnified and increased until, in the adolescent years, the sport may become the major focus of a boy's life. All other worldly matters assume secondary importance to the unashamed and open worshiper of a favorite team and favorite players. Children who have difficulty doing simple mathematical problems in school can often calculate a batting average in an instant, and students who cannot seem to remember important aspects of their reading assignments can frequently quote detailed statistics on various teams and players.

Baseball is also learned from the direct experience of playing the game in its many and varied forms. The solitary figure throwing a ball against a schoolyard wall may legitimately be said to be playing baseball, and although he appears to be by himself, he is actually not playing alone because in his imagination he has filled the empty schoolyard with teammates, opposing players, and cheering fans. In many respects, this is the finest and most rewarding baseball experience of all precisely because it is partially unreal. The pick-up game on the street corner or vacant lot, the sandlot game in the park, and the various forms of Little League, Connie Mack League, Babe Ruth League, American Legion, and interscholastic baseball constitute the remainder of the hierarchy of baseball experiences. These become more institutionalized and more selective as the less capable players are weeded out through the process of competition. Those who do not "make the teams" begin to assume roles as "armchair experts," each sure that his experiences have entitled him to survey critically the world of professional baseball with that combination of front-office adroitness and managerial savvy which is totally characteristic of the American baseball fan. One learns the state of mind called baseball, then, primarily by growing up in America, where baseball, as a national game, is a significant aspect of the culture. Baseball is a "serious business," whether one views it as simply a game or as a commercial enterprise.

Baseball is a national pastime in the United States. To argue whether or not it is *the* national pastime—as opposed to football or basketball—is to indulge in a type of mental exercise which, while it may be fun, is uninformative and indecisive. Such a debate is prompted by the same motivating influences that have caused young boys to spend entire afternoons arguing the relative merits of a Mickey Mantle or a Willie Mays. Even national polls fail to shed much light on the matter. While the Harris Poll has found baseball to be the favorite American sport—by an increasingly slim margin—for the last four years, the results do little to settle unwinnable battles such as that which annually rages between the followers of the Green Bay Packers and the backers of the New York Yankees. Whether baseball is or is not *the* national pastime, *the* national game, is not important. There are, as should be expected in such a culturally diverse nation, several national games in the United States. The American population has always demanded somewhat of a cafeteria approach to its leisure pursuits, and the number of games and sports that might legitimately be classified as national pastimes clearly reflects this facet of the American national psyche. However, it is the fact that baseball is *a* national pastime that is responsible for John Steinbeck's reference to the game as "a state of mind."

How did baseball come to occupy such a prominent position in American culture? How did it become a state of mind? The answers to these questions can be found in America's social and economic history. Baseball did not just happen. There are, we believe, legitimate explanations for the rise of baseball to a position of cultural prominence in this country.

No other American sport so closely resembles or reveals the social and economic history of nineteenth- and twentieth-century America as does the game of baseball. Baseball reflects both the good and the bad in our socio-economic history. There are both heroes and goats. There is fact, and there is myth. Indeed, one of the most accepted "facts" about baseball, the account of its inception, is a myth.

Abner Doubleday did not invent baseball, as is almost universally supposed. The game is believed to have been created in the 1840's. It is not necessarily of American origin, but rather was developed from a combination of elements found in cricket and rounders. The first official rules of the game were created by Alexander Cartwright in 1846. However, a controversy raged for years as to whether baseball was a unique American sport or whether it was merely a modified version of cricket. In 1902, A. G. Mills, the third president of the National League was ordered to conduct an investigation to answer, once and for all, questions concerning the origins of baseball. Mills had been a close friend of Abner Doubleday, and in his report he listed Doubleday as the "founder" of the game, and thus the Doubleday myth was born.

Baseball was from the beginning a sport of the people, and this is one reason why the game spread so quickly. Unlike football, baseball did not have to undergo a gradual cultural diffusion in order to become a national game. Football was at first a game for the upper classes. It originated in the monied universities of the East and only gradually diffused through the various subcultures in this country to become identified as a national game. The Civil War helped baseball to grow rapidly throughout the states, so that by 1870 it had spread widely from the New York-New Jersey area where it began.

Why did baseball appeal to people of such varying backgrounds? The Civil War helped the game to spread, but people still had to accept baseball as a pursuit that they could enjoy. It is believed that the sport's appeal came from several factors. First, the skills involved were common ones. Throwing, striking, running, and catching were all skills that men had learned as young boys. They could participate in baseball immediately because they had the necessary basic skills. Second, the equipment needed was minimal. In the early days of baseball, a ball and a reasonable facsimile of a bat were the only requisites; gloves were not used until years later. Third, the rules were flexible and not too difficult to understand or interpret. Fourth, almost any vacant field could be used as a baseball field. Fifth, the game was not overly strenuous. Many Americans had roots in England or in northern European countries where attitudes toward sports were similar to those in England. While baseball was faster paced and somewhat more strenuous than cricket, it did manage to retain some of the leisurely paced elements of that English game.

The story of the rise of baseball closely parallels the rapid growth of industrialism in America. Baseball grew in a socioeconomic climate that was increasingly conducive to the growth of a commercialized amusement. Industrialism, especially in the urban Northeast where baseball expanded most rapidly, created both the means and the need for this type of commercial amusement. As the amount of leisure time available to the American citizenry increased, national interest in baseball grew. This interest was spurred greatly by the mass media, especially the newspapers. Box scores, statistics, up-to-date standings, and stories of key players became daily news events. Baseball slang became a part of the American vocabulary, as terms such as "foul ball," "bullpen," and "rookie" came to be widely used in everyday conversation. In addition to the greater amount of leisure time available each year, a larger share of the dollar was made available for consumption in commercialized amusement as living standards rose; and baseball garnered a sizable portion of that amusement dollar. Concomitantly, the growth of professional baseball as an amusement of national significance helped the game to flourish on the amateur level. And the diffusion of this combination of professional and amateur baseball established the sport very quickly as our first national game. Professional baseball is, and basically always has been, a business. Owners of professional teams are much like other types of persons associated with American entrepreneurship. Moreover, baseball, like most other businesses, has had its share of management problems, especially in recent years. In the spring of 1969, for example, relations between professional players and the owners, traditionally rather hostile, burst into open conflict. It would be a mistake to think that this incident was without precedent; conversely, the current problems are neither new nor unusual. From 1885 to 1890, a Brotherhood of Professional Baseball Players existed as a full-fledged union. In 1890, relations between players and owners had deteriorated to such an extent that the players formed their own league and actually operated it as an opposition league for a year. The experiment was financially disastrous for both the players and the owners, but the ensuing realliance was at best an uneasy one.

Thus, the history of baseball is filled with exploitation and labor problems, not to mention the scandals that rocked the sport for a number of years. David Quentin Voigt, in his excellent book *American Baseball: From Gentleman's Sport to the Commissioner System*, has called the early 1900's the "age of the Baseball Barons." This period coincided with the most rapid spread of professional baseball as a commercial amusement. Baseball owners, like many other members of American industry, viewed labor—in this case the players—as a commodity to be bought and sold in the marketplace and exploited to the fullest. A device known as the "reserve clause" was the primary weapon of the owners in their exploitation of the players. This clause gives the owner a continuing option on the services of the player, and the player may not perform for another owner unless he has been released from the employ of the first one. The owners considered the reserve clause the backbone of baseball; indeed, it was openly known that the clause was instituted to keep salaries down and to restrict competition for players among the owners. The issue is currently before the courts, but for the present this clause remains central to the contractual agreement between the player and his employer.

Despite the fact that it has reflected some undesirable aspects of American socioeconomic history, professional baseball has provided thrilling entertainment for countless numbers of people. It has also supplied numerous heroes for the youth of the nation, although the "heroes" have not always deserved the worship accorded them.

Another important contribution of baseball to American social existence has been the provision of a socially acceptable ritual. In a nation where ceremony and pageantry were widely unacceptable, baseball provided a form of middle- and lower-class celebration that was sadly missing from the American scene. The announcement of the line-ups, the appearance on the diamond of the umpires, the entrance of the home team onto the field, and the daily exhibition of the particular idiosyncrasies of individual players all contributed to the ceremonial nature of baseball, especially professional baseball. As Howard Slusher has pointed out in his book *Man, Sport and Existence*, sport often has a significant religious element attached to it. In baseball, the combination of myths, symbols, and rituals associated with the game provides the spectator with a type of religious or spiritual experience. Moreover, the baseball stadium becomes a kind of shrine where men escape the dullness of their everyday lives and take part in the seemingly larger existence of the particular sport that holds their interest.

We are continually told that baseball is dying and no longer deserves to be categorized as a national pastime. Yet how do the forecasters of this doom account for the countless number of Little League participants or the huge number of fans who cheered those "amazing" New York Mets, the cinderella team of 1969? During the 1969 season, major league baseball experienced a great resurgence of spectator enthusiasm with the innovation of divisional play. This resurgence indicates that a widespread—and solid—base of interest in baseball still exists in this country.

During the 1967 major league season, the Boston Red Sox were the wonder team of baseball, and their path to baseball glory also created great excitement among the American people. James Reston, in a *New York Times* editorial of that year, amusingly and accurately cited the stature of this great national game!

These are hard days to write about politics in the United States. The country is in another of those lovely hypnotic trances over sports, and every time you try to write the word "Johnson," it comes out Yastrzemski. This is something more than the annual madness over the baseball World Series. When President Johnson made a major address on the war in Vietnam the other night, NBC estimated its television audience at between 9 and 10 million. The next day, when Carl Yastrzemski and his implausible Red Sox gored Minnesota in the last game of the regular season, the TV audience was estimated at 20 to 25 million. The frenzy in the capital of the Commonwealth of Massachusetts, of course, has even surpassed the excitement at the election of John F. Kennedy. And that old chestnut about Beantown has been rewritten: And this is good old Boston/The home of the bean and the cod/Where the Lowells talk only about baseball/And Yastrzemski gets signals from God.[1]

---

[1]Note: Co-author Jim Kaat was the Minnesota pitcher in the game mentioned in Reston's editorial. Kaat was seeking his 8th victory of the month of September, which is an all-time American League record. Leading 1–0, he was forced to retire with an arm injury in the third inning. Boston went on to win the game and the pennant.

Chapter 1
Throwing and Catching the Baseball

There is nothing more fundamental to the game of baseball than the skills of throwing and catching. When a father first initiates his son into the wonders of the sport, he begins by "playing catch" with the boy. Despite this early practice, however, the Little League coach and even the high school coach often find that many young players who try out for their teams still have not mastered these fundamental skills. For this reason, this chapter contains a discussion of these skills in their most elementary forms.

It would be a mistake to assume that these skills are easily mastered merely because they are the most fundamental in baseball. The skills of throwing and catching are among the most difficult of all sports skills. Any physical education teacher can testify to the fact that a first grader is far more likely to be able to do a front somersault on a trampoline than he is to be able to throw and catch a ball with any degree of skill. Thus, coaches should recognize not only the fundamental importance of these basic skills, but also their difficulty. The coach at any level should make sure that all of his players have mastered these skills and acquired the understandings needed to make use of them.

Principles of Throwing and Catching

1. The baseball should be caught with both hands whenever possible.
2. Thrown or batted balls that reach the fielder above the waist should be caught with the thumbs together.
3. Thrown or batted balls that reach the fielder below the waist should be caught with the small fingers together.
4. The fielder should "give" with the ball as he catches it.
5. The fielder should not remove his eye focus from the ball until the ball has been fielded cleanly.
6. Except in pitching, the ball should be thrown with a cross-seams grip at all times.
7. All throws should be aimed at the chest of the intended receiver, and the ball should be delivered quickly.
8. A low throw is always better than a high throw.
9. The difference among the sidearm, three-quarter, and overhand throws is in the degree of body lean and not in arm position.
10. The primary goal of the thrower (the pitcher excepted) is to throw a straight rather than a curving ball.
11. In making a throw, the player should step directly toward his target whenever possible.
12. In throwing, force is generated by efficient summation of the momenta or by the various body segments during the throwing act.

Discussing the Principles

1. The hit or thrown baseball should always be caught with both hands, unless use of both hands is not possible due to the particular nature of the situation. Whether the fielder is playing in the infield, the outfield, or in the catching position, he usually has no excuse for "one-handing" the hit or thrown baseball. The use of the one-handed catch is basically a lazy habit that can prove detrimental to effective fielding. There are certain major league fielders who one-hand the thrown or batted ball, but these players are in a very small minority. The vast majority of young players will have little success with this method of fielding. The nongloved hand contributes to the catching of the baseball in two important ways. It causes the player to concentrate more intently on making the catch and functions as a safeguard against the ball's falling out of the glove. Moreover, the two-handed method of catching the baseball enables the player to throw the ball more quickly after he has made the catch. In most baseball situations, the fielder is called upon not only to catch the ball, but also to throw it to a teammate to continue or complete a defensive play. If the nongloved hand is located

Both hands should always be used to field pop-ups and fly balls.

next to the gloved hand, the player merely has to pick the ball out of the glove and throw. If the nongloved hand is not adjacent to the gloved hand, as is the case in most one-handed catches, the player will need an extra movement to raise the nongloved hand so that it can take the ball out of the gloved hand. The time wasted in completing this additional movement could be better used in throwing the ball to the teammate more quickly, and thus having a better chance to make the defensive play successfully.

2. Thrown or batted balls that reach the fielder above the waist should be caught with the thumbs together. This is a standard technique, and it comes naturally to most young players. Some inexperienced players, however, may attempt to catch such balls with the smallest fingers of their hands together or with the hands placed in a forward-backward position. These positions are both basically unsound and should be corrected whenever they are observed being used by young players.

3. Thrown or batted balls that reach the fielder at a position below his waist should be caught with the small fingers together and the palms up. This technique should be applied to all ground balls, and to line drives and fly balls that are fielded below the waist. Again, this is basic fielding technique, and any deviations from it, particularly by young players, should be corrected immediately. Too many young players try to use the thumbs-together technique to field ground balls. This usually results in smothering the ball and knocking it down, rather than fielding it cleanly.

4. The fielder should "give" with the ball when he catches it. When players attempt to field thrown or batted balls with stiff hands that do not give, the result is too often a dropped ball or misplayed fielding chance. The thrown or batted ball has a great deal of momentum as it approaches the fielder's glove. This force must be dissipated during the fielding act, and "giving" with the ball as it is fielded accomplishes this purpose. The "giving" movement is accomplished primarily by hyper-extension of the wrists and flexion of the elbows. The trunk itself should not give. While the fielder is "giving" with his wrists and elbows, his legs and trunk can already be beginning the forward movements that will initiate the throwing motion. These two acts can and should take place at the same time. A fundamental of correct fielding technique, then, is to give with the ball in order to effectively dissipate the force of the thrown or batted ball so that it does not rebound out of the glove.[1]

---

[1]Note: The principle underlying the "give" technique deals with the absorption or dissipation of force. Force can be mathematically determined by the following formula:

$$F = \frac{2}{2d}$$

By determining that m is mass, v is velocity, and d is distance, one can clear the equation; the formula then becomes:

$$Fd = \frac{1}{2}mv^2$$

From this formula it can be easily seen and demonstrated that when mass and velocity are held constant, force can be diminished by increasing distance. Thus, when a baseball player "gives" with a catch, he is merely increasing the distance over which the force can be distributed.

5. The fielder should not take his eye focus from the ball until the ball is fielded cleanly. "Watching the ball into the glove" is a basic truism in baseball. There are two ways that the fielder may do this successfully. First, he may actually follow the ball with his eye as it comes toward him. This means focusing on the ball and maintaining that focus until the ball is fielded cleanly. As an alternative, the fielder may focus on some point in space and allow the ball to move through the full range of his vision. With this method, the eye does not actually move as it does in the previously mentioned technique. The error in technique that a fielder must avoid is shifting his eye focus to another object in the last stages before fielding the ball. This will result in his losing sight of the ball during the last hop and thus misplaying it. Fielders often do this because they are afraid of the ball, especially the hard-bouncing ground ball or the low line drive. To correct this error, the coach should help the player understand the problem, and then give him enough practice and encouragement to overcome the difficulty.

6. The ball should be thrown with a cross-seams grip at all times, unless the throw is a pitch to a hitter. Fielders should *always* throw with a cross-seams grip. The reason for this is that the cross-seams grip, with the fingers spread comfortably apart, will produce the straightest throw. Baseballs tend to "move" or "break" because of the reaction of the spinning ball to the resistance of the air. However, gripping the ball across the seams (rather than along the seams) and having the fingers comfortably spread will in most cases produce a straight backspin on the thrown ball, keeping the ball on a straight course as it approaches its target. This is especially true of the overhand throw, which is the type of throw that most fielders should strive to develop. Fielders must work to make their use of the cross-seams grip automatic, and coaches can help by insisting on their fielders employing this grip from the first day of baseball practice each year. In this regard, coaches must make their fielders conscious of the grip they are using when they pull the ball from their gloved hand to make a throw. Moreover, the coaches must place constant emphasis on this concept and must schedule enough practice to insure that it is mastered to the point where it has become a response habit. It is this habit level of behavior that the coach must strive for, because having to think about the type of grip he is to use will inhibit the fielder and slow down his delivery of the ball.

If, however, a player cannot seem to develop the use of the cross-seams grip as a habit-level technique, the coach should not require its utilization. Such a player should instead be urged to throw the ball quickly no matter what grip he is using.

7. All throws should be aimed at the chest of the target, and should be delivered quickly. Infielders should aim at the chest of the first baseman, for example, and outfielders should aim at the chest of the cut-off man. This type of throw is most easily fielded by the receiver. It is very helpful if the coach emphasizes this concept early, and makes provision for practicing the technique regularly. First basemen and cut-off men can tape brightly

colored paper targets to the front of their practice uniforms. This will provide an easily seen visual target for the other players. In addition to aiming correctly, fielders must also deliver the ball quickly. Virtually every baseball fielding play requires that this be done. A fielder's ability to get rid of the ball quickly is very often the difference between a hit and an out. The time to emphasize the quick release of the throw is at the outset of practice sessions, when the players are playing catch. Their leisurely game of catch will have little value other than the physiological warm-up of the musculature unless this time is used to practice throwing at a specific target and releasing the ball quickly.

8. A low throw is always better than a high throw. This is another old baseball adage that is an extremely valid and important concept—for both the infielder and the outfielder. Once a throw reaches a certain height, the fielder has no chance to even attempt a play on the thrown ball. The high overthrow almost always results in not only a missed put-out, but also one or more extra bases for all runners. There is, very simply, no recourse to the high throw. The low throw, on the other hand, is normally playable. This throw may also result in a missed put-out and an extra base or two for all runners; but with a low throw, the fielder has a chance to *attempt* to make a play on the ball. Players can learn to field low throws, but they can

The cross-seams grip.

never learn to project themselves very far into space to catch the high throw.

9. The difference among the sidearm, three-quarter, and overhand throws is in body lean and not in arm position. The angle that the throwing arm creates with the side of the body is similar for both the overhand throwing motion and the sidearm throwing motion. In the overhand motion, the arm is five degrees above the line of the shoulders. In the sidearm motion, the arm is five degrees below the shoulder line. Thus, only a ten-degree difference exists in these two motions when they are compared on the basis of the relationship of the throwing arm to the trunk.[2] The difference in these throwing motions is due to a difference in the body lean of the upper trunk and the inclination of the shoulders. It is the angle of the shoulders that provides the real clue to the type of throwing motion being used. In the overhand throw, the shoulders are laterally inclined toward the nonthrowing arm. In the sidearm throw, the shoulders are more nearly horizontal.

The importance of this knowledge is its usefulness to a coach in instructing his players. The coach cannot simply *tell* his fielders that they should throw with an overhand motion and expect them to pick it up immediately. His knowledge of how the motions differ will enable him to *show* each fielder the correct body lean necessary to throw the ball overhand. He can show the fielder that by thrusting the nonthrowing arm downward, the fielder can depress one shoulder and elevate the other, thus establishing the proper lean to execute the overhand throwing motion. In short, a knowledge of mechanical principles can help the coach to become a more effective teacher.

10. The primary goal of the fielder, as mentioned in the discussion of grip and throwing motion, is to throw a straight ball. By using a cross-seams grip and throwing with an overhand motion, the fielder will make the best possible throw. When executed with great force, this type of throw will rise slightly (this is the "hop" that the overhand fast ball pitcher creates). This movement of the ball will be in the vertical plane, however, and will not present great difficulties for the player attempting to catch the ball. The ball thrown with a three-quarters or sidearm grip, however, will have spin that will cause it to move in a horizontal plane. This is the "in-curve" that so many infielders and outfielders get when they employ their "natural" throwing motions. It is this in-curve that the coach should try to eliminate from the throwing motion of his fielders. Adherence to the guidelines set forth in this chapter will help him to understand the mechanics necessary to accomplish that goal.

11. In making a throw, the player should step directly toward the target whenever possible. There are situations in baseball—for example, when the third baseman fields a slowly hit ground ball—in which it is impossible for a fielder to do this because this action would take more time than the player

---

[2]Atwater and Roberts, "Cinematographic Analysis of Overarm and Sidearm Throwing Patterns," Abstracts of Research Papers, American Association for Health, Physical Education, and Recreation, 1968, p. 81.

has to successfully complete the entire play. In the vast majority of cases, however, the fielder does have time and is in position to step directly toward the target as he throws. The reason for doing this is that the fielder thereby insures that the force generated in the throw will be properly utilized. Physical science has taught the sports coach that force is most efficiently applied at right angles to its desired direction. By stepping directly toward the target, the fielder releases his throw at right angles to the line between himself and his target. If the direction of his body is away from the target, the angle of release in relation to the target changes and is either greater or less than the desired 90 degrees.

12. Force in throwing is generated by the efficient use of the specific forces created by various body segments during the throwing motion. Virtually the entire musculature of the body contributes in some way to a forcefully thrown baseball. The contractions of the various muscle groups provide movements of the joints of the body. The primary movements that contribute to throwing a baseball with great force are planter flexion of the foot, knee extension, hip rotation, medial rotation of the shoulder, elbow extension, and wrist flexion. The foot flexes very early in the throwing motion, while wrist flexion is one of the last applications of force. The total force generated is built up between the individual movements. To be efficient, each succeeding force must become operational at the height of the force which precedes it. This allows all the forces to summate, and thus, when wrist flexion is applied to the ball, it has not merely the force of this muscle group, but the resulting forces of all the previous contractions. The coach should visually check the throwing motion of each player to see that all of the body segments are contributing to that motion. If a player has difficulty throwing the baseball with force it may be due to the fact that one of the major contributors is not being fully utilized, or it may be due to the fact that the forces are not being summated efficiently. Inefficient summation of forces might happen, for example, if the wrist snap is being executed too early or too late in the movement. In either case, the application of the wrist snap will not have the force it should because it does not have the advantage of the fully summated forces of the movements that preceded it.

Chapter 2
Fielding the Ground Ball and the Fly Ball

The basic principles pertaining to catching a thrown or batted baseball have been suggested in Chapter One. An understanding of these fundamental principles is a prerequisite to mastering the principles discussed in this chapter. Fielding the ground ball or the fly ball is merely a special case of catching the ball. Both infielders and outfielders have to field ground balls and fly balls. Techniques for fielding the ground ball may be more pertinent to playing an infield position, but infielders are also called upon to field pop-ups and short fly balls. The same is true for the outfielder. While he may be primarily concerned with catching fly balls, he must possess the necessary techniques and skills to successfully field all ground ball base hits. The principles suggested below are basic in nature. A more detailed discussion of the techniques for successful play at specific positions will be considered in later chapters.

Principles of Fielding the Ground Ball and the Fly Ball

1. Once a fielder lowers his body to field a ground ball, he should remain in the lowered position until the ball is cleanly fielded.
2. It is always easier to raise your body than to lower it when fielding a ground ball.
3. The ground ball should be fielded as far in front of the body as possible.
4. Eye focus should remain on the ball until it is cleanly fielded.
5. The ground ball should be fielded with two hands whenever possible.
6. The body should be positioned so that it is in front of the ball when the fielding attempt is made.
7. The ground ball should be fielded, if possible, on the short hop or the long hop, but not in between those two points.
8. The fly ball should be caught above the shoulders with the arms extended.
9. The glove-hand can be used to shield the fielder's eyes from the glare of the sun.
10. The fly ball should be sighted so that it appears as if it will come down and hit the forehead of the fielder.
11. The fielder should, as quickly as possible, get to the place where he thinks the ball will come down.
12. Any ball hit in the air will curve toward the nearest foul line.
13. The fielder should always have in mind what he should do once he has successfully completed the act of fielding the ground ball or fly ball.

Discussing the Principles

1. Once a fielder lowers his body to field a ground ball, he should remain in that position until the ball is fielded cleanly. When an infielder or outfielder misplays a ground ball, more often than not it is because his body and glove are not low enough, thus allowing the ball to skip off or go under his glove for an error. In fielding a ground ball, the fielder should start low and stay low. The body should be flexed primarily at the knee joints rather than at the waist. By bending at the knees, the fielder can maintain a better line of vision for watching the ball and better balance for fielding. Bending at the waist lowers the center of gravity properly but inclines the body too far forward for good balance. Thus, that technique is not conducive to good fielding technique. However, bending at the knees helps keep the lowered center of gravity well within the base of support as the player moves, and this allows for well-balanced fielding techniques. The lowered center of gravity should be maintained as the fielder moves to his right or left to get his body in front of the ground ball. This is especially true for infielders. The young infielder will often begin his fielding effort in a position in which his center of gravity is sufficiently low, but as he moves to his right or left he will straighten up. This requires him to move down again once he reaches the place where he will field the ground ball. Too often, the use of this incorrect technique yields unacceptable results.

2. It is always easier to raise your body than to lower it when fielding a ground ball. This principle refers to the last-minute adjustments that fielders often have to make to field a ground ball cleanly — adjustments due

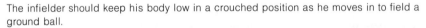

The infielder should keep his body low in a crouched position as he moves in to field a ground ball.

to a slight misjudgment on the part of the fielder or to a bad bounce from the ball due to uneven ground or pebbles. If the fielder is in the correct fielding position, with his center of gravity sufficiently lowered, he will usually have no difficulty making these adjustments. The bad bounce, for example, causes a protective reflex action in the neuromuscular system of the fielder. This protective reflex will usually cause the fielder to move in an upward and backward direction, which is exactly the direction in which he should move to make his minor fielding adjustments. If the fielder is not sufficiently low to begin with, the reflex movement will carry his body to a position of disadvantage. For both the outfielder and the infielder, then, the lowering of the body by flexing primarily at the knees is of basic importance to the successful fielding of a ground ball.

3. The ground ball should be fielded as far in front of the body as possible. Successful adherence to this principle is greatly aided by the lowering of the center of gravity, as discussed above. With the center of gravity lowered and the arms fully extended, the ground ball can be fielded far in front of the body. This is definitely to the fielder's advantage because it gives him a better visual perspective on the ball as it approaches his fielding position. The fielder who attempts to field a ground ball close to his body frequently loses sight of the ball just before it reaches his glove. This is either because the ball moves out of the periphery of his visual field or because his eye focus cannot be moved rapidly enough to maintain visual contact with the ground ball. Being able to see the ground ball during its last few feet of flight is essential because the last-minute minor adjustments in glove and body position must be made on the basis of the ball's trajectory. To field an approaching ground ball, then, the successful fielder should lower his body and extend his arms as far forward as possible.

4. Eye focus should remain on the ball until it is cleanly fielded. This principle can be executed most easily through adherence to the above technique. To keep the ball within his visual field, the fielder may want to focus on the ball and allow his eye to move with it as it bounds along the ground. This is literally "following the ball with your eye." Or, the fielder may choose to focus on one spot and allow the ball to move through the periphery of his visual field. Either technique should yield acceptable results. The important point is that the ball remain in sight until it is cleanly played by the fielder. When the fielder loses sight of the ball, there are two primary causes. One, that the arms are not extended in front of the body, is a technical error which has already been discussed. The other is that the fielder may have some fear of the ball. Most youngsters do have a fear of fielding ground balls when they first begin to play baseball. It is obvious, however, that this type of fear can be overcome by most players. The important point for the coach to recognize is that overcoming such a fear is largely a matter of learning. Thus, the coach must make the proper practice and guidance available to a fielder who has a fear of the ball so that he can gradually overcome his fear.

5. The ground ball should be fielded with two hands whenever possible. There is no excuse for "one-handing" ground balls unless they are so far

from the body that the extra few inches made available by the one-hand stretch mean the difference between fielding and missing the ball. The use of the nongloved hand to help in fielding the ground ball has two distinct advantages. First, it prevents the ball from bouncing or slipping from the glove on or just after contact. Second, having the nongloved hand that close to the gloved hand allows for the fastest possible release of the ball in the resulting throw. When a fielder one-hands a ground ball, he not only runs the risk of having the ball pop out of his glove, but he also wastes precious moments bringing his nongloved hand to the gloved hand to get the ball in preparation for the throw. When a coach sees the one-hand technique being used, he should immediately correct it.

6. The body should be positioned so that it is in front of the ground ball when the fielding attempt is made. Often a young fielder will move toward the ball just fast enough that his body is on one side or the other of the ball when he attempts to field it. Many experienced fielders also fall into this bad habit from time to time. This is a basic mistake and should be cor-

Both hands are required to field a ground ball properly.

rected whenever the coach spots a fielder using this improper technique. The reason for insisting on placement of the body in front of the path of the ball is obvious. When the body is directly in the path of the ball, a misplayed ground ball or a bad-hop ground ball can be knocked down. That is, the fielder can use his arms or chest to prevent the ball from getting through his position. This is crucial to the infielder, because if he knocks the ball down he may still have a chance to complete the play and make the putout. It is also crucial to the outfielder, because any ground ball that gets through an outfield position will result in extra bases for the hitter and other base runners.

7. The ground ball should be fielded, if possible, on the short hop or the long hop, but not in between those two points. As the ball bounds along the ground, the fielder gets a visual perspective of its path. The two points at which this path is clearest in his perception are the highest and lowest points in the trajectory, that is, the point at which the ball hits the ground and the apex of the bounce. Thus, the ball is most easily fielded in one of these two positions. Experience has shown that when the ball is in between these two points, it is more difficult to follow and, therefore, more difficult to field cleanly. The aim of the fielder, then, is to move to a position that will enable him to field the ball on the short hop or the long hop. This should be the goal whenever possible. There are times however, when this technique, no matter how desirable, cannot be used. In some situations such as when the ball is hit slowly toward the third baseman, the fielder must act quickly as he charges the ball. In this situation, the fielder will have to do the best he can to field the ball cleanly no matter where it is in its hop. If he watches the ball closely, this should not be too difficult.

Good technique, then, for successfully fielding ground balls involves a lowered body position, extended arms, eye focus on the ball until it is fielded, the use of both hands, and the fielding of the ball on either the short or long hop. Adherence to these fundamentals will yield good results in both the outfield and the infield.

8. The fly ball should be fielded above the shoulders with the arms extended. This is proper technique and should be emphasized when teaching young players. Some experienced players have developed the technique of fielding the fly ball below the waist. This is the "basket catch" made famous by Willie Mays. His success with this catch is at least partially responsible for the attempts of millions of youngsters to emulate his technique. However, it is not good technique for the majority of fielders. If a fielder catches a fly ball above the shoulders with his arms extended, he has the ball in sight until it is safely in his glove. When the "basket catch" method is utilized, the fielder will normally lose sight of the ball during the last moment before the catch is attempted. This lost of visual contact will often cause the ball to bounce off the heel or the fingers of the glove. It is the visual element, then, that is crucial and that makes the above-the-shoulder method of catching fly balls the superior technique.

9. The gloved hand can be used to shield the fielder's eyes from the

glare of the sun. There is really little excuse for a fielder's "losing the ball in the sun." He should fully extend his gloved hand to shield his eyes. Since it has already been established that the fly ball should be fielded above the shoulders, the use of this arm as a sun-shield does not detract from proper fielding technique. The key to using this method successfully is learning how to shield the eyes while keeping the ball in sight behind the shield. The main thing is that the fielder must never lose sight of the ball. Some players prefer to shield their eyes from the sun with their nongloved hand. This technique is perfectly acceptable. The important point is that each fielder must develop a successful strategy for shielding his eyes from the glare of the sun as he catches a fly ball. The technique might even change according to the type of "sun." Under "high sky," a cloudless day when the sun is high in the sky, the glare will occur when the player has to look up at a high fly ball or pop-up. The player might use one strategy to counter this type of glare. School games, on the other hand, are often played in the late afternoon, which means that the second baseman and right fielder usually have to look directly into the setting sun. In this situation, each ball hit to the right side of the infield will be "in the sun." This might require the use of another strategy.

Perhaps the first step to take when the sun is a problem for fielders is to encourage the use of flip-type sunglasses, which can be purchased relatively inexpensively at most sports stores. A note of caution is needed when discussing the use of sunglasses, however. Players need to practice a great deal with sunglasses before they can use them effectively in a game situation. Too often, the inexperienced player will pay more attention to the sunglasses than he will to the fly ball. The use of flip-type sunglasses must become a habit-level type of behavior. Then the sunglasses can be a tremendous aid in combating the glare of the sun.

10. The fly ball should be sighted so that it appears as if it will hit the

An infielder moving to his right to field a ground ball. Note that he uses good fielding technique: he keeps the ball in front of him, uses both hands to field it, and gets rid of it quickly.

forehead of the fielder when it comes down. This is especially true of the high fly ball or the infield pop-up. If the fielder will line the ball up so that it appears to be heading directly toward his forehead, he will have a relatively easy time making the catch. This is a technique that football coaches have found successful in punt return and kick-off return play. The same success can be achieved by utilizing this technique in baseball.

11. The fielder should, as quickly as is possible, get to the place where he thinks the ball will come down. An outfielder should never "drift" with a fly ball. He should, rather, run to the spot where he thinks the ball will descend and position his body for the catch. When catching a fly ball, just as in fielding a ground ball, the fielder, whether moving forward, backward, or to the side, should move quickly so that his body can be under control and in a set position by the time he makes the catch.

12. Any ball hit in the air will curve toward the nearest foul line. The spin imparted to the ball by the moving bat causes it to curve. The ball hit toward either right or right-center field will curve toward the right-field line. This is especially true for balls hit to a field opposite that of the hitter's natural power field. Thus, the ball hit to right field by the right-handed hitter will curve more than the ball hit to right field by the left-handed hitter. The direction of the curve will be the same in both cases; however, the ball hit by the right-handed hitter will tend to curve more sharply because it will have greater spin. This data must become so much a part of a fielder's knowledge that the correct response to a batted ball will be automatic for him.

13. The fielder should always have in mind what he should do once he has successfully completed the act of fielding a ground ball or fly ball. A moment of indecision after fielding a batted ball can spell the difference between a successful and an unsuccessful defensive play. The fielder should mentally rehearse the options involved in a situation *before* the pitch is

made to the hitter. He should know the number of outs, where the base runners are, and what this information means in terms of his potential responses to a batted ball. He should also have some idea of what type of hitter is at bat and what type of runner the batter is. The outfielder, for example, must know before the play begins whether the batter might attempt to stretch a single into a two-base hit. This judgment will modify to a certain degree the method by which he will attempt to field the ball and the decision as to where to throw it once it is in his hands. There are very few situations in baseball where a fielder is justified in holding the ball after fielding it; normally he must throw it to the proper place to complete the total defensive play.

Chapter 3
Hitting

It is no accident that this chapter is entitled "Hitting" rather than "Batting." These two words signify two entirely different states of mind, or attitudes, toward this important baseball skill. Much will be said in this book about hitting, and it is hoped that all of it will prove beneficial to the coach in his attempts to develop better hitters. It must be pointed out, however, that success in hitting depends, first and foremost, upon the proper attitude toward the task. The reader should keep this in mind as he digests this chapter and Chapter 9, "Coaching the Hitters."

There is a great deal of support for the idea that hitting involves the most difficult and complex set of skills in the entire realm of sport. Several research studies[1] indicate that the fast ball of a college pitcher takes .43 – .59 seconds to reach homeplate after it has been released from the pitcher's hand. Needless to say, this does not allow a hitter much time to successfully react to the pitch. To hit the ball so that it will be out of reach of the fielders, then, is a difficult task. The principles of performance suggested below are basic in nature; they may be considered fundamentals of hitting. A higher level approach to hitting may be found in Chapter Nine.

One fundamental truth about success in hitting must be considered a prerequisite to the principles of performance suggested below: Because hitting is such a difficult skill, it must be continually practiced. For almost every baseball player, a certain amount of hitting practice is enjoyable. But to become a truly first-rate hitter, a player must put in more than just a normal amount of practice. He must be prepared to put in all the extra hours of hitting that are necesssary to develop this difficult skill to a high level of competence. Coaches, too, should recognize the importance of practice in developing hitters, and they should follow the rule that *extra* hitting practice can develop *better* hitters.

Principles of Hitting

1. The hitter should use a bat that fits his capabilities and style.
2. The hitter must be aware of his team's offensive signals before he steps into the batter's box.
3. While he is waiting to bat, the hitter should observe the pitcher.
4. The three basic batting stances are: 1) open 2) parallel 3) closed.
5. The hitter should adopt a stance that is comfortable and that suits his style.
6. The stance used should be partially determined by the game situation and by the type of pitcher that the hitter is facing.
7. The grip used is a matter of personal preference and purpose.
8. In the hitting stance, the hands should be held high and away from the body.

---

[1]Scott, Gladys, *Analysis of Human Motion* (New York: Appleton-Century-Crofts, 1963); Andres and Slater Hammel, "Velocity Measurement of Fastballs and Curveballs," *Research Quarterly* 23:96–97.

9. The hitter's wrists should be cocked.
10. How the hitter distributes his weight while in the batter's box is a matter of personal preference and purpose.
11. There are three basic types of strides: 1) straight 2) open 3) closed.
12. The stride should be relatively short and to a predetermined spot.
13. The position of the back foot is not a crucial factor in hitting.
14. The hitter should have his head so that he always has the best possible view of the pitch.
15. The eyes should not be focused on the ball, but rather directed toward the pitcher, thus allowing the ball to move through the full range of vision.
16. The "hitch" need not be eliminated from the swing unless it is obviously detrimental to hitting performance.
17. The most important factor in the force of a swing is the speed at which the bat is brought into contact with the ball.
18. The hitter must learn the strike zone.
19. The coach should be aware that there are different styles of hitting, and he should make a judgment as to which style is best for each player.

Discussing the Principles

1. The hitter should use a bat that fits his capabilities and style. Too many novice players choose a bat because of the name of the player inscribed on it rather than on the basis of how the bat fits their style of hitting. The young "singles" hitter may greatly admire Harmon Killebrew of the Minnesota Twins, for instance, and want to use a bat with Killebrew's name on it, but he would be better off picking a bat with a thick handle and barrel, thus insuring greater control and a larger hitting surface. This type of hitter may also want to try a medium handle, thick barrel bat. Regardless of handle size, the thick barrel offers the singles hitter the maximum opportunity to get his bat on the ball because it has a greater hitting surface. The power hitter, on the other hand, will probably want to move to a thinner-handled bat with either a medium or thin barrel. While it offers less hitting surface, this type of bat allows for a faster swing and thus greater force. Most high-school and college squads will want to use bats that weigh one ounce for each inch in length; thus a 34-inch, 34-ounce bat is the standard for college players, while a 33-inch, 33-ounce bat is normally used by younger players. Professional quality and style bats provide more flexibility for hitters in that they come in unmatched lengths and weights, (a 35-inch, 33-ounce bat, for example) and are made of superior quality wood, which offers the best type of hitting surface. Use of such bats by other than very skilled players, however, usually results in a much higher rate of breakage, and most schools cannot afford the consequent increase in their annual budgets.

Combinations of hitting stance and direction of stride for the right-handed hitter.

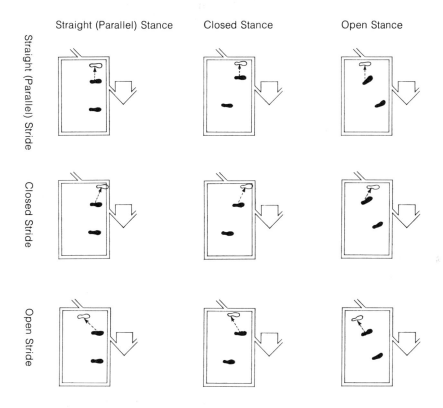

2. The hitter must be aware of his team's offensive signals — and be able to recognize them automatically — *before* he steps into the batter's box. Moreover, he should check with his coach before each pitch to obtain the relevant or new signal. Then he will be prepared to help his team offensively by attempting to perform in any way that he is called upon to do. When the hitter is in the batter's box, he must concentrate fully on the task at hand. Confusion about signals will prove detrimental to him and to his team. There is nothing more frustrating in all of baseball than to have a hitter miss a sign, thus ruining what might have been an attempted hit-and-run, sacrifice, or squeeze play. If a hitter is at all confused about what sign has been flashed, he should ask the umpire for time-out and confer verbally with his base coach. If this is standard practice for all players on a team, many unnecessary mistakes will be avoided.

3. While he is waiting to bat, the hitter should observe the pitcher. The time that a hitter spends waiting in the on-deck circle should not be wasted. In addition to preparing himself physically — by swinging a heavy bat, for example — the hitter should watch the pitcher carefully. He should watch each pitch thrown to his teammate in the batter's box; he should try to determine what types of pitches are being thrown; and he should accustom himself to the delivery style of the pitcher. This observation will not only

provide the on-deck hitter with useful information, but it will also enable him to establish his concentration by focusing his attention on the proper object, the baseball being thrown by the opposing pitcher.

4. The three basic batting stances are: 1) the open stance, 2) the parallel stance, and 3) the closed stance. The open stance is often used by hitters who want to emphasize pulling the ball. In this stance, the hitter's front foot is placed so that a line drawn through his feet would point toward his power field (left field for the right-handed hitter, etc.). Thus, a large portion of the front part of the hitter's body is visible from the pitcher's mound, and it is this fact that gives the stance its name. The principal advantage of the open stance is that it allows the hitter a good visual perspective of the pitch. The hitter's head is turned toward the pitcher, giving the batter a "straight-on" view of the pitch and enabling him to follow the ball more easily. On the other hand, with the open stance the hips are open, and this will usually prevent their becoming a powerful contributor to the force of the swing. If the hips of the batter using this stance are to contribute to the generation of force in his swing, he must rotate them backward very early in the hitting motion. (Dick McAuliffe of the Detroit Tigers uses this style.) The problem with this style is that, to allow time for the backward-forward hip movement, the stride and swing must be initiated more quickly than it otherwise would be. For this reason, the open stance is not widely used by major league hitters. Both the parallel stance and the closed stance seem to be more popular among these highly skilled players.

The parallel stance takes its name from the fact that the feet of the batter employing it are exactly parallel and are perpendicular to the inside line of the batter's box. From the pitcher's mound, only one side of the hitter's body can be seen. The parallel stance offers no single distinct advantage or disadvantage. It is a good stance for beginning baseball players because, being less extreme than the other two stances, it offers the batter less opportunity to develop major batting faults.

The batting stances of major league hitters often differ from hitter to hitter.

The third or closed stance is just the opposite of the open stance. In the closed stance, a line drawn through the batter's feet would point to the field opposite his power field (right field for the right-handed hitter). From the pitcher's mound, the closed stance reveals the rear shoulder and hip of the hitter. Regarding advantages and disadvantages, in the closed stance, the hitter's head is not naturally in a position to allow him a good visual perspective of the incoming pitch. Thus, the hitter has to turn his head. The hips, however, are actually in a cocked position in the closed stance, and when rotated during the swing, they become a powerful contributor to the force of the swing. It is not surprising, then, that the closed stance is the most popular stance among major league hitters. Reasons for this will be explored more fully in Chapter 9, "Coaching the Hitters."

5. Regardless of which stance he chooses, the hitter should adopt the one that is comfortable for him and that suits his style. Novice hitters often attempt to copy the stance of baseball players for whom they have great admiration. Not many years ago, thousands of young American baseball players were attempting to develop hitting styles like that of Stan Musial of the St. Louis Cardinals. Unfortunately, Musial's stance is a very difficult one to use successfully, and adoption of it by a novice player usually leads to serious deficiencies in the hitting performance. The coach should try to impress upon his players the fact that it is better to hit .350 using one's own style than to hit .200 with a "star's" style. The coach should also indicate to each player that the stance he chooses must first and foremost feel comfortable to him. It is difficult to hit successfully using a stance that feels cramped or stretched out. Such discomfort due to an unsuitable stance detracts from the hitter's ability to concentrate on the pitch. Moreover, the stance should fit the capabilities of the hitter. The singles hitter should have a different stance than the power hitter; and more important, the young player who possesses the capabilities to be a good line-drive singles hitter should not be using a stance that is designed to allow for maximum power.

Likewise, the young player who can generate real force in his swing should not be using a stance that hinders his power. Sometimes a young player will adopt a stance that, while it may feel comfortable to him, is, in the judgment of the coach, incorrect for him. In this situation, the coach may have to urge the hitter to adopt what seems to be an uncomfortable position. With proper encouragement and guidance, however, the player should soon begin to feel comfortable using the new stance.

6. In addition, the stance used should be partially determined by the situation and by the type of pitcher that the hitter is facing. Young players should be instructed very early in their baseball "careers," that they can modify their batting styles according to these variables. Too many hitters believe they should use only one batting style and that it should be used in every baseball situation and against every type of pitcher. However, there are numerous situations in which some change in stance and style might be warranted, including: 1) when facing an overpowering fast ball pitcher; 2) when the ball-strike count is 0–2; 3) when there is a runner on second base; 4) when nobody is on base at the start of a late inning; 5) when facing a pitcher who specializes in slow, breaking pitches; and 6) when there is a runner on third base with less than two out. The important point here is that the young hitter should be made aware that slight modifications in his stance and style might help him accomplish the immediate hitting goals that are called for by a given game situation and/or the type of pitcher that he is facing.

7. The grip that is used by the hitter is largely a matter of personal preference and purpose. Most hitters prefer to grasp the bat near the knob, leaving an inch or so between the bottom of the hands and the knob. Other hitters, mostly of the "singles" variety, prefer a choke grip, in which the hands are positioned three to six inches from the knob. The length of the grip actually determines the length of the hitting lever (in the scientific sense, the bat is a lever applying force to a projectile). A 36-inch bat, for example, becomes only a 30-inch hitting lever when it is choked up six inches by the hitter. Many singles hitters like to have the hitting surface and weight of a long, heavy bat, but are not able to exercise the necessary control over such a long bat. Therefore, to accomplish both of their goals (weight-surface and easy handling), they select a long, heavy bat but use a choke grip, thus shortening the lever and allowing for greater bat control. Some power hitters, on the other hand, have been known to actually wrap their lower hand around the knob of the bat. This makes the bat as long a lever as possible, and while it lessens the amount of control they can exercise over the bat, it does allow for the creation of a greater amount of force in the swing.

8. In the hitting stance, the hands should be held high and away from the body. Holding the hands high is good technique for two reasons. First, most hitters have the greatest success hitting a pitched ball when their swing takes a slightly downward path. This tends to prevent pop-ups and also produces the maximum number of line drives. When the bat is held high, between the chest and the shoulders, the downward path is more easily

and naturally achieved. The second reason for holding the bat high is that it enables the hitter to more easily make the minor adjustments needed for a successful hitting stroke. The bat is more easily adjusted in a downward direction than in an upward direction because of the force of gravity. The hands of the hitter should also be held away from the body to allow for maximum freedom of movement, which is necessary for the hitter to initiate his swing. This is especially important when a good fast ball pitcher throws an inside pitch. If the hitter has his bat too close to his body when such a pitch is thrown, he may be "handcuffed," i.e., unable to initiate his swing. With his hands held high and away from his body, however, he will be in the hitting position that is of maximum advantage when he actually makes his swing at the ball. While the coach should not insist on precise points or distances for holding the bat in the hitting stance, he should en-

The front leg and the back arm tend to recoil at the beginning of the hitting stroke.

courage young players to adopt a style that falls within the boundaries of the important guidelines listed above.

9. The hitter's wrists should be in a cocked position. There are several very successful major league hitters who do not cock their wrists fully. These hitters — Tony Oliva of the Minnesota Twins, for example — are called "arm swingers." Such hitters are few and far between, however, and young hitters should be encouraged to adopt a batting style in which the wrists are cocked and ready to play an important role in the swing. Thus, the coach should emphasize the cocked wrist in the hitting stance because it is through proper and vigorous snapping of the wrists during the hitting stroke that significant force is put into the swing. Over the past decade, such outstanding wrist-hitters as Ernie Banks of the Chicago Cubs and Henry Aaron of the Atlanta Braves have emerged in major league baseball. These players do not possess particularly overpowering strength or the body build normally associated with power hitting. They generate most of the force in their hitting strokes by effectively using a vigorous wrist snap — which is best prepared for by cocking the wrists in the hitting stance.

10. How the hitter distributes his weight while in the batter's box is largely a matter of personal preference and purpose. The main thing is that the distribution of weight should provide comfort to the hitter. Most young hitters would do well to distribute their weight evenly in the hitting stance. This will give them the maximum amount of balance and will tend to prevent them from developing serious batting faults early in their baseball experience. Different hitters may distribute their weight differently because they are attempting to achieve different goals. The hitter who tends to stride early, for example, may want to put more weight on the front foot, thus necessitating an extra shift of his weight in order to initiate the hitting stroke. This extra shift of weight will take time, therefore helping to curb his premature stride. Other hitters may stride too late and consequently fail to get their bats around in time to execute an effective hitting stroke. These hitters may want to try keeping more weight on the back foot, thus allowing for the quickest possible initiation of the swing. This problem will be considered in more detail in Chapter 9; it should suffice here to repeat that the distribution of weight in the hitting stance is a flexible matter that may differ for each hitter.

11. There are three basic types of strides: 1) the straight stride, 2) the open stride, and 3) the closed stride. The choice of stride should be made in conjunction with the choice of stance the hitter wishes to use. With three styles of stance and three types of stride, there are nine possible stance-stride combinations. Each of these combinations has certain advantages and disadvantages. For example, a hitter may turn an open stance into a closed hitting style with an exaggerated closed stride. Likewise, a player with a very closed stance may actually be a pull-hitter who uses an exaggerated open stride to help him pull the ball. The important thing for the coach to be aware of is that knowledge and development of a hitting style must include work on both the stance and the stride. Knowledge of and practice on one without the other gives an incomplete picture of the art of

hitting and may be very misleading to the player. The particular stance-stride combination that the successful hitter adopts after much trial and error should be the one which offers him the most advantages and enables him to achieve the best hitting performance.

12. The stride should be relatively short and to a predetermined spot. For many years it was thought that young baseball players should be taught to wait to see where each pitch was going to go and then "step to hit." In other words, the hitter was supposed to step toward the pitched ball in order to hit it. With the advent of high-speed filming in baseball, however, it became immediately obvious that this was not possible. The hitter has less than one second to react after he sees the pitch; thus he cannot possibly initiate his stride on the basis of any information he gets concerning the approximate placement of the pitch. He must begin his stride as the pitcher is releasing the ball. For this reason, good hitters stride the same distance and to approximately the same spot on each pitch. Moreover, so that they may wait as long as possible before committing themselves to the pitch, most successful hitters employ a short controlled stride. If a hitter wants to "step to hit," then, that is, if he wants to go to the opposite field, etc., he must decide this before the pitch is made. Thus, the old baseball adage that one should "go with the pitch," does not mean he should step in the direction of the pitch. Rather, it means that he should "go with the pitch" in terms of his front shoulder. Advantageous use of the front shoulder enables a hitter to successfully send the ball to the opposite field and also to "hit the ball where it is pitched." This technique will be covered in greater detail in principle seven of Chapter 9.

13. The position of the back foot is not a crucial factor in hitting. A sampling of the hitting styles of successful major league hitters immediately

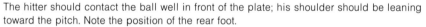
The hitter should contact the ball well in front of the plate; his shoulder should be leaning toward the pitch. Note the position of the rear foot.

reveals that there is absolutely no consistency in the use of the rear foot in the hitting action. Many hitters keep the rear foot securely planted, which has always been considered good technique. Other hitters, however, place their weight primarily on the front foot and have only the toe of the rear foot in contact with the ground. Still others allow their rear foot to leave the ground completely. It is difficult, therefore, to maintain any firm theoretical coaching position on the role of the back foot in the hitting stroke.

14. The hitter should move his head so that he always has the best possible view of the pitcher and the pitch. The best perspective from which to make judgments concerning the pitch is a direct or "head-on" view. This allows the hitter to follow more precisely the movement of the ball as it approaches the plate. Whether the hitter uses the open stance or another one, he must turn his head so that he sees the pitcher directly. Too often, a young hitter does not turn his head but merely attempts to see the pitcher and the pitch out of the corners of his eyes. This is a basic error in hitting technique and should be corrected immediately by the coach.

15. The eyes should not be focused on the ball, but rather on the pitcher. One of the most sacred of all baseball myths is the admonition to "follow the ball." The hitter is taught that good hitting technique involves following the pitch with the eyes from the moment it leaves the pitcher's hand until it is either hit or it enters the catcher's glove. The hitter is instructed to accomplish this by focusing on the ball and moving his eyes to follow it "all the way to the glove." This admonition is, unfortunately, completely

A controlled stride and proper use of the hips and shoulders are important to the generation of force in the hitting stroke.

incorrect. The hitter should never attempt to literally follow the ball with his eyes, as that method does not result in the best possible use of his vision. During World War ii, a vast amount of research was done on all topics related to vision. The research had one important implication for baseball in general and for hitting technique in particular: It indicated that one can best judge the speed and movement of a projectile by maintaining a constant focus with the eyes and allowing the projectile to move across the full range of vision, from one side of the visual periphery to the other. To the hitter, this means that he should focus his eyes on a spot somewhere between home plate and the pitcher's mound and allow the pitched ball to move through the full range of his vision. In this way, he can judge the speed of the ball and adjust to its movements as it approaches the plate. When one watches carefully major league hitters as they complete the hitting stroke, he can see that their eyes are not focused directly on the ball. Despite persistent instructions to follow the ball, they have instinctively learned to use their eyes in the most advantageous way—which seems to be the fixed-stare method.

16. The "hitch" need not be eliminated from the swing unless it is obviously detrimental to hitting performance. It had always been thought that a hitch in the hitting stroke—which, it has been discovered through high-speed filming, most good hitters have—was seriously detrimental to successful hitting performance. This, however, does not seem to be the case. Indeed, it is becoming obvious that many types of sports skills involve

some movement that is similar to what in baseball is called a hitch. In golf, this phenomenon is called the "forward press" or "waggle." The same type of movement occurs in basketball. The hitch appears to accomplish two things: It seems to aid in neuromuscular relaxation and in the prevention of the nervous "tightening" that so often occurs in motor performances; secondly, it takes slight advantage of the "stretch reflex," a neuromuscular phenomenon whereby when a particular muscle or muscle group is put on stretch, a reflex action occurs which helps that muscle to contract more forcefully. In baseball, the shoulders, arms, and wrists of the hitter are put slightly on stretch during the hitch movement, and these muscle groups respond with a forceful contraction, aiding the hitter to generate more force in his hitting stroke. Thus, while the stretch reflex is primarily a built-in protection device for the neuromuscular system, it also aids tremendously in the performance of sports skills.

17. The most important factor in the force of a swing is the speed at which the bat is brought into contact with the ball. This fact can be easily demonstrated by reference to basic physical laws. As the bat is brought forward in the hitting stroke, kinetic energy—energy of motion, or movement energy—is developed. At the moment the bat impacts with the pitched baseball, the hitter has developed a certain amount of kinetic energy in the hitting stroke. The mathematic formula for determining the development of kinetic energy is $KE = \frac{1}{2}mV^2$, where m stands for the mass (in this case the bat) and V stands for velocity.[2] Because the amount of kinetic energy developed in the bat varies directly with the *square* (V^2) of the bat, it can be easily seen that the speed at which the bat is brought around in the hitting stroke is important in the development of power. While the exact physical laws and mathematical formulas may not be well known among baseball coaches, the abovementioned principle has been well demonstrated in major league baseball during the past decade. Many hitters have become great home-run threats by using light bats and greatly increasing the velocity of their hitting stroke. The higher velocity increases the kinetic energy built up in the stroke, and when this energy is appropriately applied to the incoming pitch, the long, solid hit results.

18. The hitter must learn the strike zone. This is obviously basic to successful hitting, and young hitters should be given drills and guidance to help them master this fundamental. Two methods of teaching the strike zone seem particularly successful. First, "strings" can be used to help the hitter develop a perceptual knowledge of the zone. With these pitching strings, the hitter can determine the relationship of each pitch to the strike zone. A second method, which can be used in daily batting practice, is less precise than using strings, but it does provide frequent reinforcement to the learning of this discrimination. This method involves having the batting-practice catcher inform the hitter whenever he (the hitter) swings at a pitch that was not in the strike zone or lets a pitch go by that was in the strike zone. This should help the hitter to develop better judgment concerning

[2]John Bunn, *Scientific Principles of Coaching* (Englewood Cliffs, N.J.: Prentice-Hall, 1955), p. 95.

when to swing at a pitch and when not to swing. The hitter who does not possess precise knowledge of the strike zone will swing at pitches that are close to the zone but not in it. Thus, the pitcher can throw borderline pitches, sometimes referred to as "junk." When the hitter learns to lay off the slightly outside or slightly low pitch, he forces the pitcher to be more precise in order not to get behind in the ball-strike count. In short, the pitcher will have to make sure that his pitch is in the strike zone. The hitter will then have a chance to swing at a "fatter" pitch. (See also Chapter 9.)

19. The coach should be aware that there are different styles of hitting, and he should make a judgment as to which style is best for each player on his squad. This fact has already been stressed in terms of bat selection, stride-stance, and wrist-cocking. Both the arm-hitter and the wrist-hitter can hit for power, and both are likely to be line-drive hitters. Many hitters, however, do not have the physical capabilities to hit with these styles. This is particularly true of high-school and junior-college players. The number of genuine long-ball threats on a high-school team, for example, is usually very small. Most young hitters, therefore, would do well to adopt a hitting stroke that gives them the best chance to get good wood on the ball consistently. This usually means swinging with less force and with greater control than the line-drive hitter uses. It is the job of the coach to instruct young players in such methods. Many coaches advocate "throwing the bat at the top of the ball." This means controlling the stroke and using a firm wrist-snap to generate the force necessary to get the ball through or over the infield. Hitters who use this style are often referred to as singles hitters or "banjo" hitters. There is much to be said for the adoption of this style by the majority of high-school and college players.

Chapter 4
Bunting

The team that is well drilled in the various types of bunts can, by successful execution of these bunts, win games that it might otherwise lose. The individual hitter can add from ten to thirty points to his season's batting average by the strategic use of the bunt to achieve a base hit. In a closely contested game, there is no substitute for the sacrifice bunt in the proper situation, and the squeeze bunt remains one of the most exciting and useful plays in baseball. The weak hitter must be able to bunt both to raise his average and to successfully advance runners. The good hitter can use the bunt — or the suggestion of one — to make the third baseman wary and to cause him to move in, thus increasing the probability that a sharply hit ground ball will find its way through the infield for a base hit.

A coach must never assume that his players know how to bunt correctly. He must make sure that he instructs his entire team in the techniques of bunting. The sacrifice bunt is not particularly difficult if the bunter utilizes proper technique and is given enough instruction and practice to develop the necessary skills. Bunting for the base hit will, however, require more instruction and practice than the sacrifice bunt, since the base-hit bunt calls for a much higher level of skill. The following are suggested principles to guide performance both in the sacrifice and the base-hit bunting situations.

Principles of Bunting

1. There are two basic bunting styles: 1) the "square-around" method, in which the batter brings his rear foot forward so that he can face the pitcher; and 2) the "pivot" method, in which the batter moves his torso instead of his feet. Beginners should probably be taught the square-around method first.
2. The bat may be gripped with the hands together or with the hands apart. The beginner should probably keep his hands apart.
3. The bat should be angled upward and then brought down to contact the ball.
4. The ball should be contacted in front of the plate.
5. The bunter should not actually strike the ball; rather he should allow the force of the ball to do the work of the bunt.
6. While it is generally a good rule to bunt only strikes, there are pitches outside the strike zone which are good pitches to bunt and certain pitches within the strike zone that should not be bunted.
7. To reach down for a low strike, the bunter should bend at the knees.
8. The sacrifice *is* a sacrifice; therefore, the batter should not attempt to hide so diligently the fact that he plans to bunt that his chances to lay down a successful bunt are hampered.
9. To advance a runner from second base to third base, the batter should bunt toward the third baseman and with more than usual force.

10. Bunting for a base hit may be accomplished by a push bunt or a drag bunt.
11. The batter can hide his intention to bunt by maintaining his normal stance and just letting the bat slip down in his hands as the pitch reaches the plate.
12. The bunter must become a base runner as quickly as possible.

Discussing the Principles

1. The two basic bunting styles are the "square-around" and the "pivot" methods. The square-around method is the most popular and is probably the one that should be taught first to the novice baseball player. In the square-around method, the batter brings his rear foot forward as he turns to face the pitcher. His feet should be in a stride position rather than in the parallel position that is so often taught. The stride position allows for both side-to-side and backward movement. The parallel position, on the other hand, is a difficult one from which to move backward. If the pitch is inside and the bunter has to move quickly to get out of the way, the stride stance allows him to accomplish this movement far more easily. The feet should be comfortably spread and the bunter's knees and hips should both be flexed slightly. Most coaches feel that spreading the feet to shoulder width or slightly more is good bunting technique.

In the pivot method, the bunter does not move his feet at all, but merely twists his torso so that he faces the pitcher. Like the square-around method, this style also requires the bunter to flex somewhat at both the knees and hips. The pivot method has an advantage in that the hitter can hide his intention to bunt for a fraction of a second longer than he can with the square-around method. The pivot method should probably be reserved for the more highly skilled players, however, because most novice baseball players using it will try to hide their bunt plans too long. In order to correct this error, coaches normally encourage their players to square around quite early, and we concur with this strategy. The sacrifice bunt is, after all, a sacrifice of the bunter in order to advance a teammate. To attempt to hide the bunt for too long a time serves no useful purpose, and too often results in a missed attempt or a badly bunted ball. The pivot method, then, is for players who are able to bunt well and know the purposes of the sacrifice.

2. In executing the bunt, the bat may be gripped with the hands together or with the hands apart. Beginners should probably grip the bat with their hands spread apart. From the normal grip, the bunter should move his top hand up the bat to a position just below the trademark. Here he should hold the bat firmly, but not tightly, with his thumb on top of the bat and his first two fingers on the underside. The bottom hand does not actually move up the bat, but merely spreads with a firm, but not a tight, grip. The advanced player may want to experiment with a hands-together grip. In this

method, both hands slide up the bat to a position just below the trademark. Again, the bat is gripped firmly, but not tightly. For advanced players, the grip adopted is mostly a matter of personal preference, and they should be allowed to use whatever grip they feel can best help them to get the job done.

3. The bat should be held so that it is angled upward. While this is contrary to the method suggested by many coaches (who favor holding the bat parallel to the ground), it seems to be a superior method because it forces the bunter to bring the bat downward in order to bunt the ball. This downward action is helpful in insuring that the bunt becomes a ground ball rather than a pop-up. Most pop-ups on attempted bunts are caused by a last-minute upward movement of the bat. Since most players will not adopt the upward-angle technique on their own, it will be necessary for the coach to continually remind his players that this is the desired method. He should emphasize that this technique best accomplishes the goal of getting the bunt on the ground. By offering some small reward for each bunt hit on the ground and a small punishment for each bunt popped-up, the coach will quickly establish the proper emphasis in his practices.

4. All bunters should attempt to contact the ball in front of the plate, reaching out somewhat to accomplish this. The arms should be almost fully extended when the bunt is made to prevent "stabbing" at the ball. There are two important reasons why the ball should be contacted in front of the plate. First, the more quickly the bunt is executed after the pitch has been

When bunting, the hitter should keep his arms extended, his knees bent, and his bat angled downward.

thrown, the better chance the bunter has to advance the runner or beat out the bunt. Second, and more important, contacting the ball in front of the plate insures that the batter will have the best chance to see the pitched ball clearly and, therefore, to bunt it successfully. There is approximately a two-foot difference between bunting the ball in front of the plate and waiting to bunt it over the plate. It is within this two-foot span, however, that bunters lose sight of the ball, in most cases ruining their chances to lay down a successful bunt. Coaches should encourage players to contact the ball in front of the plate, extend their arms to bunt, and bend at the knees so that they can "sight" the incoming pitch over the top of their bats.

5. The bunter should not actually strike the ball, but rather allow the force of the ball to do the work of the bunt. The bunter must also remember not to recoil from the bunt to soften it. If the proper grip is assumed (see above), the bunter should merely be able to allow the ball to hit the bat in order to execute a good bunt. The force of the pitch will be ample to power the bunt, and it will also push the bat back into the "V" between the thumb and the first finger, thus dissipating enough force to insure a successful bunt. Striking at a bunt hampers its accuracy and creates too much force. Recoiling from the contact also hampers the accuracy of the bunt and has a tendency to cause the bunter to pop the ball up. The force or speed of the bunt should be primarily determined by the tightness of the grip. To bunt the ball hard, the bunter should tighten his grip. To execute a soft bunt, he should use a loose grip. The loose grip absorbs much of the force of the incoming pitch, making the equal and opposite reactionary force less. The tight grip insures just the reverse. By utilizing the grip to accomplish these tasks, the bunter can be far more accurate than he can by striking at or recoiling from the pitch.

6. The bunter should not only bunt strikes, although he should be hesitant about going for the high fast ball. The old adage to "bunt only strikes" is not always good strategy. Many pitches that are outside the strike zone are good pitches to bunt. The low curve ball is easy to bunt on the ground. The outside fast ball is a good pitch for the left-handed hitter to bunt down the third-base line in an attempt to get a base hit. On the other hand, some pitches that come within the strike zone are very difficult to bunt. The high fast ball is a good example of this; there is a great tendency to pop-up when bunting such a pitch. In the sacrifice-bunt situation, the hitter has a definite job. By not being overly choosy about what pitch he bunts, he guarantees himself three attempts to make a successful sacrifice. When bunting for a base hit, the hitter wants to surprise the infield. In this situation, he should look primarily for a good pitch to bunt, but he, too, must keep in mind that a "good pitch" does not necessarily mean one within the strike zone.

7. To reach down for a low strike, the bunter should bend at the knees. Many bunters get themselves into difficulty when trying to bunt the low pitch that is in or near the strike zone because they attempt to reach for the pitch by bending at the waist. This creates an unfavorable visual situation

whereby the bunter is no longer able to view the incoming pitch from a good angle. By bending at the knees to get down to the low pitch, however, the bunter can maintain a favorable line of vision and thus see the ball accurately as he attempts to bunt it.

8. As mentioned previously, the sacrifice-bunt situation calls for the hitter to actually sacrifice himself to advance his teammate. Many young players attempt to hide their intention to bunt too long and therefore are not in the best position to execute the bunt when the time comes. The sacrifice bunter should not allow this to happen. He should, rather, put himself in good bunting position so that he has the best possible chance to bunt successfully. Moreover, in most cases, he should not be trying for a base hit. His job is to lay the ball down in such an area of the infield that the fielders will have to attempt to put him out at first base rather than try to cut down his advancing teammate.

9. To advance a teammate from second base to third base, a bunter should bunt the ball toward the third baseman and with more than the usual amount of force. The third baseman will then have to try to field the ball and thus will be unable to make the putout at third base. Instead, he will have to try for the putout at first. The bunter's job will then have been accomplished. Since, in this situation, pitchers move over to cover the third-base line in anticipation of a bunt in that direction, the bunter must apply more force than usual to his bunt. This will insure that the rolling bunt will get by the pitcher before he can move over, thus forcing the third baseman to field the ball. Occasionally, if your coach knows the opposing personnel well, he may call for a bunt to the poorest of the opposing fielders, regardless of which position that person plays. On many high-school and college teams, for example, the first baseman is not an outstanding fielder. He often occupies the first-base position because he is a good hitter who cannot really play the outfield. In such a situation, it is good strategy to bunt toward this player. He is not likely to field the ball cleanly or execute the play to third base correctly. While this ignores the traditional strategy of bunting the ball toward the third baseman in these circumstances, it does make good sense. It also points up the fact that no baseball strategy should ever become so iron-clad that it cannot on occasion be revised or replaced.

10. There are two primary methods of bunting to achieve a base hit: push bunting and drag bunting. There are also two areas that are especially good targets for the bunter seeking a base hit. These are the third-base line, where the bunt is very difficult for a charging third baseman to handle, and the area between the pitcher's mound and second base, where the same is true for a charging second baseman. For a right-handed hitter, the drag bunt is aimed down the third-base line and the push bunt is aimed toward the second baseman. For a left-handed hitter, the opposite is true. When bunting for a base hit, most of the abovementioned principles of bunting hold true. Again, the bunter should not strike at the ball, but rather let the force of the ball and the momentum of his body propel his bunt toward the desired area

of the infield. However, the bunt for the base hit will have more force because the bunter should already be moving toward first base when he bunts the ball. This movement adds an additional component of force to the bunt. As in all bunting situations, the ball should be contacted well in front of the plate.

The push bunt most often refers to the attempt of a left-handed hitter to bunt the ball down the third-base line. The left-handed hitter, of course, is more likely to bunt for the base hit simply because he is approximately four feet closer to first base when he initiates his bunt than is the right-handed hitter. To execute a good push bunt, the bunter should extend his arms fully to contact the ball in front of the plate. He should hold the bat so that it is angled toward the target area. For example, the right-handed bunter should line up his bat in a closed position. The right-handed hitter should bunt the ball while his weight is on his left foot so that he can begin his movement toward first base most quickly. The left-handed bunter should almost be taking his first step toward first base as he attempts to push the bunt down the third-base line. He can do this either by crossing over with the left foot to start toward first base or by using the right foot for the first step toward first. The cross-over technique is probably the better of the two because it keeps the bunter closer to home plate, thereby giving him a greater chance to bunt the outside pitch. Needless to say, the push bunt is very difficult and requires much practice to master completely.

The drag-bunt technique is much the same as the push-bunt technique. Here again, the bunter should start his movement toward first base as he is executing the bunt. The left-handed hitter should attempt to bunt the ball

In a bunt situation, the hitter, in this case a right-handed batter, must start toward first base *immediately* after bunting the ball.

relatively hard and directly toward the second baseman. He must make sure, too, that the bunt gets past the pitcher. This is important. If the first baseman is able to field the ball, the bunter has a chance to beat the play out for a base hit. But if the pitcher fields the ball, the bunter will almost always be thrown out at first base. The perfect drag bunt, of course, is the one that has to be fielded by the second baseman just on the edge of the infield grass. This makes for a difficult defensive play, and the bunter should be able to reach first safely even if he possesses only normal speed.

11. The bunter seeking a base hit will want to hide his intention to bunt as long as possible and still be able to use proper techniques. One method to accomplish this is to let the bat slip down in his hands while in his normal batting stance. Infielders will have a hard time seeing this movement, yet it allows the hitter to move his hands into proper bunting position while remaining in his normal stance without tipping off his intention to bunt.

12. Whether a bunt is a sacrifice or an attempt for a base hit, the bunter must become a base runner as quickly as possible. To do this, he must practice bunting and running in the same motion. The immediate running movement must become a reflex action that is a part of the total bunting motion. This requires that the hitter practice at some length. It is good policy to run a few steps each time a bunt is attempted during batting practice. Moreover, the coach should make sure that no bunter ever stands to admire his well-placed bunt, when he should be running hard to first base. This is inexcusable and should be corrected whenever seen either in practice or in a game.

With proper technique and adequate practice, almost every player can be a good bunter. Coaches should allot sufficient practice time to the development of players' skills in this important area of offensive baseball. The bunter should be encouraged to use a method that is comfortable for him. He will have his best chance for success if he feels comfortable executing the bunt. Moreover, bunters should practice their skill against "live" pitching. To bunt fast balls and curve balls successfully, bunters need to practice against good pitching. If a bunter learns to bunt against half-speed pitching, he will not be able to transfer his skill to the game situation. Thus, the coach must use good pitchers during practice if the bunting portion of practice sessions is to be of real value.

Chapter 5
Running the Bases and Sliding

The importance of base running to the success of a baseball team has been underscored in recent years. A resurgence of interest in the running type of offense in the major leagues has caused baseball coaches at all levels to move away somewhat from the emphasis on power that has dominated baseball for over a decade. Coaches have begun to reconsider the basic importance of the hit-and-run, the stolen base, and the extra base for their offensive strategy. Unfortunately, interest has centered around the one or two best runners on each team. This has led to fantastic individual base-stealing records in recent years, but has done little to improve the overall quality of running by the team as a whole. The coach would be wise to teach his entire squad the fundamentals of good base running. Moreover, he must encourage his players to run at every opportunity in actual game situations. This will kindle enthusiasm among the players that will result in interest and improvement in this part of the game. Also, it will allow them to gain the experience that is absolutely essential if they are to become first-rate base runners. The following are suggested principles for instruction in base running.

Principles of Base Running

1. The batter becomes a base runner as soon as he hits the ball; the first thirty feet from home plate are the most important part of the run to first base.
2. When running to first base, the runner should follow a straight line, tag the front part of the base, and "run through" the base instead of lunging during the last step.
3. When he hits a ball through or over the infield, the runner should always round first base as if he were going to continue to second base.
4. The "Rickey" method or the "angle" method of rounding first base may be superior to the "round-out" method.
5. Before a runner leads-off from a base, he should know the sign, the situation, and whether the pitcher has the ball and is on or astride the rubber.
6. In taking his lead-off, the runner should keep his eyes on the pitcher, lead-off gradually, and proceed on a line of maximum advantage for advancement to the next base.
7. The upright, crouching, and walking stances are the three basic strategies in leading-off from a base.
8. The good base stealer is the player who gets the jump on the pitcher.
9. A runner must never hesitate once he has committed himself to attempt to steal.
10. The first step toward the next base should be long and low with the body leaning forward in the acceleration phase of the run.
11. In the all-out running that comes next, the body should be upright.

12. When attempting to steal, the runner must check to see if his teammate at bat has hit the ball, unless he has prior knowledge that the hitter is taking the pitch.
13. During a steal attempt, the runner should move in a straight line and watch the opposing fielder when approaching the base.
14. The secondary lead-off is very important to good base running.
15. The base runner should make optimal use of the bases as pivot points.
16. Generally speaking, the base runner is on his own when the play is in front of him; he should watch the coach if the play is behind him.
17. There are two methods that can be used in tagging-up for advance to the next base after a fly ball has been caught.
18. The situation should determine whether the runner tags-up or leads-off on a fly ball hit to the outfield.
19. The same principles are involved in stealing third base and home plate as in stealing second base; the strategies differ.

Discussing the Principles

1. The batter becomes a base runner as soon as he hits the ball. Accelerating to full running speed as quickly as possible after the ball is hit must become automatic. In fact, immediate acceleration must become part of the swing itself. The batter cannot afford to wait to see if the batted ball is fair or foul, or if it is going to be an easy out. He must accelerate during the first thirty feet of the run to first base as if every ball he hits were going to be a base hit. The first thirty feet of that are the most important. How quickly the batter accelerates in those few feet might be the difference between an infield hit and an infield out; between a force play at second and a double play; between the possible two-base hit and the easy single. The time to develop this automatic start to first base is during batting practice. Coaches should have their hitters run after every two or three swings rather than only after the last swing. In addition, the coach should insist that the hitter try to accelerate quickly on every run to first base. If this behavior is required in practice, it is likely to take place during the game. If, however, the coach does not insist that his players run hard in practice, he will find that in game situations they will have a tendency to watch the ball and then run.

2. When running to first base, the base runner should attempt to follow a straight line. If the basepaths have had proper maintenance, he can run directly along the chalked baseline. This will prevent the wobbling from side to side that cuts down running speed and will help the runner to reach first base in the shortest possible distance. The base runner should attempt to "run through" first base instead of lunging at it during the final step of his run. The lunge is an unnecessary movement that slows down the runner.

Seymour[1] experimented with the run-through and lunge methods of tag-

---

[1]Emery W. Seymour, "Comparison of Baserunning Methods," *Research Quarterly* 30:321.

ging first base. He noted that the mean running time of the run-through group was 0.0117 seconds faster than the mean time of the lunge group. This suggests that the runner's horizontal speed is less when the vertical component (the lunge) is added. Thus, the runner should if possible avoid rising into the air.

The base runner should attempt to tag the front part of first base, i.e., the portion that is closest to home plate. Running in a straight line, running through the base, and tagging the inside edge of the base will only cut the runner's time to first base by a fraction of a second, but that instant could mean the difference between being safe and being out.

The left-handed batter has an obvious advantage in running to first base. Garner[2] reported that right-handed batters have to run 92.3158 feet after contacting the ball, while left-handed batters must run only 88.7080 feet. The right-handed batter has a further disadvantage if he is a pull-hitter. When attempting to pull the ball, the right-handed hitter will shift his weight toward the third-base side of the diamond when he swings. After contacting the ball, he then must shift the momentum of his body back toward first base in order to begin his run. This extra shift of weight costs the right-handed pull-hitter an additional fraction of a second in running time. The left-handed hitter, however, is often aided in the initiation of his run by the momentum of his swing. That momentum carries him in the general direction of first base, and no further shift of his weight is necessary.

3. When he hits a ball over or through the infield, the runner should always round first base as if he were going to continue to second base. Once he has rounded the base at full speed, he can then decide whether to go on to second base or return to first. If the ball is hit to center field or right field, the runner will be able to see the play and thus he will know whether to actually proceed toward second base. If the ball is hit down the third-base side of the diamond, the runner should be told by the first-base coach whether or not to continue. If the runner decides or is told to return to first base, he must stop his forward momentum and move quickly back to the base. A good way to accomplish this, especially if the runner feels that an outfielder might attempt to throw behind him to first base, is to allow the center of mass of the body to move backward—actually almost fall backward—break the fall with an arm, and then scramble back to first base.

4. The "Rickey" method or the angle method of rounding first base may be superior to the "round-out" method. The most widely used method, however, is the "round-out." With this technique, the runner runs straight toward first base until he reaches a point approximately fifteen to twenty feet from the base. He then makes a semi-circle to his right and crosses the base headed in the direction of second. In the angle method, on the other hand, the runner moves directly to a predetermined point that is approximately six feet short of first base and five feet to the right of the baseline. At this point, he makes a fairly sharp pivot and crosses first base already headed for second. The "Rickey" method differs from both of these in that

---

[2]Charles W. Garner, *Difference in Time Taken to Reach First Base in Right- and Left-Hand Batting,* unpublished master's thesis, University of Iowa, 1937.

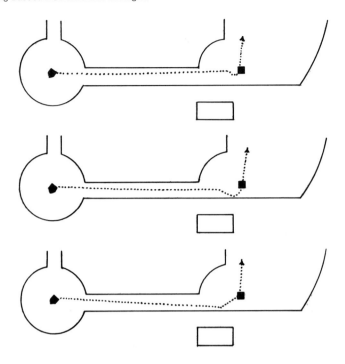

Three Methods of Rounding First Base.

in this method, the runner runs directly along the base line toward first base. In his last running stride before reaching the base, he makes a slight loop to his right and uses the bag to pivot sharply and continue toward second base. The major difference between the Rickey and the other methods is that with the Rickey method the runner uses the base as a pivot point. When he is in the stride that will carry him into contact with the base, the runner leans strongly to the inside, thus using centrifugal force to change the angle of his momentum and transfer it toward second base. Research done on this subject has yielded inconclusive results. Francis[3] experimented with two styles of the round-out method and the Rickey method. He found the Rickey method to be superior to the round-out method, and the round-out method described above to be superior to a second round-out style that carried the runner toward the right-field edge of the infield. Browder[4] used the Rickey, round-out, and angle methods in his study, but found no significant difference among them. Kaufman[5] examined two styles of the angle method and two styles of the round-out method; he found the

[3]Joseph S. Francis, *A Study to Compare Three Methods of Running From Home to Second Base*, unpublished master's thesis, Springfield College, 1955.
[4]John T. Browder, *A Study to Compare Four Methods of Rounding First Base in Baseball*, unpublished master's thesis, Ohio State University, 1955.
[5]Wayne S. Kaufman, *A Comparison of Two Methods of Rounding First Base in Baseball*, unpublished master's thesis, Ohio State University, 1961.

two angle methods to be superior to the two round-out methods. He could find, however, no difference between angle styles that used four feet and six feet from the baseline, respectively, as their pivot points. While further research is needed on this subject, it would appear that both the angle and Rickey methods may be superior to the round-out method. The first two methods take greater advantage of the use of centrifugal force and they entail slightly less distance to be covered than does the round-out method.

5. There are several things that a base runner should do before he leads-off from a base. He should check with his coach to obtain any sign or signs that are intended for his knowledge. He should acknowledge the receipt of the signs to avoid mix-ups. The base runner should also be aware of what the game situation is and what defensive capabilities his opponents have. He should know the number of outs and the score of the game, and he should think about these factors in terms of previous instruction from his coach on early-game or late-game strategy. He should be aware of the weather conditions and the conditions of the field. A windy day, a wet out-field, a muddy infield, or very bright sunlight affect any decision he has to make concerning base running. He should also know the strength and accuracy of the throwing arms of the opposing outfielders. When the base runner has made a quick mental check of these items, he should then make sure that the pitcher — not an opposing infielder — has the ball in clear view or is on or astride the pitching rubber. In this way, he will avoid the embarrassment of being picked off a base through the use of the old hidden-ball trick. When all these factors have been checked, the runner can begin to take his lead-off.

6. Lead-off techniques are largely a matter of personal preference; how-

When leading-off from third base, a runner should move into foul territory and be ready to run quickly toward home plate when the ball is hit.

After taking a long lead-off, the runner makes his break for second base.

ever, there are certain fundamentals that should be observed by all base runners. In taking a lead-off, the runner should keep his eyes on the pitcher. (Thus, as mentioned above, he must get his signs from the coaches *before* leading-off.) This attention is important, for if he does not react immediately when the pitcher attempts to pick him off, he will have extreme difficulty getting back to his base before a tag is made. After the first step off the base, the base runner should avoid crossing his feet during succeeding steps. The reason for this is that there is a point during the cross-step in which body balance is precarious, making any return movement to the base difficult to initiate. It is recommended that base runners use a sliding step to avoid this situation. The runner should lead-off on a line that maximizes his advantage in starting and moving quickly to the next base. At first base, especially, this means finding that part of the baseline that is firmest and in which the base runner feels most comfortable. It does little good to instruct a base runner to lead-off on a straight line between his base and the next if this places him in a section of the infield dirt that is soft or loose. This will merely slow him down. In short, then, he should move in as straight a line as possible and still have the firmest footing available.

7. The upright, crouching, and walking stances are the three basic strategies in leading-off from a base. Most players use the crouch stance, in which the feet are kept fairly wide apart, the knees are flexed, the body is bent at the waist, and the center of mass is quite low with the weight evenly distributed. Some players, though, prefer an upright stance, in which the feet are not spread nearly so far apart and there is less flexion at the knees and waist. Still other players take a walking lead-off, using almost an up-

right walk. While one cannot take nearly as long a lead-off with the walking style, it allows the runner to make the quickest start for second base. This is because he need not waste time overcoming inertia as runners who start to run from the other stances must do. Thus while a runner using one of the first two styles can take a wider lead-off and, therefore, start closer to second base, he cannot run there as quickly as the man who gets a good jump on the pitcher with a walking lead-off. For this reason, the latter method seems to prevail among the best base stealers in the major leagues. It is impossible to name a certain distance and suggest that this would constitute a good lead-off. Each player should attempt to take that length of lead-off which he feels will put him in the best position to be a successful base runner. Good base stealers constantly study the stretch motion of the opposing pitcher in an attempt to pinpoint the exact moment at which the pitcher commits himself to either a throw to the base or to a pitch to the plate. It is this knowledge that gives the base runner his best chance to steal a base or otherwise help his team.

8. The good base stealer is the player who gets the jump on the pitcher. Outright speed is a great asset, but it is not the only requisite for stealing bases. As mentioned above, the runner must also be able to detect, through observation of the mannerisms and early movements of the pitcher, just exactly when the pitcher has committed himself to throw to home plate. There is a point in the pitching motion when it is obvious what the pitcher's intention is. By that time, however, the good base runner should be off and running toward second base. He should have spotted an early cue in the pitcher's motion which allowed him to begin his advance. This cue will differ with each pitcher. But this is precisely why studying pitchers' man-

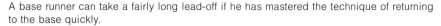

A base runner can take a fairly long lead-off if he has mastered the technique of returning to the base quickly.

nerisms and delivery is such an important part of good base running. One
cue to look for is the direction of movement of the pitcher's pivot foot on
the rubber. Many runners feel that the movement of this foot is a much better indicator of a pitcher's plans than the movement of his stride foot. With
a right-handed pitcher, the base runner would do well to watch either the
pitcher's hips or his shoulders. If these move forward, the pitcher is likely
to throw to home plate. To throw to first base, he would normally have to
rotate his hips and shoulders first. The intentions of a left-handed pitcher
are more difficult to detect. There is no easy way to learn his plans, and hip
rotation is no longer a potential cue. In this case, the runner will have to
look for individual mannerisms which will give him the needed tip-off.

9. A runner must never hesitate once he has committed himself to attempt to steal. Often, a runner will get a signal to steal and will start his
movement toward second base but will momentarily hesitate because he is
not sure where the pitcher — especially if he is a left-handed hurler — is
going to throw the ball. This is a basic error in base-stealing technique. The
base runner who hesitates is very likely to be thrown out by several feet at
second base — and this is just as humiliating for him as being picked off first
base. The good base stealer will occasionally be picked off; this is one of
the hazards of the trade. But it must not be allowed to hinder his base-
stealing technique or affect his coach's instruction in this important skill.

10. Once the desired lead-off is achieved, the base runner must be concerned with getting the quickest possible start toward the next base. In

As a base runner breaks for second, his body leans forward.

this regard, the first step of his run is very important. The base runner should take a long, low first step and thrust his upper torso forward. He should maintain this forward lean in the acceleration phase of the run. This technique has been shown to be the fastest, most efficient way to initiate movement.

11. After the first thirty feet of his run, the base runner will probably have completed his acceleration and will be approaching his all-out running speed. In all-out running, he should keep his body upright and make optimal use of the bases as pivot points, leaning heavily toward the inside of the diamond and making as short a turn as possible toward the next base. At all times during the run, he should keep his head up so that he may obtain the information he needs to make decisions about his base running.

12. When attempting to steal, the runner must know if his teammate at bat has hit the ball, unless he has prior knowledge that the hitter is taking the pitch. There is no excuse for a base runner attempting to steal to be doubled up at first because he did not see the ball hit. Occasionally, the base stealer will be doubled up because a line drive is unexpectedly caught. This cannot be avoided, but the runner must, as he runs, always turn his head to watch the hitter. While this might slow him down slightly, it is a necessary cautionary technique. With a runner on base, the coach should flash any take signs to the hitter. This allows the base runner to obtain the information he needs and to run "full out" without looking back at the hitter. Coaches should take this into consideration when deciding whether to give the steal sign to base runners.

13. During a steal attempt, the base runner should move in a straight line, and he should watch the opposing fielder when approaching the base. Thus, he can obtain information about what kind of slide to use. Some fielders will attempt to decoy the base stealer by giving false cues, but this strategy is used effectively only at the highest level of skilled baseball performance. Most high-school and college infielders will probably not attempt to use a decoy strategy, even though they may be aware of its value.

14. The secondary lead-off, or the movement the base runner makes after the pitcher delivers the ball to the plate, is very important to good base running. The runner has an opportunity to take a good secondary lead-off after every pitch. This puts him closer to the next base in case the batter hits the ball. The extra step or two that the aggressive base runner takes in his secondary lead-off results in his being able to move from first to third on a hit to the outfield instead of having to stop at second base. Many major league base runners use the secondary lead-off to draw a throw from the opposing catcher or to rattle the opposing pitcher. Occasionally, the secondary lead-off can be made into a fake break toward second base. At other times, it can be used to lull the catcher into the false opinion that the runner will not attempt to steal. The secondary lead-off is a skill that is not often emphasized in practice sessions, but it is important and can be used to great advantage in the total base-running effort of the team.

15. The base runner should make optimal use of the bases as pivot points. When running from first to third, for example, he should use the in-

side corner of second base as a pivot point and lean toward the infield as he turns. In this way, he can make a sharp turn at second without cutting down on his speed. Thus he will be using the physical and mechanical elements of the situation in the most efficient manner.

16. Generally speaking, the base runner is on his own when the play is in front of him. This means that when the ball is hit into left field, a base runner at first base is on his own in deciding whether or not to attempt to advance to third base. When the ball is hit to center or right in the same situation, the base runner must look to the third-base coach for a decision on the play. But, whoever makes it, a decision must be made, made quickly, and carried through regardless of the consequences. Hesitation too often results in the runner's being stranded in "no-man's-land," that middle section of the baseline in which he is liable to be put out regardless of whether he attempts to advance to the next base or return to the base he has just rounded.

17. There are two methods that can be used in tagging-up for advance to the next base after a fly ball has been caught. One method places full responsibility on the base runner. He tags-up in a semi-crouch position and watches the fielder who is catching the ball. Immediately after the catch, the runner must turn his head and start for the next base. The second, probably superior, method calls for the base coach to signal the runner when the fly ball has been caught. The coach can best do this by raising his hand and bringing it down forcefully as a signal for the base runner to start. This method has the major advantage of dividing the responsibility for successfully executing the play. The coach must decide when to start his runner; the base runner has to make a quick start. Each can devote full attention to his appointed task. The second method also enables the base runner to employ a "track start" using the base as a starting block. The four-point stance of the track start is far better for making a quick start than the crouching stance used in the first method.

18. The situation should determine whether the runner tags-up or leads-off on a fly ball hit to the outfield. Most often it is good strategy to tag-up because most fly balls are caught – not dropped. Moreover, the runner may want to tag-up and bluff a start to the next base in the hope of drawing a throw. Drawing a throw from the outfielder is good strategy because a wild throw is often a possibility. On days when there is a high wind or a very bright sky, however, the possibility of a dropped fly ball is increased. In this situation, the "half-way" or lead-off strategy may be used. On the other hand, one of the opposing outfielders might have such a weak arm that the tag-up strategy is always best on a fly ball hit to that player's area. The coach should discuss this phase of his strategy with his team before each game because his plans in this regard are likely to change from game to game.

In recent years, it has become obvious that the good base runner is not necessarily the fastest runner or the player who happens to take the longest lead-offs. The good base runner is the one who gets the jump on the pitcher.

who always knows the situation, who does not allow himself to fall into any one base-running pattern, and who knows when to take the calculated risk. He is aggressive without being foolhardy. He does not dare the pitcher too much; rather he subtly lulls the pitcher—or the outfielder—into a false sense of security and then takes advantage of the momentary lapse by bursting into action. With proper instruction and practice, and with the use of heads-up technique, every player can become a better base runner.

19. Most of what has been said thus far in this chapter concerns the base runner's attempts to steal second base. The principles which apply to that situation also apply to attempts to steal third base and home plate. The primary differences are in the strategies involved, especially as they apply to receiving cues from the pitcher. When attempting to steal third base, the base runner can take a much longer primary lead-off than he can when trying to steal second. Also, he can concentrate on determining whether the pitcher falls into a definite pattern in his attempt to hold the runner close to the base. Many pitchers will look at home plate to get the sign, take their stretch, look back to second base, look again to home plate, and then throw to the plate. If the base runner can detect this pattern, he can actually begin to run when the pitcher looks back to home plate. Stealing home, more than any other attempted steal, depends upon how well the base runner knows the mannerisms of the pitcher. This attempted steal also requires that the runner commit himself and not hesitate at all once he decides to break for home plate.

Base running and stealing can become a highly skilled art, but the high level of skill is always based upon a mastery of the fundamentals. Since most coaches do not have a great deal of time to devote to the practice of this skill, they would be well advised to spend the bulk of the available time on the important fundamentals.

Sliding

Sliding is a form of collapsing in which a player falls down, feet first, without losing the momentum that he has built up in his run. It is perhaps the most difficult baseball skill to teach. We believe that a coach cannot "tell" a player how to slide. He must instead provide a good model on which the players can pattern their own attempts to learn the various slides. If the coach cannot demonstrate the skill well, he should find someone who can. One of the major stumbling blocks that must be overcome is the hesitancy to slide or the fear of the slide. To learn to slide well, the player must practice the skill until he can do it automatically and without any hesitation.

Principles of Sliding

1. Good results rather than precise form should be emphasized in teaching sliding.
2. The two basic styles of slides are the bent-leg and the straight-leg slides.
3. The straight-leg slide is usually called a hook slide, and players who can make this slide to either side of the base have an advantage.
4. The bent-leg slide with the lead leg carried high is the best slide to use to break up a double play.
5. The head-first slide is the quickest form of sliding but should be used judiciously.
6. Methods for practicing sliding should be such that they encourage players rather than inhibit them.

Discussion of the Principles

1. Most baseball texts suggest that the slide should be made on the rear and back, rather than on the side, of the buttocks. Secondly, these texts often indicate that the hands should not be used in "breaking" the slide, but should rather be held high to avoid injury. These two suggestions are sensible and theoretically correct. In reality, however, it is almost impossible to find a player who exhibits these characteristics in his slide. We believe that coaches should concentrate on results rather than on form in sliding. If the coach can get his players to overcome their hesitancy to slide when running full speed, he will find that the question of form tends to take care of itself. Many players slow down a bit to initiate a slide, and their hesitancy not only costs them a good slide, but also makes the difference between their being safe and being out.

2. There are two basic types of slides: those in which one leg is bent under the buttocks and those in which both legs are kept out in front of the body. The bent-leg slide is perhaps the more natural of the two. The bent leg has one distinct advantage in that it allows the player to spring quickly to his feet again. Often a player will use a slide primarily as a precautionary measure to insure his stopping at, rather than overrunning, a base. In this case, he will want to spring to his feet immediately. This type of bent-leg slide is generally known as the "come-up" slide.

3. The slide with both feet in front of the body generally takes the form of a "hook" slide. The runner in this case will slide to one side of a base and actually hook the base with one of his legs. If he slides to the right side of the base, he hooks the base with his left leg and vice versa. This slide is usually used to elude a tag. Theoretically, the player is supposed to be able to make this slide to either side of the base, although most players can slide

well to only one side. If young players are taught slides early in their careers, however, they can usually master hook slides to either side of the base, and this added skill is entirely to their advantage.

4. A runner from first base often has to slide into second in an attempt to break up a double play. Either the bent-leg or the hook slide can be effectively used for this purpose, although the bent-leg slide often works best. The only adjustment that has to be made is to lift the lead leg off the ground slightly more than usual. This leg is used to "bother" the shortstop or second baseman as the pivot is made at second base. No attempt should ever be made to spike the defensive player.

5. Most baseball texts discourage utilization of the head-first slide. It is generally felt that this slide is too dangerous and the chance of injury to the hands, arms, and face too great. While it is no doubt good policy to use it only occasionally and with a certain amount of caution, this slide should not be completely neglected, however. The head-first slide tends to allow the player to get to the base more quickly than any other slide because he does not lose any of his momentum. On the other hand, the head-first slide should not be forced on any player who has reservations about using it.

6. The baseball coach must schedule practice in sliding as this skill requires much development. However, it is generally not good policy to allow players to practice sliding to any great extent on the regular diamond. Even if sliding pads are provided, sliding can take its toll in scrapes and

A runner's feet actually leave the ground as he begins his slide.

bruises. This type of minor injury is not terribly harmful physically, but it does tend to inhibit players psychologically and they will begin to shy away from sliding. Thus, sliding should be practiced in such a way that these minor scrapes and bruises can be avoided. One possibility is to have a sliding pit with sawdust or fine sand in it. If this is adjacent to the field, players can use it during daily practice. Another method is to schedule sliding practice on those days when rain has dampened the grass. The players can wear older clothes and practice sliding on the wet grass. Another possibility is to hold sliding practice indoors during the early part of the season. An old surplus parachute plus a few gymnasium mats (ordinarily used for gymnastics) can be used for this purpose. The parachute will provide a slick surface and the mats are cushioned enough so that sliding on them is not too uncomfortable for the players. Regardless of the methods used in practicing slides, the coach should make sure that the players take off their spiked shoes. This will eliminate the most dangerous source of injury in sliding.

Chapter 6
Coaching the Infielders

A strong defensive infield can turn a mediocre baseball team into a good, winning team. A good infield can make an average pitcher good, and a good pitcher great. Turning potential hits into outs and taking pitchers out of jams with timely double plays become the trademarks of a good defensive infield. The value of such play cannot be overestimated.

The first section of this chapter deals with techniques of defensive play that are common to all infield positions. This section is a natural extension of Chapters 1 and 2, which are concerned with the fundamentals of throwing, catching, and fielding. The next four sections of the chapter deal with the infield positions individually. In these sections, the special techniques specific to the playing of third base, shortstop, second base, and first base are dealt with in greater detail. Because the double play is so important in defensive baseball, a separate discussion of the techniques involved in its execution is included at the end of the chapter.

There is perhaps no area of baseball coaching which requires more detailed attention than defensive play in the infield. The successful baseball coach spends a great deal of practice time helping his players to perfect the techniques of sound play and to learn the special situations that require a defensive strategy.

GENERAL INFIELD PLAY

The team that has reasonably sound pitching and strong defensive play in the infield will make a good showing in game situations. However, in high-school and college baseball, a disproportionate number of errors occurs in infield play. We refer here to both physical and mental errors, even though the record book shows only the physical ones. Frequently, the mental error is a far more crucial mistake. Coaching the infielders, then, becomes especially important. The coach must consider technique, execution of plays, and basic infield strategy. If his players receive good instruction in these areas, physical errors will to a large extent be avoided. With good coaching and a minimal amount of experience, mental errors, too, will be virtually eliminated.

Certain elements of performance are common to all infield positions. The material covered in Chapters 1 and 2 is of an even more fundamental nature than the techniques considered in this section. But, the coach must be certain that the basics of throwing, catching, and fielding have been covered before he proceeds to the fundamental aspects of infield play and the specific techniques that pertain to the individual infield positions.

Principles of Infield Play

1. All throws made in the infield should be aimed at the chest of the target player.
2. It is always better to knock down a hard-to-handle ground ball than to allow it to get through to the outfield.
3. The infielders should always allow the outfielders to field all short fly balls that are accessible to both positions.
4. When acting as a cut-off man, the infielder should stand with his arms spread and up, and he should listen for directions from the infielder covering the base for which the throw is intended.
5. Relay throws made by infielders should be low.
6. In tagging a runner at a base, the defensive infielder should straddle the rear part of the base and place his glove-hand, containing the ball, in front of the base, thus forcing the runner to "tag himself out" as he attempts to reach the base.

When fielding a ground ball, the infielder should keep his eyes on the ball, extend his arms in front of his body, and use both hands to make the play.

Discussing the Principles

1. Infielders should always aim at the chest of the teammate for whom a throw is intended. To make this method of throwing a habit, coaches should insist from the first day of spring practice that all infielders throw at targets. It takes five to twenty minutes for infielders to warm up their arms each day before practice. This time can be merely a physiological warm-up period, or it can be a learning period in which infielders concentrate on making correct throws.

Most high-school and college teams face a full schedule of baseball games each spring without the benefit of extensive spring training. Infielders, especially third basemen and shortstops, normally need a significant amount of time to get their throwing arms in shape so that they can make the long throws required of them. Therefore, many of the errors committed in the early games are throwing errors made by infielders. Thus, in addition to daily warm-ups, it is also important that infielders get their arms in good shape prior to the opening of the season. This is particularly difficult to accomplish in the colder climates where early practices have to be held indoors. Coaches are normally mindful of the necessity for pitchers to get their arms in shape early, but they often fail to recognize that the infielders also need time to get their arms in shape. Like pitchers, infielders should start slowly, gradually moving further back and throwing harder as the spring season progresses. There are many phases of baseball technique and strategy to be covered during early practices, but the coach must also allow time for purposeful throwing practice. He must recognize that the techniques and strategies will be of little value if players constantly commit throwing errors because their arms are not in good shape.

2. It is always better to knock down a hard-to-handle ground ball than to allow it to get through the infield and into the outfield. The infielder should never give up on a ground ball. If he keeps his eye on the bounding ball, he will have a good chance to reach it with his glove either by stretching or by diving for it. But the infielder must not take his eye off the ball or it may bound either over or under his outstretched glove and roll into the outfield. Instruction and practice in this fielding art may pay off in actual games by preventing a runner on second base from scoring an important run.

3. The infielders should always allow the outfielders to field all short fly balls that are accessible to both positions. The short fly ball or the "Texas-league" line drive is always easier for the outfielder to field than for the infielder, because the outfielder has the ball in clear sight in front of him at all times. The outfielder is also in a much better position to throw to a base because his weight is moving toward the infield as he makes the catch. Moreover, when the outfielder calls for a ball, the infielder should automatically move away from the play. Among other things, this will prevent collisions.

A word signal should be decided upon between outfielders and infielders to aid in preventing fielding mishaps on such plays, and this signal should always be used. A team may decide to use "I've got it" as the terminology for this situation. This means that the fielders should not use "mine" or "I'll take it." While this may seem to be a minor point, the use of consistent terminology will be beneficial in the long run. The same policy should be followed when giving directions to a cut-off man. When the catcher, for example, is receiving a throw from center field, he must instruct the first baseman (the cut-off man in this situation) whether to cut the ball off or let the throw go all the way to home plate. Precise consistent terminology, such as "cut" and "go," will help players to execute this play efficiently. For instance, if the catcher always uses "cut" when he wants the ball cut-off, the infielders will be able to make a consistent response to the situation.

4. When an infielder acts as a cut-off man on a play from the outfield, he should stand with his arms spread and above his head, and he should listen for directions from the infielder covering the base for which the throw is ultimately intended. The man covering the base will inform the cut-off man whether he should cut the ball off and throw it to another base, or whether he should let the ball go. Most importantly, the cut-off man must make himself as large and as obvious a target as is possible.

5. Often, the infielder has to go into the outfield to act as a relay man (see Chapter 13). When he receives a relay throw, the infielder must turn quickly and throw to a base. If there is a cut-off man in the infield, the relay man should throw for his chest. But more often than not, there is no cut-off man on this type of play. In this case, the relay man must throw the ball low, attempting to get it to the intended target on a low first bounce. This will give the target fielder the best possible chance to field the ball and make the putout. There is no such chance when the throw is too high.

6. In tagging a runner at a base, the defensive infielder should straddle the rear part of the base and place his glove-hand, containing the ball, in front of the base after he receives the throw. The runner will then be forced to "tag himself out" as he attempts to reach the base. The infielder should

When tagging a runner, particularly at second or third base, the infielder should straddle the base and place his glove-hand down in front of the bag, virtually forcing the runner to tag himself out.

not make the mistake of trying to reach out to tag the approaching runner. Too often when this type of tag is attempted, the runner slides, and while the infielder is tagging the sliding runner on the hip or chest, the runner's lead foot reaches the base and the umpire will (correctly) rule the runner safe. The defensive player covering the base should wait as long as possible before initiating his movements to field the thrown ball and tag the runner. This type of "decoy" might lure the runner into a false sense of security and actually cause him to slow up a little.

Principles for Playing First Base

1. While good play at first base is important, there are fewer necessary qualifications for successful play at this base than for any position in baseball.
2. Infielders must have confidence in the ability of the first baseman to field all throws.
3. There are two basic styles of receiving throws: 1) the shift style, and 2) the crossover style.
4. The first baseman should attempt to field low throws on either the short hop or the long hop, but not in the middle of a hop.
5. The first baseman must be able to judge when to move off the base to save a bad throw.
6. The first baseman should present a suitable target for a pitcher who is holding a runner on first base.
7. The first baseman must be able to move off the base quickly to get into good fielding position.
8. First basemen normally use one of two methods of throwing the ball to a pitcher who is covering first base: 1) the lead method, or 2) the straight method.

9. The first baseman must decide instantly on the best way to make the 3–6–3 double play.
10. Right-handed first basemen should make a short turn when throwing to second base.

Discussing the Principles

1. There are fewer necessary qualifications for successful play at first base than for any other position in baseball. For this reason many different types of players can become good first basemen. It is probably advantageous for a first baseman to be tall, but there are outstanding major league first basemen who are of average height. It is also a slight advantage — especially in holding a runner on base and in making throws to second base — to have a left-handed first baseman, but, again, there are many outstanding right-handed first basemen. The first baseman does not need the speed of a shortstop, the quickness of a third baseman, or the mental alertness of a second baseman. Most players, then, can learn to play this position adequately in a relatively short period of time. This statement is borne out by the experience of major league teams. Many players who performed suc-

Proper fielding technique for making a force out. The infielder keeps his rear foot on the bag, stretches to take the throw, and makes the catch with both hands.

cessfully at other positions have made the transition to first base in the twilight of their careers when their speed and reactions began to slow down. Ernie Banks of the Chicago Cubs and Mickey Mantle of the New York Yankees are outstanding examples of players who made this transition late in their careers.

2. There is one qualification, however, that the successful first baseman must have. He must be able to catch all types of throws, and his teammates in the infield must have confidence in his ability to do this. If infielders lack confidence in their first baseman, they will feel too great a need to be perfectly accurate with their throws and the resulting tension will often cause bad throws. Moreover, this "need" for pinpoint accuracy will cause the players to take more time in throwing to first and thus result in fewer putouts. Soon the entire infield will establish a mental block that will mediate against successful defensive play. The first baseman must be able to leap to take a high throw, stretch to field a low throw, and perhaps most important of all, "dig" the ball out of the dirt on the low throw that cannot be fielded on the fly. When the first baseman can help his infield teammates in these ways, the entire infield tends to play "loose" and the result is a considerably improved defense. There is only one way to learn to field bad throws at first base, and that is to practice taking such throws. The coach should see that time is set aside for practicing this part of infield defense. Regular infielders should probably not be asked to throw bad throws to first base, but the coach should choose a reserve player to make high, low, and wide throws to the first baseman.

3. There are two basic styles of receiving throws: 1) the shift style, and 2) the crossover style. The shift style is the more popular and is most often taught as "correct" technique. In this method, the first baseman moves so that he will take the throw on his left. He does this by shifting both feet to the left with a short shuffle step, avoiding any crossing of the feet. He then fields the throw with his left leg stretched out and his right foot on the base. With the crossover method, the shuffle step is eliminated; this may be the better method for the first baseman who is not especially agile. In this method, the first baseman again fields the throw on his left by keeping his left foot on the base and crossing over with his right leg to stretch for the ball. While this method prevents the first baseman from stretching as far as he can with the shift method, it has the advantage of being easier to master. Thus, there is less likelihood of error with this style. Regardless of the style used, however, the first baseman must make sure to always tag the base. To do this, he must place his toe securely against the side of the base and keep it there even though his stretching body tends to pull it away. Frequently, a novice first baseman stands with his heel on the base in anticipation of the throw. But, when he steps out to field the incoming throw, his heels leave the base. This player must remember that as the heels come off the base, the toe of the tagging foot must be thrust back so that it is securely in contact with the base — and remains in contact with the base even during a long stretching movement.

4. The first baseman should never field a ball in the middle of a hop.

When a low throw comes to him, he has the choice of stretching to field the ball on the short hop, that is, just after it has bounced, or of backing up and waiting for the ball to reach the top of its bounce. The latter course may even entail moving to the foul side of first base to field the ball. Either method can be successful with practice. Where the first baseman gets into trouble, however, is when he attempts to field a low throw in the middle of its hop. To avoid this situation, the first baseman must be prepared to stretch or to move back to play the ball at its proper height, rather than remain stationary and "let the ball play him." Whether to stretch to get the short hop or move back to get the long hop usually depends on how close the base runner is. If the play is going to be close, the first baseman will naturally want to stretch to get the ball on the short hop. If the runner is slow and there is ample time to make the play, many first basemen prefer to play the ball on the long hop.

5. The first baseman must learn to judge when to move off the base to field a bad throw. This is a difficult judgment to make because the moment he leaves the base to secure the throw, he almost always forfeits his chance to make the putout. There are situations, however, when it might be better to forfeit the putout than to allow other runners to advance, on a misplayed overthrow or bad throw. For example, if the winning run is on second base in the late innings and a putout is being attempted on a ground ball at first base, a bad throw will usually allow the runner on second to score the lead or winning run. In this case, the putout at first becomes secondary. The first baseman must, above all else, make sure that he fields or blocks the ball, thus holding the runner on second to a one-base advance.

The throw that is on the home-plate side of first base can be particularly difficult to field. When the base runner is close, this throw can cause a collision and almost always results in a lost chance at a putout. The first baseman should move off the base to field this kind of throw. By doing that and moving slightly to the inside of the diamond, he can get in position to field the throw easily and then make a swipe-tag at the runner as he goes by. Many first basemen master this play to such an extent that the catch and the tag seem to be made in one smooth motion.

Another difficult throw for the first baseman to field is the throw from the catcher. This occurs most often when a batter has bunted the ball. In this situation, the first baseman should move to the inside part of the diamond with his left foot on the base and his right foot in the baseline between first and second base. He should then raise his hand and present as large and as clear a target as possible for the catcher. Use of this technique will optimize the chances for a good throw.

6. The first baseman should present a suitable target for the pitcher who is holding a runner on first base. To accomplish this, the first baseman should stand facing the pitcher with his feet in a parallel position near the inside corner of the base. His gloved hand should provide a pinpoint target for the pitcher. Some first basemen hold the gloved hand low, by their right knee, thus shortening the distance to the base where the putout might be

made. Other first basemen prefer to present a waist-high target. Pitchers should constantly practice with their first basemen to arrive at a suitable target position. Regardless of where the gloved hand is held, the technique for attempting to tag the runner is always the same. The ideal throw from the pitcher is, of course, one that comes in somewhere between the first baseman's knee and ankle. After catching the ball, the first baseman should "swipe" his gloved hand down very quickly so that it covers the entire inside edge of the base. In this manner, the runner attempting to return to first will literally tag himself out. Novice first basemen too often attempt to tag the runner on the hip or shoulder. However, this type of tag may not catch him until after he has touched the base with his foot. In this case, the umpire will correctly rule the runner safe.

The left-handed first baseman has a natural advantage in making the pick-off play at first base. His glove is on his right hand, meaning that he must move it a shorter distance in order to make the tag. The right-handed first baseman has to reach across his body to catch the ball and make the tag. Whether the first baseman is right-handed or left-handed, however, he should not hesitate to move off the base to catch a throw which he thinks will be difficult to field. A bad throw or a missed catch in this situation will usually result in the runner advancing two bases.

If a base runner is slow, the first baseman can sometimes play four to six feet behind him and three to six feet off the baseline. This puts the first baseman in a much better fielding position, but it should be done mostly when a left-handed hitter is at bat, and *only* when the runner is not likely to steal second base.

The pitcher and first baseman can develop a planned pick-off play to be used when there is a runner on first base. Such a play, which is especially useful in bunt situations, should be keyed to a signal agreed upon between the two players. For example, the first baseman might fake a move toward home plate as if he were positioning himself to field a bunt. After taking several steps, however, he would move quickly back to the base to take a throw from the pitcher. The pitcher would actually have begun his move to first base before the first baseman had returned to the base. This type of play should not be used in games until it has been fully mastered in practice sessions.

7. Even when holding a runner, the first baseman must be able to move off the base quickly to get into a good fielding position. After the pitcher has initiated his delivery to home plate, the first baseman must get to the defensive position that will enable him to contribute most to the play. Whether this is in on the infield grass or back toward the outfield grass, the move must be made quickly. The first baseman must hustle. The move is usually best made with a kind of shuffle step, so that the first baseman can keep his eyes on the hitter and the ball while he is moving.

8. First basemen normally use one of two methods of throwing the ball to a pitcher who is covering first base. These methods are: 1) the lead method, or 2) the straight method. Most major league teams seem to prefer

the lead method, but only practice will determine which method is best suited to a particular group of players. In the lead method, the first baseman makes an underhand toss to the pitcher as the latter runs toward the base. This toss actually "leads," or is ahead of, the pitcher. This method requires practice so that the first baseman can learn the necessary timing adjustments to make with the various pitchers. The straight method entails a more forceful throw that is overhand rather than underhand. The throw is made directly toward the chest of the pitcher. Regardless of the method used, several basic rules should be followed. It is ideal for the pitcher to have the ball well before he arrives at the base. If this is not possible, the first baseman should wait to throw until the pitcher actually reaches the base. When the pitcher reaches the base without the ball, he should position himself on the base just as a first baseman would (See Principle 3.) The first baseman can then make a hard overhand throw to the pitcher. That throw should not be "looped" to the pitcher. Underhand or overhand, it should be a hard throw on a direct plane. The pitcher will often signal for the ball by extending his glove. This is a good practice because it prevents confusion as to when the first baseman should throw the ball.

If the first baseman fields a ball close to the baseline, he should tag the runner whenever possible. In doing this, the first baseman should hold the ball in his glove with his bare hand to prevent the base runner from knocking it out of the glove. The first baseman should never chase the runner, however. If the runner stops or retreats toward home plate, the first baseman should immediately turn and throw to first base to complete the putout.

9. When a double-play situation exists, the first baseman has two options in fielding ground balls hit to his position. He can initiate a 3 – 6 – 3 double play, i.e., he can throw the ball immediately to the shortstop, who should always cover second base in this situation. The shortstop will then return the ball to first base so that the second putout can be made. After throwing to the shortstop, the first baseman should return to his base at once so that he can catch the return throw. If he is too far away to return in time, the second baseman should receive the throw. In option number two, the first baseman can make the putout at first base before throwing to second base. In this situation, the shortstop then has to tag the runner sliding into second base because the force out is no longer possible. Naturally, the decision as to which method to use is determined by how close the first baseman is to the base when he fields the ball. Normally, he should opt for the 3 – 6 – 3 double play unless he is within two short steps of the base. The important factor to remember, of course, is the necessity to put out the lead runner.

10. Right-handed first basemen should make a short turn when throwing to second base. When a first baseman wants to attempt a force-out play or initiate a double play, he should always turn to his right to make the throw toward second base. If he turns to his left, he will lose sight of the target. When fielding a ground ball in front of first base, the first baseman should make his throw to the home plate side of second. When fielding the ball in back of first base, however, he should make his throw to the outfield side

of second base. These two situations should be practiced with the shortstop to insure proper timing and anticipation.

Playing first base is not inordinately difficult, but it does require practice. The first baseman must work particularly on fielding throws from other infielders. Infielders must be confident that their first baseman can field all throws within reach. To practice this skill, the first baseman should have a teammate stand thirty to sixty feet away from him and make throws of all kinds. In this way, the long hop, short hop, high throw, and other situations can be practiced. When the first baseman becomes skilled in fielding difficult throws, and displays confidence in his skill, the entire infield will improve. The first baseman should also be prepared to get rid of the ball quickly after making a putout at first base. He should never be caught off-guard by a second runner attempting to advance an extra base after the putout.

Principles for Playing Second Base

1. The primary qualifications for successful performance at second base are speed, alertness, and a strong throwing arm.
2. The second baseman must constantly make adjustments in his fielding position according to the strengths and weaknesses of the hitter and the defensive situation.
3. The second baseman must cover first base on all bunt plays.
4. In making a play on a ground ball behind second base, the second baseman must plant his right foot firmly and throw as quickly as possible.
5. In fielding the slow grounder, the type of play the second baseman can make will depend on how much time he has.
6. In initiating the double play, the most important factor is getting rid of the ball.
7. The second baseman must know how far he can be from second base and still use the underhand toss for the double play.
8. The second baseman should make a short turn when throwing to second base from the first-base side.
9. There are three basic methods of pivoting on the double play at second base: 1) the quick method, 2) the across method, and 3) the back method.
10. When forcing a runner out at second, the second baseman should play the base just as a first baseman would play first.
11. The second baseman should use the "tag out and throw" double-play method only when the runner approaching second is very close to where the ground ball is fielded.
12. The second baseman's role in pick-off plays at second base is largely that of a decoy.

Discussing the Principles

1. The primary qualifications for successful performance at second base are speed, alertness, and a strong throwing arm. The second baseman must possess speed because he must cover more total territory than any other infielder. He is expected to cover second base on the steal play, the force-out play, and the double play. He must also cover first base on all bunting situations. This means that he must be ready to move quickly to either first or second base from his normal position between the bases. His speed, however, is not always enough to get the job done. He must also display mental alertness. Because of the many defensive situations to which the second baseman must react, he must constantly be aware of these situations, and he must be able to anticipate the possible movements which might be required of him in any particular situation. When mental alertness is combined with speed, the result is good defensive play at second base. When either of these qualities is lacking, however, the result is too often inadequate defensive play at this very important infield position. Speed can be improved only to a certain degree, but mental alertness can be increased through serious attempts to learn the various situations and the movements necessary to cope with each. The coach, therefore, should concentrate on practice methods to increase the mental awareness of his infielders in general and his second baseman in particular.

When covering first base, the second baseman must move over quickly in order to position himself on the inside of the base and present a clear target for his teammate making the throw.

The second baseman should also possess a strong throwing arm. To complete double plays successfully and to throw out runners on difficult plays, the second baseman must have a strong arm. The weak-armed second baseman is particularly limited in his ability to complete the double play after making a pivot at second base.

2. The second baseman must constantly make adjustments in his defensive position according to the type of hitter at bat. Against the right-handed pull-hitter who is not a fast runner, he will want to play well toward second base. This means that he may take up a defensive position almost directly behind second base near the edge of the infield grass. Against the left-handed pull-hitter, however, the second baseman may need to play as much as two or three steps toward the right-field line from his normal position. He may also want to play deep, even one or two steps out on the outfield grass. This would still give him time, however, because of the short throw involved, to make a play at first base. For all other hitters, the second baseman will normally assume a defensive position somewhere in between these two extremes, and he will make minor adjustments in position as the defensive situation demands. Thus, the second baseman should constantly make mental notes about opposing hitters. This will enable him to build up the reservoir of knowledge from which he can draw to make his defensive adjustments.

3. The second baseman must cover first base in all sacrifice bunt situations. Whenever a bunt is made, he should immediately initiate a quick movement toward first base. He should *never* assume that the first baseman will cover the base, even if it appears that that player will be able to do so. It must be emphasized that the second baseman should *run* to first in

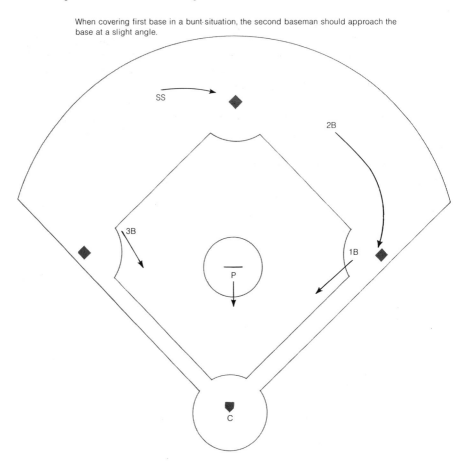

When covering first base in a bunt situation, the second baseman should approach the base at a slight angle.

this situation. If possible, he should move to a point on the first-base line about six to ten feet behind the base. He should then turn and approach the base along the base line. There are two reasons for using this technique. First, the second baseman is easier to throw to if he is still moving when the ball is thrown. Second, use of this technique will prevent any collision between the second baseman and the base runner. Such a collision might occur if the second baseman were to run directly to the base because his momentum might carry him across the base into the approaching runner. There will be occasions when the second baseman will judge that a play is so close that he will have to move directly to first base. But on most plays, he will have time to employ the safer method of approaching the base. As soon as he reaches first base he should place himself in a defensive position much like that which the first baseman assumes when taking throws at first.

When a ball is bunted down the first-base line and either the pitcher, the catcher, or the first baseman makes the defensive play, the second baseman, who is covering first base, should provide a good target for any throw to the inside part of the baseline. In this way, the player throwing the ball can avoid hitting the runner coming down the baseline.

4. In making a play on a ground ball hit behind second base, the second baseman should, after fielding the ball, plant his right foot firmly and throw to first base as quickly as possible. This is one of the most difficult plays for a second baseman to make. Novice players usually try to make a very strong throw to complete this play. To gain the necessary momentum to do this, however, the second baseman must plant his right foot and then take a shuffle step. The problem with this method is that the shuffle step takes too much time. Therefore, top-flight second basemen usually make this play by planting the right foot firmly, stepping out with the left foot, and throwing the ball. While a throw made in this manner does not have as much velocity as one made via the shuffle-step method, it is executed much more quickly, giving the defensive team a better chance of getting the runner out at first base.

5. Another difficult play for the second baseman occurs when the batter hits a slow ground ball that just gets by the pitcher. In fielding the slow grounder, the type of play the second baseman can make will depend on how much time he has. If the runner is not fast, the second baseman may be able to reach down to field the ball, stand up, plant his right foot, and throw to first base. If the hitter has any speed, however, the second baseman will have to pick up the ball and throw from the underhand position in an attempt to get the runner out at first. This play takes a great deal of practice to perfect. The second baseman should avoid a bare-handed pick-up if at all possible, because such a pick-up is risky and does not save enough time to warrant its use. Moreover, as with other types of ground balls, he should use both hands to field the ball. The underarm throw that he uses in

When making a short, underhand throw, the ball should always be kept in full sight.

this situation should be made across the body and toward the target (the first baseman) who is somewhat to the rear of the second baseman.

6. In initiating the double play, the most important factor for the second baseman is to get rid of the ball quickly. He must anticipate his double-play partner, i.e., he must not wait to complete his throw until the shortstop is at second base. He must turn and throw to the shortstop as quickly as he can, and he must throw the ball without using a shuffle step to gain momentum. The coach must emphasize quickness so his players understand what is important in this situation. However, a note of caution should be added at this point. The infielder must make sure that he has fielded the ground ball completely and successfully before initiating his throw. But once he has done this, he must release his throw as quickly as possible. All of this requires that double-play partners practice together and know each other's playing style.

7. The second baseman and the shortstop must know the area around second base within which the underhand throw can be used to initiate the double play. This is a rather arbitrary distance, and the two players may, with the advice of the coach, set their own limits. The important factor is not what the distance is, but that each player knows exactly where the underhand-toss area is. To enable the players to develop a knowledge of the desired distance the coach can draw a semi-circle around the second base area using the base as the center point and the desired distance as the radius. For example, if fifteen feet, which is a common distance, were used, a fifteen-foot semi-circle would be drawn in the infield dirt during practice sessions. After several such sessions, the two players will instinctively recognize the area within which they should use the underhand throw.

8. Another difficult play for the second baseman to complete successfully occurs when he has to throw to second base after having moved toward first base to field a ground ball. This throw may come when the second baseman is attempting a force out at second, or when he is initiating a double play by way of second base. The problem arises because the second baseman has built up momentum toward first base, and he must halt this

When the second baseman fields a ground ball within fifteen feet of second base, he should use the quick underhand toss.

momentum and turn it in an opposite direction to aid his throw toward second base. Young second basemen often make a long turn rather than a
short turn to complete this throw. The long turn means a pivot to the left,
and the short turn means a pivot to the right. The second baseman should
always use the short turn because it enables him to keep both the base runner and his throwing target in sight. If he uses the long turn, both the base
runner and target are lost from view for a moment, and this can result in a
bad throw.

9. There are three basic methods that the second baseman may use to
pivot on the double play: 1) the quick or straight method, 2) the across
method, and 3) the back method. Which one he should choose depends on
the total defensive situation. Regardless of his choice, however, the second
baseman should move to his base as quickly as possible. This is important.
The second baseman should time his movement so that he arrives at the
base ahead of the ball. Once he has reached the base, he should assume a
straddle position, placing one foot on each side of the bag. He should not
wait behind the base, but rather on the base.

The quick or straight method is, as the name implies, the most direct and
speediest of the three methods of pivoting. In this method, the second
baseman takes the throw, steps on the base with his right foot, pushes off
from that right foot while stepping directly down the baseline with his left
foot, and throws to first base. Second basemen who become adept at this
method often modify it by using a shuffle step which involves identical
footwork as described above but is done more quickly. The major advantage of the straight method is its quickness. It is most often used when the
throw from the shortstop has been good and the approaching runner is not
too close, since it leaves the second baseman open to collision with the
sliding runner. To avoid this problem, the second baseman usually must
jump up into the air after releasing his throw. It would seem that the approaching base runner might try to interfere with this throw, but normally
the runner will get himself out of the way of the throw.

The across method of double-play pivoting is also popular with major

leaguers. It is often used when the approaching base runner is close to second base, when the batter is a slow runner, or when the shortstop must field a ground ball that is hard hit. With the across method, the second baseman receives the throw, steps on the base with his left foot, crosses over toward the inside part of the diamond with his right foot, plants and pushes off with the right foot, steps toward first base with the left foot, and makes the throw. This method should always be used when a throw from the shortstop or third baseman is to the first-base side of second.

The back method is used less frequently than either of the other two.

When throwing to second base after fielding a ground ball at his normal position, the second baseman should make a short turn and an overhand throw.

The across method of pivoting used by the second baseman in this double-play attempt will carry him to the inside part of the diamond and away from a sliding runner.

Here, the second baseman receives the throw, tags the base with his left foot, pushes back with his left foot, steps to the outfield side of second base with his right foot, plants the right foot and pushes off from it, steps toward first base with his left foot, and completes his throw. This method is perhaps the slowest of the three since it involves a complete shift in momentum. This method should be used whenever a throw is to the outside part of second base.

The decision as to what method to use should be made on the basis of the total defensive situation. The second baseman must take into account

the following information: 1) the speed of the base runner approaching second base, 2) the speed of the hitter, 3) the type of throw that is received from the shortstop or third baseman, and 4) how hard hit the ground ball was that originally started the double play. To learn how to handle all this information quickly and make an instantaneous decision requires practice. Perhaps no other aspect of defensive play calls for as much practice time as the pivot at second base. When initiating practice on the various pivots, the coach should set up situations that are as much like game situations as possible. This means having base runners approach second base at all times during double-play practice.

10. When forcing a runner out at second, the second baseman should play the base just as a first baseman would play first. This means that instead of straddling the base, the second baseman should actually step across the base and be ready as quickly as possible to tag the base and stretch to secure the throw. Whether to attempt the force out or the double play must be decided instantaneously. Once the decision is made, the second baseman must adhere to it and complete the play. Any change of mind or hesitation usually results in a bad play or a missed putout.

11. The second baseman should use the "tag out and throw" double-play method only when the runner is very close to where the ground ball is fielded. In that case, the second baseman should hold the ball in his glove-hand, cover it with his bare hand as he makes the tag, and then complete his throw to first base. If, however, the runner tries to avoid the tag by running out of the baseline, the second baseman should not chase the runner. He should, instead, complete the double play by throwing to first base and assume that the umpire will call the runner out. If the base runner stops and retreats toward first base, the second baseman, again, should not chase the runner but should throw immediately to first base to put out the batter. The first baseman can throw back to the shortstop covering second base, who should then have no difficulty tagging the base runner out. The important point is that the second baseman should use the "tag out and throw"

In a double-play attempt, this second baseman uses the straight pivot, the quickest to execute, to position himself for a throw to first. Note that he catches the ball with both hands.

method only when it is the most obvious method. If there is any doubt, he should choose another method of making the double play.

12. The second baseman's role in pick-off plays at second base is largely that of a decoy. The second baseman is almost always within full view of the base runner on second and therefore cannot "sneak up" on the base and work the pick-off play. He can, however, act as a decoy to bluff the runner back to second base, and he should always assume that he has a major responsibility in completing this task. To work this play, the second baseman may move toward the base and then run quickly to his regular defensive position. The base runner, who is usually watching the second baseman, will sometimes become careless when he sees the second baseman retreating to his defensive position. When that happens, the shortstop can sneak in behind the runner and attempt to pick him off the base.

Principles for Playing Third Base

1. The third baseman must possess quickness as much as outright speed; he must be mentally tough and have a strong throwing arm.
2. The fielding stance of the third baseman is wider and lower than that of any other fielder.
3. The third baseman must constantly make adjustments in his fielding position according to the batter and the defensive situation.
4. The third baseman should always be "foul-line conscious."
5. The third baseman should field every ground ball hit to his left that he can reach.
6. The third baseman should block the hard-hit ball and keep it in front of him so he can retrieve it quickly and throw the runner out.
7. The slow roller is the most difficult ball for the third baseman to field,

and the way he plays it will depend on how much time he feels he has.

8. The throw to second base should be made sidearm across the front of the body.
9. The third baseman should allow the shortstop to take all pop-ups that are hit down the left-field foul line.
10. With a runner on second base, the third baseman must make adjustments in his defensive play.
11. The double-play strategy used by the third baseman depends upon the defensive situation and, particularly, on the batter.
12. When the third baseman is covering his base but has no chance for a putout there, he should leave the base to catch a batted ball in the air if possible.
13. When receiving a throw from the catcher, the third baseman should straddle the inside part of the base.

Discussing the Principles

1. The third baseman does not need the speed required of the shortstop or second baseman. He is called upon to move only short distances to field batted balls, and therefore it is quickness as much as speed that is necessary for successful performance at this position. The third baseman must move quickly—to his left to cut off ground balls, to his right to cover the baseline, and forward to field the slowly moving ball. The third-base position is also no place for the timid player. The third baseman must possess mental toughness. It is not easy to maintain eye focus and correct body position on the sharply hit ground ball to third base. The body's natural reaction is to pull away from such a ball; however, the third baseman must learn to stay with these balls, to knock them down with his body if necessary, to quickly retrieve them, and to throw to first base for the putout. Like the shortstop, the third baseman must have a reasonably strong throwing arm. The distance across the infield from the deep third-base position is significant. Moveover, the shorter throw to first that the third baseman must make after fielding the slowly hit ground ball also requires a strong arm. In sum, quickness, mental toughness, and a strong arm seem to be the most important qualifications for successful performance as a third baseman.

2. The fielding stance of the third baseman is wider and lower than that of any other fielder. By spreading his feet farther apart than other fielders, the third baseman lowers his center of mass and increases his stability. He also bends at the waist and extends his arms down in front of his body. The extra stability afforded him by this stance enables him to stay with the sharply hit ground ball and it allows him to move quickly in the three directions (left, right, and forward) he must cover. The lowness of this stance is beneficial because the third baseman often would not have time to move down from a more upright position to field a batted ball. This is particularly

true in the case of the sharply hit ground ball. Further, when moving to his left or right, the third baseman must be able to stay low as he moves, and the initial lowness of the stance aids in this technique. To help in assuming the proper stance, some third basemen take a step toward the hitter as the pitcher releases the ball.

3. The third baseman, more than any other infielder perhaps, must constantly make adjustments in his fielding position according to the batter and the defensive situation. These adjustments will be determined by the type of hitter (a pull-hitter, a punch-hitter, etc.), whether he is left- or right-handed, the speed of the batter, the number of outs in the inning, the number of men on base, the score of the game, and the ball-strike count on the batter. For example, with two out and a slow, right-handed pull-hitter at bat, the third baseman may want to play deep to protect the foul line. On the other hand, with no outs and a fast, left-handed punch-hitter at bat, the third baseman may want to play a full four to six feet in on the infield grass and away from the foul line. These two extremes may call for initial positions that are twenty feet apart. In less extreme situations, the third baseman has to make constant minor adjustments to put himself in what he feels is the most advantageous defensive position.

A correct preparatory fielding stance—low and well-balanced—allows the third basemen to move quickly in any direction when a ball is hit to his position.

It is, of course, a great advantage for the third baseman to be able to play deep. The deep position enables him to field balls that would get by him were he in a more shallow fielding position. Defensive baseball is, however, a compromise between what is theoretically most advantageous and what the situation demands. When a fast, left-handed hitter is at bat, the third baseman will have to play shallow. This means that any sharply hit ground ball from such a hitter that is not hit directly at the third baseman will probably get through to the outfield for a base hit.

In a potential sacrifice bunt situation, the third baseman must also play a shallow position. With a runner on first, the third baseman should play three to five feet wide of the base and on the edge of the grass. As soon as the hitter indicates that he is going to bunt, the third baseman should rush in toward the hitter. With runners on first and second bases, the situation is somewhat different. Most teams prefer to use a defensive strategy whereby the third baseman covers third base in this situation. To accomplish this and still be able to field a bunt that gets by the pitcher, the third baseman has to be particularly alert. He should assume a beginning position that is identical to that mentioned above. When the hitter squares around to bunt, the third baseman should take two quick steps toward home plate. From this position, the third baseman must judge whether or not he will have to field the bunt. If he decides that a teammate (the catcher, pitcher, or first baseman) will be able to field it, he must quickly move back to cover third base.

With a runner on third, the third baseman must assume the same defensive position that he would if the runner were not there, but he should never ignore the runner. He must constantly bluff the runner back to the base so the runner does not get too big a lead on the pitcher or too big a jump on the play. His defensive position is still determined by the defensive situation (the hitter, the number of outs, etc.), but the third baseman has the added responsibility of keeping the runner close to third base.

4. The third baseman should always be "foul-line conscious." Regardless of the small adjustments in his defensive position, he should always make sure that the foul line is reasonably well protected. Defensively, it is always better if a ground ball gets through to the outfield by passing between the third baseman and the shortstop than by passing on the foul-line side of the third baseman. The position of the ball in this case usually means the difference between a double and a single. This strategy becomes especially important in a close game or in the late innings when the defense must protect against the extra-base hit in order to keep opposing runners out of scoring position.

5. The third baseman should field every ground ball hit to his left that he can reach. He should not hesitate to cut in front of the shortstop to field this type of ball. He can almost always reach such ground balls more quickly than the shortstop, and this saving of time can mean the difference between an out and a hit on a close play at first base. When making the throw after fielding this type of ground ball, the third baseman must make a shuffle half-pivot and throw across his body to first base.

6. The third baseman should make sure that he is in position to block all sharply hit ground balls. Moreover, he must keep these balls in front of him so that he can retrieve them and still throw the base runner out. This kind of fielding requires mental toughness on the part of the third baseman. He must keep his eye on the ball and the plane of his body perpendicular to the path of the oncoming grounder—no matter how sharply it is hit. Thus, if the ball bounces off his arms or chest it will bound directly in front of him where he may keep it within sight and quickly retrieve it. The third baseman who pulls his head away at the last moment on this type of play also changes the plane of his body. The ball may then bounce off his body at an angle and go into foul territory down the left-field line. This will allow the hitter to continue to second base, thus turning a potential putout into a two-base hit.

7. The slow roller is the most difficult ball for the third baseman to field, and the way he plays it must depend on how much time he feels that he has. This means that the third baseman must make a judgment about the speed of each hitter before the play begins. The slow roller is difficult when the hit is a good bunt, but it is even more difficult on the "swinging bunt," the slow rolling ground ball that results when the batter swings full but only catches a piece of the ball and tops it down the third-base line. The third baseman must first decide if he has sufficient time to pick up the ball with both hands. If he does, he should field the ball with his left foot forward as he does any other ground ball. He should then step on his right foot and throw across his body to first base while he is still in the down position. If, however, he decides that he does not have this much time, he must attempt to pick up the ball with his bare hand. This maneuver is best accomplished by fielding the ball just off the right foot when the right foot is forward in the run. The throw must then be made in almost the same motion as the ball is picked up. It takes a great deal of practice to fully master this type of quick throw. Brooks Robinson, the great third baseman of the Baltimore Orioles, prefers to make this play by fielding the ball with both hands and always straightening up to make the throw—no matter how close the play is. His reasoning is that he can make a much stronger throw after having straightened up and the stronger throw makes up for the time he loses in straightening. There is a great deal of merit in his technique. In particular, it lessens the risk of a bad throw; the third baseman who throws from the down position is more likely to throw inaccurately.

Regardless of what technique is used to field slow rollers, several things should be remembered. First, the third baseman should use both hands to field the ball whenever possible, i.e., nearly all the time. The time saved with the bare-handed pick-up is negligible compared to the risk of error involved. Secondly, the third baseman should remember to pick up, or at least touch, all foul balls. Often the slow roller or bunt rolls into foul territory. When it does, the third baseman should immediately touch it so the umpire will call it a foul ball. Often times such slow hit balls will roll back into fair territory unless they are touched when in foul territory.

8. Often, the third baseman must throw to second base either to force

out a runner or to initiate a double play. Again, the key to the success of
this play is to get rid of the ball quickly. To do this, the third baseman must
field the ground ball, push off from his right foot, make a very short pivot at
the hips, and throw sidearm across his body to second base. He must not
take the time to make a full pivot or use a shuffle step to add power to the
throw. Novice third basemen often assume that the important aspect of this
play is a strong throw. Thus, they pivot and use a shuffle step to "wind-up"
before making the throw. This technique takes too much time. The third
baseman must learn to throw with only the short step taken with the left
foot after he has fielded the ground ball.

9. The third baseman should allow the shortstop to take all pop-ups that
are hit down the left-field foul line. The shortstop has a better view of this
kind of pop-up. When a third baseman attempts to field such balls, he often
gets caught in a back-pedalling movement and cannot maintain good balance. Furthermore, when the third baseman hears the shortstop call for this
type of pop-up, he should move quickly away from the play to avoid an
unneccesary collision. He should, however, always move to field pop-ups
and if no other players call him off the play, he should field the ball. But,
if the left fielder or the shortstop calls for the ball, the third baseman should
take himself out of the play.

10. With a runner on second base, the third baseman must make adjustments in his defensive play. First, he must always "look" the runner back
to second base after fielding a ground ball and before throwing to first. This
will usually prevent the runner from advancing to third on the put out at
first base. Second, with a runner on second base, the third baseman must
not allow himself to be bluffed into moving in by a fake bunt. He must always return to third base to be ready to cover in case of an attempted steal.
It is important that the third baseman do all he can to keep a runner from
reaching third base. With a runner on second, a base hit is usually needed
to produce a run. With a runner on third base, however, a fly ball, a passed
ball, or even an infield out can mean a run.

11. The double-play strategy used by the third baseman depends on the
defensive situation and, particularly, on the batter. With a runner on first
base, the strategy is clear. The third baseman merely initiates the $5-4-3$
double play. With runners on first and second base, however, there are options. The third baseman can elect to touch third base and then throw to
first base, or he can initiate the $5-4-3$ double play. Generally speaking,
the latter play should be used except for two special situations. The first
occurs when the batter is a left-handed pull-hitter. In this situation, the
second baseman should be playing deeper and closer to first base than he
normally would. Thus, he would have difficulty moving to second base to
receive the throw from the third baseman. In this case, the third baseman
would do well to make the putout at third base if at all possible and then
complete the double play by throwing to first base. The second situation
when the third-to-first strategy should be used is when a ground ball is
fielded near the third-base line. Then, the third baseman is close enough to
the base to touch it quickly and throw to first base to complete the double

play. In all other situations, the 5 – 4 – 3 strategy is probably best because it is the quickest. It takes more time for a third baseman to run a short distance and touch third base than it does for him to throw quickly to second base to start the around-the-horn double play.

12. There are several situations that call for an attempted putout at third base. For instance, when the shortstop or second baseman is trying to cut down a runner attempting to take third on a ground ball, the defense should always try for a putout. Also, as happens frequently, when a runner is attempting to move from first to third base on a hit to the outfield, a putout attempt is called for. This is often a close and exciting play. It is, however, a difficult defensive play to make, and the cost of a misplay is almost always a run scored by the opposition. When such situations occur, the third baseman must at some point in the play make a decision as to how likely he is to be able to complete the putout. If he thinks that his chances for making the putout are slim, he should leave the base and attempt to catch the throw on the fly, or at least make sure that he fields the ball cleanly. This will keep the ball from getting by the third baseman and thus giving the runner an opportunity to score.

13. When receiving a throw from the catcher, the third baseman should straddle the inside part of the base. By taking this position, he leaves the base open, thus almost eliminating the possibility of a collision with an approaching runner in which the third baseman might get spiked or the play might be broken up. This defensive position also enables the third baseman to move to take a wide throw without being hindered by the oncoming runner.

Principles for Playing Shortstop

1. The primary requirements for shortstop play are range, a good arm, and mental alertness.
2. The shortstop must have a fairly upright stance that enables him to move relatively long distances to either the left or the right.
3. After making a fielding play in the "hole" the shortstop should get rid of the ball as quickly as possible.
4. When making a play behind second base, the shortstop must throw across his body while moving.
5. In initiating the double play, the shortstop should throw quickly and forcefully with a sidearm throw aimed at the chest of the second baseman.
6. There are several pivots available to the shortstop in making the double play, but he should use the "drag" method almost exclusively.
7. In fielding the softly hit ground ball, the shortstop should pick up the ball and make his throw from the down position.
8. The shortstop must cover third base whenever a defensive situation

arises which requires the third baseman to vacate his normal position.
9. The shortstop has the primary responsibility for holding a base runner on second base.
10. The shortstop will be the player most involved in attempted pick-off plays at second base.

Discussing the Principles

1. There are several attributes that a coach should look for when selecting players for the shortstop position. The shortstop must have a good arm. A good arm in baseball terminology means an arm strong enough and accurate enough for the position. When the shortstop goes into the "hole" to field a ground ball, he must make a long throw to first base. To make this throw, and any other throws from such a distance, he must have both strength and accuracy. Since the shortstop will probably handle more ground-ball chances than any other infielder, his accuracy is important. Without it, numerous errors will result. The potential shortstop must also have range. Range for the shortstop means speed (whereas range for the third baseman is more related to quickness). To cover all the territory from the "hole" to the area behind second base requires a certain amount of speed. Shortstops are often among the faster runners on the squad (major leaguers Maury Wills, Bert Campenoris, Luis Aparicio, and Don Kessinger are good examples). The shortstop must also possess mental alertness. He must make many judgments, and this requires a heads-up knowledge of particular situations and of overall baseball strategy. Most of all, perhaps,

When a shortsop moves to his right to field a ground ball in the hole, he should plant his right foot and throw quickly to complete this difficult play.

the shortstop must be a player upon whom the coach and the rest of the team can depend. He must be steady and sure. Traditionally, his is the only position on a baseball team that a player can earn or nail down solely on the basis of his fielding ability. Along with the catcher's spot, the shortstop's position is the one position where defensive ability far outweighs whatever contribution the player might make to the offense. However, if a player can play shortstop well and also contribute substantially to the offensive production of the team, his value is unmatched.

2. The shortstop should use a fairly upright stance that will enable him to move with speed in either direction. When going to his right or left, he should begin with a long, low first step; this is the best way to gain speed quickly. While a shortstop can usually glide to pick up a ground ball, he should always make sure that his position enables him to get his body in front of the baseball as he makes the fielding play. Young shortstops too often acquire the bad habit of fielding ground balls to one side of their body. They do this primarily when they move too lazily and just glide over to make the play. This should be avoided unless it is the only way to reach the ball. The shortstop should get to the ball quickly so that he can move in on it. Thus, the coach should instruct the shortstop to run if that is the only way he can get into the proper fielding position.

3. After making a fielding play in the "hole," the shortstop should get rid of the ball as quickly as possible. This is particularly difficult to do because he must make a very long throw while the momentum of his body is carrying him away from his intended target. Throwing forcefully in this situation is therefore a problem. Often a shortstop will take one extra step after fielding this type of ball, plant his back foot to halt his body momentum, and push off from this foot to make a forceful throw to first base. While this results in a stronger throw, it also takes a great deal of time. It is usually

better for the shortstop to get rid of the ball quickly rather than to worry about throwing forcefully. As the ground ball is fielded, the shortstop should plant his back foot as best he can and make his throw—all in one motion. This strategy will yield a less forceful throw, but it will take less time.

When a ground ball is hit to the shortstop, there may be a runner on second base. If that runner does not attempt to move to third on the ground ball, the shortstop should automatically throw to first base. But he should first "look the runner back" to second base. A glance in the runner's direction is usually sufficient. If the shortstop does not do this, the runner might move on to third base *after* the shortstop has thrown to first. This is serious because a runner on third base can score in many ways. If the runner on second attempts to run to third on the ground ball, the shortstop must decide whether to throw to third base or to go to first for the sure putout. Generally, he is better advised to throw to first base, especially if the ground ball is hit near second. If, however, the ball is hit in the "hole," the shortstop should attempt the putout at third base. There are two reasons for this. First, the play at first base is always difficult and close when made after a ground ball is fielded in the hole, and second, the throw from the hole to third base is much easier than the throw from the hole to first. Moreover, there is less chance of hitting the runner when the throw is to third base. Another situation that might call for a putout attempt at third base is when the runner on second is the lead run in the game, especially if the play occurs in the late innings.

4. When making a play behind second base, the shortstop must throw across his body while moving in the direction of his run to the ball. The idea behind this strategy is the same as that behind the suggested strategy for making the play in the hole: the shortstop frequently cannot spare the time to stop the momentum of his body, make a complete turn, and step

In a double-play situation, the shortstop can use an inside pivot after taking a throw on the left side of second base. Note that the player's right foot is firmly planted and that he uses that foot to step directly toward first base as he throws.

toward first base before he throws. He should therefore adopt the strategy of throwing across his body. Again, a less forceful throw results, but the total play takes less time.

5. In initiating the double play, the shortstop should throw quickly and forcefully with a sidearm throw aimed at the chest of the second baseman. Both the quickness and the forcefulness of the throw are important. Novice shortstops tend to hold up on this throw, with disastrous results. First, even if the throw is good, the play has been slowed down and the chances of completing the double play are lessened. Second, holding up on the throw may lead to a bad throw, which could cause the defense to lose the chance for either the force out or the double play. The shortstop and second baseman must know each other well enough to avoid these pitfalls. The shortstop must know that he can throw forcefully without any fear that his partner at second base will be surprised by the throw. This takes purposeful practice, and the coach must see that time is set aside to perfect this aspect of infield play. The sidearm throw is a far more natural throw in this situation than the overhand throw. This is true because the sidearm throw can be made without the pivot. The shortstop need only twist his trunk at the hips as he throws.

Like the second baseman, the shortstop must decide whether to use a sidearm throw or an underhand toss. It is suggested, as before, that within a certain, predetermined distance the underhand throw should be used. The shortstop should always be alert to the possibility that he can make the force out at second base himself and then complete the double play with a throw to first base. For instance, if the shortstop is moving toward second base when he fields a ground ball, he can, with just a few extra steps, easily touch the base and then complete the play by throwing to first. The great advantage of this, of course, is that it eliminates one throw from the total play and thereby reduces the chance for error.

6. There are several pivots available to the shortstop as a middleman in the double play. One option is to tag the base with the right foot, step onto the left foot on the outside of the bag, and leap off that foot to throw to first base. This is tricky to master; in addition, it leaves the player in a position from which it is most difficult to throw to first base. A second option is the inside tag, which might be used when the throw from the second baseman is to the inside part of the base. To execute this pivot, the player tags the base with his left foot, pushes backward and shifts his weight to the right foot, pivots on the right foot, and steps toward first base as he makes his throw to complete the double play. This technique takes a great deal of time, but it is a safe technique, especially when the throw is to the inside of the diamond. A third possibility is the outside tag, which may be effective when the throw is slightly wild and to the center-field side of the base. With this technique, the shortstop tags the base with his right foot, steps across to his left foot, pivots on the left foot, brings the right foot behind the left, shifts his weight to the right foot, and steps toward first base to complete his throw. This technique is also time-consuming, but some shortstops like to use it when the base runner is very close to second base. The step across the base in this situation usually takes the shortstop away from the slide of the runner, thus preventing a collision that might break up the double play. The fourth option is the drag technique, and it is this one that should be used most of the time. This technique takes considerably less time than either the inside or outside method, and it can be easily mastered by young players. With this technique, the shortstop approaches the outside part of the base on a slight angle toward the right-field line. As he receives the ball from the second baseman, he makes a half-pivot so that he crosses the base sideways. His feet are now in a position to shuffle or slide

Shortstops frequently use the "drag" method when making the double-play pivot at second base. In this method, the shortstop tags the base with his right foot as he takes the sliding or "drag" step.

across the outside corner of the base. He steps across the base with his left foot and slides his right foot, touching or kicking the corner of the base as he moves. He then completes the sliding or shuffling movement by bringing the right foot up to the left but not crossing his feet. Using the momentum of his movement, he steps out with his left foot and throws across his body to first base. This drag or shuffle pivot is the quickest and most natural of the techniques available to the shortstop, and he should use it more than any other. Nevertheless, he must remember that he should to some extent let the throw determine what kind of pivot he will use. A throw to the pitcher's-mound side of second base will require an inside pivot. A throw to the center-field side of the base will require an outside pivot.

In addition to his other duties, the shortstop serves as the middleman in the 3 – 6 – 3 double play. He receives the ball from the first baseman, tags second base, and throws back to first base. In this situation, the shortstop must be certain that the first baseman has not already made the putout at first. If the first baseman has done that before throwing to second, the shortstop must tag the approaching base runner. In the true 3 – 6 – 3 double-play situation, however, the shortstop should move to the base and straddle it facing the first baseman. As noted above, he must make his pivot according to the kind of throw he receives. Most often, the shortstop will want to tag the base with his left foot, then step off and plant the right foot before throwing to first base.

7. As with the third baseman, one of the most difficult plays for the shortstop to execute involves the slowly bounding ground ball that gets by the pitcher. The shortstop must attempt to play this ball with the same general technique that the third baseman uses in fielding the swinging bunt. He must charge the ball aggressively, field the ball, and throw—all in the same

motion. Whenever possible, the shortstop should use his glove-hand to field the ball, as he would do with any other ground ball. The "bare-handed pick-up" is a sensational play for television fans to watch, but it does not pay off in the long run. If, however, the shortstop feels that the only way he can get the runner at first base is to field the ball with his bare hand, he should attempt to do so by picking it up off his right foot as he runs in. Regardless of how he fields the ball, the shortstop will not be able to straighten up to throw; he must throw from the down position if he is to have time to complete the putout at first base.

8. There are several situations that call for the shortstop to cover third base. One such situation arises when the third baseman has moved to catch a pop fly either in foul territory or in fair territory near home plate. Another occurs when the third baseman has had to move in to field a slow roller. Frequently, a runner on first base will try to move all the way around to third on this type of play. He will be successful unless the shortstop is alert enough to cover third base. Another occasion that sometimes calls for the shortstop to cover third base occurs when the third baseman has moved off his base to act as a cut-off man on a throw from the outfield. Alertness in these kinds of situations is the mark of a veteran shortstop.

9. The shortstop has the primary responsibility for holding a base runner on second base. When a runner on second base takes his lead off the base, he cannot see the shortstop without twisting around. This puts the short-stop in the best position to "bother" the runner. As the runner leads off, the shortstop should bluff him back to the base by making several quick but short movements toward second. Occasionally, the shortstop should move almost all the way to second base so that the runner does not become in-ured to the bluff movements. This is a tedious but important and necessary job. If the shortstop, by his active movement, can cause the base runner to

The shortstop must complete his throw quickly and accurately, even if an approaching base runner is almost on top of him.

stay two steps closer to second base than he normally would, he may prevent a run from scoring since these two steps can mean the difference between being safe or out on a play at home plate.

10. The shortstop will be the player most involved in attempted pick-off plays at second base. A pitcher may turn and throw to second base at any time before he begins his actual pitch. The pitcher also has the right to move off the rubber and fake a throw to second. Pick-offs at second base, therefore, can often be bluffed, and this is good strategy. The actual throw probably should not be made very often, however, as this pick-off play is seldom successful, and it creates a situation in which the probability of error is high. Such error is harmful because it almost always allows the runner to advance to third base, from where he is much more likely to score.

There are two primary methods of working a predetermined pick-off play: 1) the "daylight" method, and 2) the "count" method. The "daylight" pick-off play may be executed when the pitcher can see between the shortstop and the base runner—with the shortstop in a normal fielding position. As soon as the shortstop sees the pitcher begin to turn, he should break quickly for second base to take the throw. The "count" method is initiated by some predetermined signal between the pitcher and the shortstop. The play usually begins when the pitcher comes to his "set" position. The count should be "one thousand one, two thousand two, three thousand three, etc." When the count reaches two, for example, the shortstop should break for the base. When the count reaches three, the pitcher will turn to start his throw. A variation of this method is to use the second baseman as a bluff man on the play. This play can begin with the second baseman moving over to second to draw the runner back to the base. As the second baseman returns to his normal position, the runner is likely to move off the base again. Precisely at this moment, the shortstop should break to cover second base. The advantage of this play is that the base runner is sometimes caught moving toward third base, and it takes time for him to shift his momentum and return to second base.

Making the Double Play

Double-play techniques for each infield position have been discussed in this chapter. There are several important aspects, however, which seem to be common to all double-play situations. These techniques and strategies are so important that they warrant consideration in a section devoted solely to making the double play.

Nothing in baseball can kill a rally as quickly as the double play. Every coach knows that the double play is the defensive coup that can change the complexion of an inning and a game in short order. The double play, however, is not easy to make. It normally requires proper techniques and timing on the part of three players. Double-play possibilities that occur most often are the 5 – 4 – 3 double play, the 6 – 4 – 3 double play, the 4 – 6 – 3 double play, the 3 – 6 – 3 double play, and the 1 – 4 – 3 double play. Each of these situations demands a coordinated effort by the participants. If one of the three players involved does not complete his assignment satisfactorily, the double play is lost. Below are principles of performance which should aid the coach in developing good double-play combinations.

Principles of Performance

1. The most important rule for a player to remember when initiating a double play is that he must see that the first putout is made successfully.
2. Infielders should establish their double-play positions according to the type of hitter at bat.
3. The most important aspect of double-play technique is the first throw. The player who initiates the double play must get rid of the ball quickly and accurately.
4. The type of throw used to initiate the double play will depend on the distance between the infielder and the base he is throwing to.
5. The technique by which the double play is made should be determined by the speed of the base runner, the batter, and the ground ball.
6. The type of pivot used in the double play will depend on the proximity of the base runner, the speed of the batter, and the type of throw received from the teammate.
7. All ground balls and throws should be caught with two hands; however, the player initiating the double play should make sure that his teammate sees the ball as quickly as possible.
8. The middleman on the double play should move as quickly as possible to a position just behind the base he is covering.
9. If, due to the circumstances of the play, the middleman decides that he can get no better than a force out, he should take a position on the base and play as if he were a first baseman.
10. The shortstop and second baseman should always inform the pitcher as to who will cover the base on a ground ball to the latter.

Discussing the Principles

1. The most important rule for a player to remember when initiating a double play is that he must make sure the first putout is made successfully. While it may sound trite, it is nevertheless true that "you can't get two unless you get the first one." The accuracy of the first throw in the double play is, therefore, important and should be stressed constantly. It is also important that the middleman catch the ball and tag the base before he

throws to first to complete the double play. Too often, the middleman will drop the first throw because he is in a hurry to get his own throw to first base and actually starts to make his throw before he is in full possession of the ball thrown by his teammate.

2. There is no fixed "double-play depth" for infielders. The shortstop, second baseman, third baseman, and first baseman will each establish his defensive position according to the total defensive situation, giving primary emphasis to whatever position makes the most sense in terms of the hitter. The infielders should consider what type of hitter he is, whether he is left- or right-handed, and how fast he can run. The double-play defense against a slow, left-handed hitter will be different than that against a fast, right-handed hitter. In the first situation, the second baseman can play deeper and closer to first base than he can in other double-play situations, and the first baseman can perhaps play slightly behind the runner on first base. In the second instance, however, the second baseman and the first baseman will have to move to what is normally considered an average double-play depth. This means that the shortstop and the second baseman should position themselves somewhat closer to second base than they would if there were no runners on base. They should move quickly (one step over, and one step toward second base) to their double-play depth, from which each can get to his respective base in time to receive a quick throw from his partner.

Infielders at double-play depth to defend against a right-handed power hitter.

3. As emphasized above, the most important aspect of the double-play technique is the first throw. The player who initiates the play by throwing to the middleman must get rid of the ball quickly, and his throw must be accurate. A common error committed by novice infielders is to wait until the middleman has established his position near the base before throwing the ball to him. This slows down the initiation of the double play unduly and often makes the throw to first base late. Just as the good quarterback must know enough about his receivers and the planned plays to throw quickly to "spots" that the receivers are moving to occupy, the baseball player who initiates the double play must know his teammate's abilities well enough to allow him to throw to second base before the teammate actually reaches the base. In other words, he must accurately anticipate the movement of his teammate. This must be done quickly and the throw must be accurate, with the optimum being the chest-high throw.

4. The type of throw used to initiate the double play will depend on the distance between the initiating infielder and the base he is throwing to. The shortstop and second baseman should come to some agreement as to what distance from the base will be the dividing line for determining whether they will use the underhand toss or the normal throw. Many infielders have found that the underhand toss works best within fifteen feet or so of the base. (See the section in this chapter on Playing Second Base for suggestions on teaching players to recognize this distance automatically.) When the infielder decides to throw the ball with a normal throw, however, he should throw it forcefully and not attempt to hold up on his regular throwing motion. Holding up leads to more bad throws in this situation than any other cause. If the fielder feels that he cannot throw the ball forcefully because of his close proximity to the base, he should use the underhand toss.

5. The technique by which the double play is made should be determined by the speed of the base runner, the batter, and the ground ball. The infielder should have some knowledge of the running ability of both the base runner and the hitter. With a slow base runner, a slow right-handed hitter, and a sharply hit ground ball, a good deal of care and caution can be taken by all infielders involved in the double play. The players can take that extra fraction of a second to insure that their throws will be accurate. With a fast base runner, a speedy, left-handed hitter, and a slowly hit ground ball, the situation is reversed. The man who initiates the double play must throw with almost the same motion that he fields the ball. The middleman must then decide whether he should go for the force out or attempt the double play. If he elects to try for the double play, he must use the fastest pivot to complete the play.

6. The type of pivot used by the middleman in the double play will depend on the proximity of the base runner, the speed of the batter, and the type of throw received from the initiator of the play. The types of pivots recommended for the shortstop and second baseman are described in the sections of this chapter dealing specifically with those positions. It is our opinion that the speed of the batter may be the most important factor for

the infielders to consider in choosing a pivot style. When a fast runner is at bat, especially a fast left-handed hitter, the middleman on the double play must make the fastest pivot possible regardless of the proximity of the approaching runner. This, of course, assumes that the throw from the first man in the double play is reasonably good. If the throw is not good, the middleman should just make the force out and forget about attempting to complete the double play; the chances are that he would have no chance to put out the fast runner at first, and any attempt to hurry his throw to first from a position of disadvantage might well result in a wild throw that would allow the batter to continue on to second base. For the second baseman, the fastest pivot is the straight method. (See the section on Playing Second Base.) When the base runner is close to second base, the second baseman will have to execute a slight jump at the end of his pivot in order to avoid a collision and possible spike injury. The middleman must always be aware that the approaching base runner has only one task: to break up the double play by sliding hard into the middleman.

7. As has been previously mentioned, all ground balls should be caught with two hands; however, the player initiating the double play should make sure that his teammate sees the ball as quickly as possible. This means that once the ball has been fielded cleanly, the infielder should pull his glove-hand away so that the ball is in clear view in this throwing hand. This will enable the middleman in the double play to follow the ball easily as it is thrown to him. This is especially necessary if the throw is an underhand toss. All infielders, and particularly the shortstop and second baseman — because they are so close to each other during the execution of the double play — should heed this principle.

8. It is important that the middleman in the double play get to the base he is to cover as *quickly* as possible. In the case of the second baseman, he should move quickly to the base and straddle it in anticipation of a throw from the shortstop or third baseman. When the shortstop is to be the middleman, he should run to a position just behind the base in anticipation of the throw from the second baseman or the first baseman. Many infielders do not practice this aspect of double-play technique. But running to the proper position gives an infielder several advantages over another player who merely trots to the double-play position. First, he can play farther away from the base and thus cover more territory. This is particularly important for the shortstop who should never "over-cheat," but should always protect the hole between third base and short. Second, by running to the base, he can complete the pivot aspect of the double play more quickly and thus have more time to throw to first base. Finally, more real hustle at this point will result in more successful double plays.

9. If, due to the circumstances of the play, the middleman decides that he can get no better than a force out, he should play the base as if he were a first baseman. He should present a clear target and stretch to catch the throw. This decision must be made quickly and, once made, adhered to. Any change in plans during the execution of the play is liable to result in

the loss of both the force out and the putout at first base. In short, each infielder must keep in mind that getting the force out is of primary importance.

10. The shortstop and second baseman should always inform the pitcher as to who will cover the base on a ground ball to the latter. There should never be any mix-up on this play. The decision as to who should cover the base usually depends on the type of hitter at bat. With a left-handed hitter, the shortstop should cover the base. With a right-handed hitter, the second baseman should cover. The shortstop and second baseman, however, should not hesitate to make exceptions to this rule. If a right-handed batter is primarily a right-field push-hitter, then the shortstop should cover the base. (This, of course, is another good example of why it is so important for defensive players to know as much as possible about their opponents.) When the decision is made, it should be communicated clearly to the pitcher so there is no doubt in the pitcher's mind. When a ground ball is hit to the pitcher, he should be able to turn and throw to second base knowing which of his teammates will be there to take the throw and act as the middleman in a double play.

Chapter 7
Coaching the Outfielders

The outfield positions are too often the most neglected positions on the baseball team in terms of instruction and practice. Frequently, coaches do not provide adequate instruction for their outfielders. Thus, a player may perform in the outfield for years without ever substantially improving his skills. However, attention to outfield play is important. Outfield errors are serious because they occur so far from the infield that base runners often advance two or more bases when such errors are committed. The missed ground ball in the infield is a major error, but the incorrectly played ground ball in the outfield is a disaster, simply because it often clears the bases. At the major league level, the defensive value of a Curt Flood, Carl Yaztremski, Willie Mays, or Al Kaline has never been underestimated. A good defensive outfielder can provide the same boost for a team at the little league level that he does at the professional level. Below are principles of performance that will help the baseball coach to develop better defensive outfielders.

Principles for Playing the Outfield

1. Each outfield position requires different skills, and the coach should carefully place his players in the various outfield positions so as to best meet his defensive goals.
2. The outfielder should be aware, before a pitch is made, of what defensive options he will have if a ball is hit into his territory.
3. The outfielder should make preliminary adjustments in his position according to his knowledge of the pitcher and the hitter.
4. The outfielder can get a "jump on the ball" by anticipating the direction of the hit according to the type of swing the hitter makes.
5. The outfielder should move quickly to the position where he can best field the ball; he should never "drift" with a fly ball.
6. The outfielder should move into his fielding play whenever he thinks he will have to throw after making the catch.
7. If at all possible, the outfielder should be facing the infield when he catches the ball.
8. An outfielder, particularly a center fielder, should not play his position too deep.
9. The outfielder should always call — loudly — for any ball that he feels is in his territory.
10. The center fielder should have preference on balls hit to right-center field and left-center field.
11. All outfielders should use the overhand throw as exclusively as possible for throws to the infield.
12. The outfielder should aim his throw at the chest of the cut-off man.
13. The outfielder should throw low when no cut-off man is being used on the defensive play.

14. The outfielder should never hold the ball after fielding it.
15. Outfielders should always back each other up.
16. The outfielder should not attempt a shoe-string catch unless the ball is a pop-fly or unless such a catch would prevent a tying or winning run from scoring.
17. The outfielder should keep the ball in front of him as he charges it.
18. The outfielder must learn how to use his glove-hand to shield his eyes from the sun on bright days.
19. The outfielder must learn how to play a ball which caroms off the outfield fence.

Discussing the Principles

1. Each outfield position requires different skills. The baseball coach should place his players in the outfield so as to take their abilities into account and yet meet his defensive goals. The best fielder should be placed in center field. The reason for this is that the center fielder is called upon to handle more fielding chances than either the left fielder or the right fielder. Center field is difficult to play, although many coaches would argue that right field is the most difficult of all the outfield positions. The center fielder needs good range to cover all the many balls hit to his immediate left and right. He also needs to have a strong throwing arm because he is required to make numerous crucial throws. The most difficult ball for the center fielder to field successfully is the line drive that is hit directly toward his position. He must judge how far this type of drive will carry. An all too familiar sight at the lower echelons of competitive baseball is the young center fielder charging in on a line drive, only to have the ball carry over his head for a home run.

Right field is also a very difficult position to play, but because the right fielder does not handle as many chances as the center fielder, the coach should generally avoid placing his best outfielder in this position. If a coach is fortunate enough to have two good defensive outfielders, he may wish to put the faster of the two in center field and the player with the better throwing arm in right field. The right fielder should have a strong throwing arm because he must frequently make the long throw from right field to third base. To add to the difficulty of playing this position, right field is the "sun" field – if the baseball diamond is laid out according to the rule book. In the late afternoon, the right fielder has to look almost directly into the setting sun on each ball hit toward his position. Moreover, many right-handed batters hit to the opposite field, and their drives and fly balls are difficult to field because they often curve sharply away from the right fielder and toward the right-field foul line. A left-handed right fielder has an advantage in such cases because he has an easier time throwing after playing a ball hit toward the foul line. In center field, on the other hand, it makes little difference whether the player is right-handed or left-handed.

Left field is the least difficult of the outfield positions. The left fielder can be reasonably successful at his position without having a strong throwing arm. The only long throw he has to make is to home plate; throws from left field to second base and third base do not require an exceptionally strong arm. The most difficult play for the left fielder is, again, the ball hit toward the foul line. For this type of ball, the right-handed left fielder has a slight advantage since he can make his throw more easily after fielding the ball. While it has been suggested that there may be some slight advantage to having a left-handed or right-handed player in a particular outfield position, the coach should not consider this a primary factor when deciding where to place which players in the outfield. The other factors mentioned above are far more important than which arm the player uses when throwing.

2. The outfielder should be aware, before a pitch is made, of what defensive options he will have if a ball is hit into his territory. He should, before each pitch, mentally review what he will do with the ball if it is hit to his position. He should know, beforehand, where to throw after fielding either a ground ball or a fly ball. A review of his options should prevent the harmful "mental errors" that plague many baseball teams. Physical errors are to be expected at times; but no coach should long condone repeated mental errors by his players. Mental rehearsal of the defensive options available to the outfielder will also tend to prevent the momentary time lag that often occurs when a fielder is "making up his mind" after he fields the ball. Such a time lag can occasionally mean the difference between winning and losing a baseball game.

3. The outfielder should make preliminary adjustments in his position according to his knowledge of the pitcher and the hitter. With sufficient experience, he should be able to assume a preliminary defensive position that will give him maximum defensive advantage most of the time. He does this by learning how certain pitchers pitch and how certain hitters hit. If one of his teammates is an exceptionally good fast ball pitcher, the outfielder will want to shade almost every hitter slightly to the opposite field. If his pitcher throws a lot of breaking pitches, the outfielder may want to shade toward the power field. When the outfielder combines this knowledge of his teammate's pitching with knowledge of the opposing hitters, he will be able to determine his best defensive position. Some right-handed hitters prefer to hit to right-center field. Others attempt to pull every pitch down the left-field foul line. The outfielder must make his preliminary adjustments on the basis of such facts. He will not be right 100% of the time, but he will be playing the percentages, and this is intelligent baseball.

4. The outfielder gets a "jump on the ball" by anticipating the direction of the hit according to the type of swing the hitter makes. Getting a jump on the ball is not done by means of some special sixth sense. The good defensive outfielder gets a jump on the ball because he concentrates on the swing that the hitter is making and anticipates the direction of the ball on the basis of how the batter is swinging. With adequate experience and proper concentration, the outfielder will come to know what kind of swing will produce an opposite-field hit and what kind of swing will result in a pulled

hit. This anticipation enables the outfielder to begin his defensive reaction before the ball leaves the bat, thus giving him a jump on the ball.

5. The outfielder should move quickly to the position where he can best field the ball, whether it be a fly ball or a ground ball. He should never "drift" with a fly ball; normally, he should run to the fielding spot. Moving quickly to the spot where the ball will be fielded has two distinct advantages over the "drifting" method. First, the outfielder will be able to set his body and move into the catch. Second, he will be better able to make the last-moment adjustments that might be needed to field the ball successfully. Young outfielders often fall into the habit of drifting with fly balls, especially ones for which they have to move back to make the catch. This is not good technique. The outfielder should turn and run to the spot where he will catch the fly ball. As he runs, he can look over his shoulder to keep the ball in sight. To field a ground ball, the outfielder should also move quickly to the spot where he wants to make the play. Then he can set his body and field the ball. If he attempts to field the ball while moving with a jogging step, the play will be much more difficult than it should be.

6. The outfielder should move into his fielding play whenever he thinks he will have to throw after making the play. When a base runner may attempt to advance after a fielding play in the outfield, the outfielder must combine his fielding of the ball with the beginning of his throw to the infield. On a fly ball, this means that the outfielder, after moving to the spot where he expects the ball to come down, should take three or four steps backward. He can then move his body forward to catch the ball. This forward movement will give him adequate momentum to throw forcefully and quickly to the infield after the catch. If the outfielder catches the fly ball while in a stationary position, he must first build up momentum before he can throw the ball forcefully enough to prevent an advance by a base runner. The time he wastes building momentum lessens the chance for a successful defensive play. By moving into the catch, however, he builds his momentum prior to catching the ball, and, therefore, he can throw to the infield more quickly. The same basic technique should be used when fielding a ground ball. While maintaining correct fielding technique (he should avoid fielding the ball off to the side of his body), the outfielder should move into the ground ball, again building up the momentum for his throw *before* he makes the fielding play.

7. If at all possible, the outfielder should be facing the infield when he catches the ball. In that way, there is less chance that a misplayed ball will get through his position; moreover, he will be in a far better position to make a throw back to the infield. While it is true that some balls will go to one side of the outfielder's body as he moves sideways, or over his shoulder as he moves away from the infield, it is also true that, with a little extra hustle, the outfielders could be facing the infield when they field these balls. Hustle by the outfielder is the key on such a play. The coach must explain to his players why it is to their advantage to field the ball while facing the infield, and he must then constantly encourage the outfielders to put forth the necessary effort to accomplish that goal.

8. The outfielder, especially the center fielder, should not play his position too deep. An outfielder often plays deep because he fears that the ball will be hit over his head and prove embarrassing to him. However, most balls fall in front of the outfielder rather than behind him. Thus, especially if the baseball field has an outfield fence, the outfielder is more effective if he plays a fairly shallow position. The short fly ball, the low line drive, and the "Texas-leaguer" can be more often turned into outs if the fielder plays a relatively shallow outfield position. This is especially true for the center fielder. Center field is not a power field normally. That is, the right-handed and the left-handed power hitters will hit most of their long balls to their power fields (right or left). While there are long balls hit to center field, the great majority of hits to that section are not long drives. The center fielder can, therefore, afford to play even more shallow than the right fielder or the left fielder. If there is no outfield fence, this strategy cannot be used. In that case, the outfielder must be cautious and protect the deep part of the outfield. With or without a fence, some balls will go over the outfielder's head. These balls will be of two kinds: long fly balls, that might stay in the air long enough for the outfielder to move back and field them; and a few long line drives. The latter will go over the fielder's head if he plays shallow, but might be out of his reach anyway. If there is an outfield fence, that will hold the long drives in the park and prevent the hitter from circling the bases.

9. The outfielder should always call — loudly — for any ball that he feels is in his defensive territory; he should never assume that a fly ball, particularly, is his fielding chance alone without informing his teammates. Waving one's arms is not a sufficient method of communication. Whenever there might be some question as to who should field a fly ball, both outfielders and infielders should be communicating with each other. The outfielder has preference over the infielder if the outfielder yells loudly enough for the infielder to hear him. The outfielder should continue to yell "I've got it" or "I'll take it" over and over again; he should not just yell once and assume that his teammates have all heard him. This practice will help prevent collisions between two outfielders, or between an outfielder and an infielder. Such collisions are costly because they occur on batted balls that should be routine putouts for one of the fielders. Adequate communication among the team players is the only way to avoid this type of mistake.

10. The center fielder should have preference on balls hit to right-center field or left-center field. It has already been suggested that the coach should place his best fielder in center because more balls are hit to that position than to either of the other two outfield positions. Thus, it would make sense to have the center fielder field all the balls that he can get to. When there is a question — for example, between the center fielder and the left fielder as to who will handle a ball hit to left-center field — the center fielder should automatically be allowed to field the ball. When the left fielder or right fielder hears the center fielder call for a ball, he should move away from the play and let his teammate handle the fielding chance. This should be team policy, just as giving an outfielder preference over an infielder in

taking a fly ball should be automatic team policy. If such policies are clearly established, and the players yell loudly to each other, the chances of a collision, and therefore an error, are minimized.

11. All outfielders should use the overhand throw as exclusively as possible for throws to the infield. Very few young players throw overhand naturally. Almost all of them throw the baseball with a three-quarters throwing motion. Some even learn to throw sidearm. When a young player begins to participate in competitive baseball, however, he will have to make some adjustments in the skills that he has already developed. One of these adjustments will probably be learning how to throw with an overhand motion. All outfielders should learn this. The reason is obvious. The sidearm and three-quarters throwing motions produce throws which spin in a plane that is different from the vertical plane in which the overhand throw spins. This three-quarters or sidearm spin causes the ball to break or "tail-off," especially when the throw is a long one. While pitchers may find this break desirable, outfielders will not. The outfielder is called upon to throw to a cut-off man or a base; in either case his throw must be as straight as possible. Therefore, he must get the "tail" off his long throws. He does this by throwing with an overhand motion. The coach can aid his outfielders with some technique pointers. He should tell them, for instance, to depress the shoulder of the nonthrowing arm. This will cause the shoulder of the throwing arm to be elevated, thus making it easier for the player to throw with an overarm motion.

12. The outfielder should always aim his throw at the chest of his target—usually the cut-off man. On throws from center field to home plate, for example, the first baseman will be stationed somewhere near the pitching mound to act as a cut-off man. The cut-off man should be aligned so that a throw that reaches him chest high will also be a perfect throw to the base behind him. Therefore, he may catch the ball and throw to any base, or he may let the ball go through to the base behind him. The throw made to his chest has given him these options. If the throw is aimed directly at a base, however, it may or may not give him the option of fielding it. In short, the outfielder contributes to the total defensive play by aiming his throw at the chest of the cut-off man. If he does this, he has done his job well.

13. The outfielder should throw low when no cut-off man is being used. In this case, he must use the base and the player at that base as his target. He should not attempt to throw the ball to the target on the fly. If the ball comes in too high, there will be no chance to field it and the base runner will almost assuredly be safe. On the other hand, the player always has a chance to field the low throw. Thus, the outfielder should throw low enough that the ball will reach the base on the first or second bounce. Even if the ball bounces several times, it will still have some velocity and can be fielded by the player at the base.

14. The outfielder should never hold the ball after fielding it. This is a basic rule of outfield play. There is no situation where an outfielder should hold the ball rather than throw it to a teammate in the infield. He does not necessarily have to rush the ball back to the infield after each play, but he

should not keep it in the outfield. Moreover, if before each play the outfielder has mentally reviewed the defensive options he will have if the ball comes to his position, he should have no trouble throwing to the correct player in the infield.

15. Outfielders should always back each other up, especially on plays in left-center and right-center fields. When the center fielder fields the ball in left-center field, the left fielder should back up the play. The same is true for the right fielder in the right-center field. The center fielder should attempt to back up the left fielder and right fielder also. If this is done as a matter of habit, the defense can often prevent base runners from taking extra bases when a ball gets through one of the outfielders. If an outfielder is backing up his teammates, he can quickly retrieve a misplayed ball and return it to the infield.

16. The outfielder should not attempt a shoe-string catch unless the ball is a pop-fly or unless such a catch would prevent the winning or tying run from scoring. Should he miss such a catch on a pop-fly, the ball would not be far from his position and the situation would not be too serious. He could quickly retrieve the ball and prevent any base runners from advancing. If, however, the ball is a sinking line drive, the outfielder should not attempt a shoe-string catch unless the tying or winning run is at stake. Should be miss the catch on this type of hit, the ball would probably roll all the way to the outfield fence and permit the runners to advance several bases. The number of successful catches on such attempts does not warrant taking this chance unless it will prevent a crucial run from scoring.

17. The outfielder should keep the ball in front of him as he charges it. An outfielder often has to charge a ground ball, field the ball, and make a quick throw to a base. Some outfielders fall into the bad habit of attempting to field these ground balls to one side of their bodies. This is incorrect. The ball should be kept squarely in front of the outfielder's body as he charges it. He can then use good fielding technique to pick up the ball. The outfielder should always remember that he must first cleanly field the ground ball before he can throw it to a teammate. If he does not field it correctly, his second task, throwing, will be meaningless.

18. The outfielder must learn how to use his glove-hand to shield his eyes from the sun on bright days. During the early afternoon, outfielders often encounter what is called a "high sky"—i.e., a cloudless sky with a high sun that can bother all fielders. The right fielder in particular will have to learn how to shield his eyes with his glove-hand, for he will have difficulty not only on the "high-sky" days, but also with a late afternoon sun. If a baseball field is constructed according to the rule book, right field will be the sun field. For high-school and college teams, this is particularly meaningful because they play so many of their games in the late afternoon when the spring sun is going down. During the late innings of such games, the sun will be almost directly in the right fielder's eyes on each play. Shielding one's eyes from the sun with the glove-hand is not a terribly difficult skill, but it must be practiced a great deal because when fielding a fly ball in the sun it is crucial that the fielder have the confidence to stay

with the ball even though it might momentarily be lost from his view. To shield his eyes properly, the outfielder should put his glove-hand straight up and extend his arm fully so that his glove is as far away from his face as possible. This will increase his ability to use the glove and still allow him to scan a wide range with his eyes.

Many outfielders like to use sunglasses. Sunglasses can be a great asset to *those players who have learned how to use them.* It should be emphasized, however, that sunglasses should not be used unless the players have mastered the skills necessary to use them effectively. This requires practice before games. Nothing is more frustrating to a coach than to see an outfielder misjudge a fly ball because he is busy trying to adjust his sunglasses. The sunglasses that a major leaguer uses are far different from those sold inexpensively in a sporting goods store. The major league type will come down into place with a mere nod of the head, but the inexpensive ones need to be pulled down, and sometimes they stick. A basic coaching attitude toward the use of sunglasses by novice players should be "be careful."

19. The outfielder must learn how to play a ball which caroms off the outfield fence. Most high-school and college baseball fields have either snow fences or chain-link fences. Neither of these fences will cause a hit baseball to bounce very far. Many players and coaches have seen a great major league outfielder determine where a ball that has been hit over his head will land after bouncing off the outfield wall and make a great play. Such a situation is not likely to arise on fields that have snow or chain-link fences. In any case, the outfielder will have to find out how each fence plays. The most important thing for him to look for is how tightly the fence is attached to its posts. Often snow fences or chain-link fences can become fairly loose, and in these situations there will be almost no bounce. Then, the outfielder can run right up to the fence and not worry about a ball bouncing off it and rolling toward the infield. When the fence is very tight, however, it will have to be approached with much more caution.

Generally speaking, the outfielder is only called upon to make a limited number of plays during a game. Thus, he must make the most of each play. This means that he must play intelligently. Very few runners, for example, are thrown out at home plate by throws from the outfield. Outfielders, therefore, should concentrate primarily on keeping runners from advancing an extra base on balls hit to their positions. Consequently, hustle and intelligence are the major traits to look for when choosing an outfielder.

Chapter 8
Coaching the Catchers

It is difficult to recall a major league pennant-winning baseball team that did not have a top-flight catcher performing behind the plate. Great teams are often best characterized by their outstanding catchers; Bill Dickey of the Yankees and Roy Campanella of the Dodgers come immediately to mind. Good performance from the catcher is vital. The catcher is the quarterback of the baseball team; he is the leader of the pitching staff; and he is also often a very important team leader. Moreover, he must have good defensive technique, because his defensive play has to win him the confidence of his pitching staff. He must know how to "handle" a pitching staff collectively and each pitcher individually. He must have a great knowledge of opposing hitters as well. If a catcher can master all these techniques and in addition can produce base hits and drive in runs periodically, he will be a huge plus factor for any team.

The baseball coach needs to spend a great deal of time working with his catchers. He must instruct them in effective catching techniques and, perhaps more important, in pitching strategy. If the coach and the catcher have confidence in each other, the catcher can actually act as a "coach on the field." Below are listed principles of performance which should aid coaches in developing good catchers. Additional important information for catchers can also be found in Chapter 14, Pitching Strategy.

Principles of Catching

1. The primary qualifications for successful performance as a catcher are mental and physical toughness, authority, confidence, and a strong throwing arm.
2. With no runners on base, the catcher should use a stance that is comfortable and will provide the best possible target for the pitcher.
3. With runners on base, the catcher should adopt a stance that allows him to make the quick movements needed to stop wild pitches and to release throws quickly.
4. Signs given to the pitcher must be understandable and protected from detection by the opponents.
5. Signs should be simple and adjustable to the situation.
6. There are several methods that catchers can use to provide target areas at which the pitcher can throw.
7. In throwing to a base, the catcher should release the ball as quickly as possible.
8. The pattern of footwork used by the catcher when throwing to a base will depend on the hitter.
9. The catcher must shift his body quickly to block the low pitch and keep it in front of him.
10. The catcher should turn around to field all pop-ups.
11. The catcher should not discard his mask until he knows where the pop-up is coming down.

12. The catcher should field all bunts with both hands and make his throws to the inside part of the first-base line.
13. The catcher should catch each pitch as close to the plate as possible.
14. In bunt situations, the catcher should call the defensive plays in the infield.
15. When tagging a runner out at home plate, the catcher must block the plate.
16. The catcher must move quickly in order to get himself into position to catch a pitch-out or a pitch made during an intentional pass.
17. The catcher is sometimes called upon to force a runner out at home plate and to act as a middleman on a double-play attempt.
18. The catcher must be in charge of the game and instill confidence in his pitchers and teammates.

Discussing the Principles

1. The primary qualifications for successful performance as a catcher are mental and physical toughness, authority, confidence, and a strong throwing arm. A catcher cannot be a timid personality or a person who is physically weak. The position is so demanding that he must be a physically strong person who has a considerable amount of endurance. His legs must be particularly strong. The constant up and down movements and the amount of time spent in the catching stance, which is a squat position, put a great deal of physical stress on the muscular system. The position also requires mental toughness because the successful catcher must be constantly alert and able to quickly recover from the minor setbacks that occur in a baseball game. The foul tip off the bare hand, the ball in the dirt that bounces off the body, and the sore hand from catching too many fast balls are all minor irritations that must be overcome if a catcher is to be successful and inspire confidence in his teammates.

The catcher must also be an authority figure. This does not necessarily mean that he must be a "holler-guy" who exerts a great deal of overt authority, although there are many great catchers who have exhibited this personality characteristic. Authority may also be generated by a quiet personality who merely does his catching job consistently and without fanfare, a person who is the "boss" as a result of quiet and firm handling of pitchers. Regardless of his personality type, however, if the catcher lacks authority with his pitchers and teammates, he will have a difficult time performing successfully in his position. The team must have confidence in its catcher, and to command the respect of his teammates, the catcher must handle his position in an authoritative manner.

In addition, the catcher must have a strong throwing arm. There are methods that catchers who have only fair throwing arms can employ to compensate for the absence of arm strength but there is no compensation for a weak arm. The catcher simply cannot perform adequately if he cannot throw the ball to the various bases with some force.

2. With no runners on base, the catcher should use a stance that is comfortable and will provide the best possible target for the pitcher. First and foremost, the catcher must provide the necessary target for pitchers. As long as his stance accomplishes that, he may catch from whatever position is most comfortable and requires the least physical effort. With no runners on base a comfortable stance can save the catcher a great deal of energy over a nine-inning period. He can thus remain strong and alert for these situations in which he has to move quickly. Some catchers prefer to use a stance in which their weight is evenly distributed, while others favor shifting their weight from one side to the other at various times. Some even go so far as to place one knee on the ground. If the catcher can provide the necessary target in this position, there is no reason why it cannot be used.

3. With runners on base, the catcher should adopt a stance that allows him to make the quick movements needed to stop wild pitches and to throw quickly to bases. With runners on base, the catcher must sacrifice comfort in his stance for efficiency. He cannot be resting or conserving strength. He must be alert and ready, and therefore his stance must be fairly well balanced with his weight evenly distributed so that he may move easily in either direction to block a low pitch. The right foot should be slightly behind the left to enable the catcher to initiate his throwing motion more quickly. In the squat position with no men on base, it is acceptable for the catcher's hips to be below his knees, but with runners on base he must have his hips above the knees for the best mobility. This is a position of readiness. It cannot be emphasized too strongly that when there are runners on base the catcher must catch every pitch as if he were going to throw to a base. He should take the first step of the throwing motion after every pitch. If this procedure becomes automatic, the catcher will always be ready to throw.

4. Signs given to the pitcher must be understandable and protected from detection by the opponents. The basic rule is that the signs should be easily visible to the pitcher but not to the opponents, notably the base coaches, and they should be given slowly. To keep the signs from being seen by the opposing coaches, the catcher, in his squat position, should hang his glove-hand below and outside of his left knee. His right leg should be slightly in front of the left leg to protect the signs from being seen by the first-base coach. If the signs are given with the hand, they should be flashed well back in the crotch, rather than out toward the knees. If these procedures are followed, and the catcher gives the signs slowly enough, no problems should occur.

5. Signs must be simple and adjustable to the situation. The most popular signs are: one finger for the fast ball, two fingers for the curve ball, three fingers for the change-up, and a fist for the pitch-out. Although a coach may choose different signs, there is very seldom any need for more intricate ones. If a team desires intricacy because of a particular situation, such

as when there is a runner on second base who can also see the signs, the objective is best achieved by flashing more than one sign. For example, the catcher might flash one finger, then two fingers, then two fingers again. If his team is taking the first of three signs, the pitch would be a fast ball. If the team is taking the second or third sign, the pitch would be a curve ball. Using multiple signs will generally prevent a base runner from stealing the sign and relaying it to the hitter. When a pitcher throws a change-up fast ball and a change-up curve, more than one sign for the change-up pitch must be used. In that case, the catcher can wiggle his finger or fingers to indicate a change-up. For example, wiggling one finger would signal the change-up fast ball, and wiggling two fingers would mean that a change-up curve ball is wanted.

Frequently, teams will flash one sign telling the pitcher what pitch to throw and another sign telling him where to throw it. This causes the pitcher to concentrate on where he is going to throw the pitch and allows for closer communication between the catcher and the pitcher. The second sign is generally flashed by moving the hand to indicate where the ball should be thrown. To indicate that he wants the pitch to be high or low, the catcher can turn his palm either up or down. To indicate inside or outside, he can touch the leg that corresponds to the side he wishes the pitcher to aim

When flashing signals to the pitcher, the catcher should use his glove-hand to shield the signals from the opposing base coaches.

for. To call for a low, inside fast ball to a right-handed hitter, for example, the catcher would flash one finger, turn his palm down, and finally touch his hand to his left leg.

If a team feels its signals are being stolen by the opponents, the catcher might want to use his glove to flash the signs for a short period of time. The reader will recall that when he is in the squat position, the catcher uses his glove-hand to protect the signs from being seen by the third-base coach. This hand can also be used to flash signs. The glove straight out could signal a fast ball, for instance, and the glove laid flat across the front of the knee could indicate a curve ball. Thus, the catcher can be flashing all sorts of signals with his fingers, but the pitcher will be looking at the glove for his signs. This system is acceptable for limited use but is not flexible enough to be the primary system of flashing signs to the pitcher.

A team should have one set of signs to use when there is no runner on second base, and another set to use when there is a runner on that base. It has been suggested here that the multiple-sign system (with the pitcher ignoring all the signs except the predetermined signal) is probably the easiest and least confusing method to use. However, the coach must make sure that the catcher and pitcher agree on the sets of signals before each game begins. A mix-up early in the game could prove very detrimental until it is corrected.

6. There are several methods that catchers can use to provide target areas at which the pitcher can throw. Most often, a catcher uses the glove as the target, positioning the glove at the spot where he wants the pitcher to throw. This is probably the best method because it is flexible and familiar to most pitchers. The catcher must remember two things when using the glove as a target, however. He must get the target (glove) into position early so that the pitcher sees it all during his pitching motion. He must leave the glove at the desired position until after the pitcher releases the ball. If the glove is brought into position too late or taken away too early, the purpose — helping the pitcher concentrate on where to throw the pitch — will be defeated. Some pitchers prefer to use parts of the catcher's body and equipment as target areas. For example, the shin guards worn by the catcher may be used. Most shin guards are painted in bright colors around the knee area and thus make good targets, especially for pitches aimed at the lower part of the strike zone. When the catcher is in his receiving stance, the knee guard is generally in the lower part of the strike zone, and by aiming at either the left or right knee guard the pitcher can attempt to pitch to the low-inside or low-outside corner of the strike zone. Regardless of what target is used, the important thing is to *have* a definite target and to accustom the pitcher to that target. The catcher must remind his pitchers that this is the function of the target, and he must make sure that his target is in place soon enough and long enough that the pitcher can use it effectively.

7. In throwing to a base, the catcher should release his throw as quickly as possible. Young catchers too often attempt to imitate the hard "clothesline" throw made by strong-armed professional catchers. To do this, the young catcher will take an extra sliding step before he releases his throw.

The extra step enables him to build up momentum and thus throw the ball harder. While this technique may result in a "picture-book" throw, it does not often lead to a putout because the time expended in taking the extra step is usually sufficient to allow the runner to reach his intended base safely. Therefore, the catcher should make his primary goal a quick release of the throw. To accomplish this, he can seldom afford to take more than one step in this throwing motion, and his stance should be such that he will always be ready to throw after each pitch. If he uses these guidelines, he can be a good throwing catcher without necessarily being able to make the "clothesline" throw to the base. Moreover, once he has developed a technique that enables him to release the ball quickly, then he can begin to work on making a more forceful throw.

It is difficult to tell exactly when a catcher should begin to shift his feet in preparation for throwing to a base. The professional catcher probably begins to shift his feet a fraction of a second *before* he catches the pitch, especially if he sees or is informed that the base runner is attempting to steal. (His teammates should always inform the catcher whenever a base runner is attempting to steal, and they should do this in loud and clear terms.)

8. The pattern of footwork used by the catcher when throwing to a base will depend on the hitter. In the catching stance, the catcher's right foot is frequently placed slightly behind his left foot. In most throwing situations, the catcher will want to plant his right foot as he catches the pitch and step

In certain situations, the catcher should provide a relatively low target for his pitcher.

forward with his left foot to throw. Additional steps will only increase the total time it takes for the ball to get to the base. There are situations, however, when a catcher needs to use footwork that is slightly more intricate than the one-step method generally recommended. Against a left-handed hitter, for example, the catcher will often have to take a quick side step with his rear (right) foot in order to avoid colliding with the hitter while making his throw. Another situation that requires an extra short step with the rear foot occurs when a pitch is far outside. The catcher will have to shift his feet to move over and catch such a pitch. Moreover, the catcher will no doubt have to take the side step in almost all situations when throwing to third base. With a right-handed hitter, the side step will be to the right, and with a left-handed hitter, the side step will be to the left. Again, this is done in order that the catcher will be far enough away from the hitter that the hitter will not interfere with the throwing motion. The extra side step is always detrimental time-wise, but it is not so serious when the throw is to third base because that throw is relatively short.

9. The catcher must shift his body quickly to block the low pitch and keep it in front of him. Pitchers often throw curve balls that break downward so sharply that they go into the dirt. Such pitches are also often outside the strike zone, thus requiring the catcher to move to either the right or the left to block them. If the catcher is lazy and does not reposition himself quickly so that his body is directly in front of the ball, the ball may bounce off his chest protector or glove and go back toward the screen, thus allowing an advance by any runners on base. In order to block the ball correctly, the catcher must move so that the front of his body is perpendicular to the path of the incoming pitch. Then if the ball bounces off his chest protector, it will go directly in front of his body where he can keep it in clear view, retrieve it quickly, and prevent a base runner from taking an extra base. To achieve this correct position, however, the catcher must hustle and he must move his entire body. If he steps out with just one foot, his body will not be perpendicular to the path of the incoming pitch, and the blocking of the ball will not yield favorable results.

10. The catcher should turn around (so that he is facing the same direction as the other fielders) to field all pop-ups. This is because any ball popped-up in the general area of the catcher's position will have a great deal of spin on it. This spin will cause the ball to move toward the infield. Thus, if the catcher does not turn around to field the pop-up, the ball will curve away from him, and such a ball is always more difficult to catch than one that is curving toward him. The catcher should follow this rule even for the pop-up in front of the plate, where he might attempt to field the ball by merely moving forward without turning around.

11. The catcher should not discard his mask until he knows where the pop-up is coming down. Once he has determined this and has turned around to make the play, then, and not before, he can discard his mask by throwing it far to one side of his body. If a catcher does this before he sees where the pop-up is going, he runs the risk of stumbling over the discarded mask. This basic technique should become automatic with even the youn-

gest catchers; it should be taught as the only correct method for fielding pop-ups from the catcher's position.

12. The catcher should field all bunts with both hands, and he should make his throws to the inside part of the first-base line. The catcher's glove is not designed for fielding ground balls, nor is it good technique for a catcher to attempt to field a bunt with his bare hand. Rather, he must use both his glove-hand and his bare hand. He should bring his hands together as he fields the ball so that the fielded bunt does not pop out of the glove-hand. In throwing to a base, he should always use the short turn instead of the long turn. If he has moved toward third base to field a bunt, he should turn to his right to set himself for the throw. If he turns to his left, he will lose sight of his target. The throw should be to the inside part of the first-base line. This will prevent the ball from hitting the runner moving toward first base, and it will also give the player covering first base the easiest play. If the first baseman has to cross over in front of an approaching runner to field a throw to the foul side of the baseline, he will have a difficult time following the ball and may commit an error.

13. The catcher should catch each pitch as close to the plate as possible, i.e., he should catch the ball as quickly as possible. This will enable him to throw to a base quickly, and perhaps more important, it will make the ball appear to be farther inside the strike zone than if it were caught at a greater distance behind the plate. This is especially true for breaking pitches, which will often curve well outside the strike zone if not caught until they have neared the catcher's body. To make sure that the umpire gets the truest picture of the pitch, then, the catcher should catch the ball near the strike zone and with his arms extended.

14. In bunting situations, the catcher should call the defensive plays in the infield. Whenever a bunt occurs with men on base, the defense is faced with several options. The biggest decision concerns whether an attempt should be made to put out the lead runner or whether the throw should be made to first base. The throw to first is usually the safest out, and this important consideration should never be neglected. The catcher is the player who should make the decisions in all such situations. When the third baseman, pitcher, or first baseman fields the ball, the catcher should tell him immediately and clearly where to make his throw. The decision must be made instantaneously and with no hesitation. Any hestiation or timidity will often result in losing the chance to make a putout. The catcher must make sure that he yells loud enough so that there is no confusion. It is usually enough merely to yell out the base to which the throw should be made—"third," for example, or "first."

The coach should work with his catchers so much that their decisions on the field reflect his defensive philosophy. Some coaches prefer to be aggressive on defense and to take the chance to cut down the lead runner in bunt situations. Other coaches prefer to play it safe and get the sure out at first base. The important point, as far as the coach is concerned, is that the catcher's decision should reflect the coach's defensive strategy.

15. When tagging a runner out at home plate, the catcher must block the

plate. The rule book states that the catcher may not block the plate before he has the ball. As he fields the throw, therefore, he must move into the baseline and drop to one knee, using his shinguard to block the baseline. This will enable him to block the incoming runner without getting spiked in the process. The ball should be held securely in the glove-hand and covered with the free hand. The catcher should put the glove down with the back of it facing the incoming runner. It the throw comes from the left-field side of second base, the catcher should stand inside the diamond to take it. Once he has the throw, he should move into the baseline, drop to his right knee, and use his right shinguard for protection. When the throw comes from the right-field side of second base, he should stand in foul territory along the third-base line. In blocking the plate after a throw from the right, he must drop to his left knee.

16. The catcher must move quickly in order to get himself into position to catch a pitch-out or a pitch made during an intentional pass. Both the pitch-out and the intentional-pass pitch are purposely thrown far enough outside of the strike zone that the hitter cannot hit them. The catcher knows about each situation before it occurs and he must move quickly to catch the ball in front of his body. The pitch-out is, of course, the more difficult for the catcher as he has to hide his intentions until the last moment. The pitch-out should always be a high, outside fast ball. This pitch is the easiest for the catcher to field and to throw quickly after fielding. The intentional pass is not as serious a situation although it, too, requires hustle. When a batter is being walked intentionally, the catcher should use his arm to provide an outside target for the pitcher. He should stand up rather than go into his crouch, and he should hold his arm straight out to the side so the pitcher will know where to throw the ball. After the pitcher has released the pitch, the catcher must move quickly outside to field it. He must hustle so that he will catch each pitch in a good defensive position.

17. The catcher is sometimes called upon to force a runner out at home plate and to act as a middleman on a double play. When such situations occur, the catcher should stand in front of homeplate. As he catches the ball, he should tag the plate with his left foot, step out with his right foot, and make a half-pivot so he is facing first base. This will enable him to keep any throw to first well inside the baseline, thus avoiding any possibility that the ball might hit the runner.

18. The catcher must be in charge of the game and instill confidence in his pitchers and teammates. This can be accomplished partially if the catcher merely follows the principles of technique suggested in this chapter. In addition to good technique, however, the catcher must also command the respect of and have authority over his teammates, especially the pitchers. The timid catcher will find it difficult to successfully execute his responsibility as a team leader. While the catcher does not necessarily have to be an outgoing, aggressive personality, he does have to assert himself. His relationship with his pitchers must be one of mutual respect and confidence. If he does not have the confidence of his pitching staff, the pitchers will tend to "second guess" him whenever an opposing player gets

a key hit. The catcher must also be able to communicate with his pitchers not only before games when they should discuss pitching strategy, but also during the game. A pitcher may have a streak of wildness, and it is the catcher who can do the most to bring him back on target. A pitcher may get upset after an error by a teammate or a key hit by an opponent. Again, the catcher must be able to calm him down and get his mind back on the task at hand. To do all this, the catcher must know his pitchers well and be able to treat them as individuals, and he must have their respect and confidence so that what he says to them will be effective.

It is impossible to list principles to direct the catcher in his attempts to psychologically relate to his pitchers and to his teammates so that he may better command the game. Each situation that arises will call for a different strategy. Perhaps it is most important that the catcher recognize his role in the total team defense, especially as it relates to his handling of the pitching staff.

The catcher must sometimes choose between developing his strategy on the basis of the hitter or on the basis of the pitcher. When a hitter is jittery and nervous, the catcher should handle him slowly. When a hitter likes to take his time, the catcher should attempt to speed up the game. The catcher cannot, however, ignore his pitcher when making such decisions. He must know how speeding up or slowing down the game will affect the pitcher.

The catcher must also make decisions about individual pitches. When the pitcher's strength is the hitter's weakness, the proper course of action is easily determined. When the hitter is a good fast ball hitter, however, and the pitcher is a fast ball pitcher, the decision becomes more difficult. (Most baseball coaches feel that when all is said and done, the pitcher must pitch with his strength—even if this means challenging the strength of the hitter.) Needless to say, all these factors make the position of catcher one of the most important positions on the baseball team.

Chapter 9
Coaching
the
Hitters

This chapter deals primarily with methods and techniques for improving performances in the complex baseball skill of hitting. The fundamentals of hitting have already been discussed in Chapter 3. Basic consideration in that chapter was given to batting stance, hand position, head position, the hitting stride, vision as it relates to hitting, and other matters of direct concern to a fundamental understanding of the factors influencing successful performance in hitting. This chapter takes the reader beyond those fundamentals and into the realm of coaching hitters to achieve a higher level of performance. Here, we will deal with the coach as an aid in the total "feedback" mechanisms present in the learning environment. Feedback refers to information about performance that can be immediately or latently returned to the performer so that he can better modify his skill strategies and improve his performance. If the coach is to act as the primary source of *beneficial* information feedback, he must be able to separate important information concerning performance from unimportant information. This is true because too much information feedback to the sports performer will tend to inhibit his performance rather than improve it. The coach must choose his information carefully, and make sure that it is the kind of information that will aid, not inhibit, the hitter in his attempts to improve his performance. Below are suggested principles of performance that can act as guides for the coach as he attempts to bring about a higher level of skill in his hitters.

Principles of Coaching Hitters

1. The hitter must think aggressively.
2. Part of becoming a good hitter is overcoming the fear of being hit by a thrown baseball.
3. Young hitters should place great emphasis on bat control.
4. The successful hitter learns what pitches he should attempt to hit.
5. Good hitters compensate for different pitchers, game situations, field conditions, and weather elements.
6. Hitting power may be increased in three important ways.
7. Hitting the ball where it is pitched requires moving the front shoulder in the direction of the pitch during the hitting stroke.
8. There are several methods by which the hitter can increase his ability to hit the curve ball.
9. The successful hitter picks up information about the incoming pitch at the earliest possible moment.
10. Guess hitting, or attempting to outguess the pitcher, is acceptable for all hitters in certain situations, but should vary according to the pitcher.
11. There are at least seven major batting errors, which, when spotted, should be corrected by the coach as quickly as possible.
12. Research studies have detected certain consistencies in the hitting strategies of successful baseball players.

Discussing the Principles

1. The hitter must think aggressively. It is for this reason that both Chapter 3 and this chapter talk about "hitting" rather than "batting." The important question for the coach is how does he help his hitters become more aggressive without having them turn into overswingers who go after any pitch regardless of how good or bad it is. We believe that the attitude of the coach is crucial to the player's attitude toward hitting. Thus it is important that a constructive attitude be displayed by the coach and reflected in his coaching strategies. He must make absolutely sure that his players know what type of attitude he wants them to have. This must be made clear in what the coach says and does. A good start can be made in batting practice. The hitter who allows a good pitch (to be defined more fully later in this chapter) to go by in batting practice ought to face some mild penalty such as a reduction in the number of swings allotted to him. Aggressive hitting must also become automatic in actual game situations. No coach can hope to instill and maintain a team attitude toward aggressive hitting if, for example, he has his hitters constantly take the 2 – 0 pitch and the 3 – 1 pitch during a game. This attitude must also be a consideration in how the coach expects his team to hit when the count is 0 – 0. While the "take-up-to-one-strike" strategy might be appropriate for certain game situations, it is difficult to employ this strategy often and still expect the team to maintain an aggressive attitude toward hitting. Both in practice and in games, then, the coach must be sure that a belief in an aggressive attitude toward hitting is reflected in his coaching techniques and strategies.

2. Most young baseball players have an outright fear of a hard thrown ball. The neuromuscular system of the body reacts with a protective reflex mechanism whenever a projectile is thrown at or near the body. The overwhelming majority of players who advance to the higher levels of competition, while maintaining a respect for a baseball thrown near to their bodies, have overcome this fear of the ball, however. They have conditioned themselves not to reflexively pull away from a pitch unless they know that that pitch is dangerously close to their body. What is obvious and important for the coach to know is that these players have *learned* to inhibit this reflex movement. Therefore, he must aid and encourage this learning process, particularly with younger players who have not had enough experience in baseball to be able to discriminate between a pitch that is potentially dangerous and one that is not. Young hitters who tend to pull away from the curve ball also have to learn this discrimination.

The coach can help his players overcome this fear in several ways. First, he can verbally explain several informative facts. For example, he can state that a player with normal vision and normal neuromuscular coordination can usually react quickly enough to avoid being hit by a ball. He can add that the protective helmets used in today's competition greatly lessen the chance of any serious injury. These admonitions, however, are usually not effective by themselves. The reason for this is that the necessary discrimination cannot be learned through verbal instruction alone. The player must also have guidance in experiencing the situations. One effective method is to have each hitter stand in the batter's box and watch pitches go by without swinging at them. He can thus watch the curve ball, for example, without having to worry about hitting it. He can concentrate completely on learning the perceptual discrimination. After this is learned, he can then attempt to hit the pitches. The coach must realize that making the perceptual discrimination and hitting the pitch are two separate tasks. They are closely related in terms of total performance, but they can, and probably should, be learned separately — particularly by the young hitter.

3. Young hitters should place great emphasis on bat control, that is, the ability of the hitter to control the use of his bat in order to meet differing needs and situations. First of all, the young hitter should use a bat that he *can* control. The bat should not be so long or so heavy that it prevents him from exercising control over it during the hitting stroke. Bat control also means using the bat differently to meet differing situations. It means that the hitter can, when he wants to, alter his batting stroke to either pull the ball or hit the ball to the opposite field. The concept of bat control is of fundamental importance to successful hitting. When there is a runner on second base and nobody out, the hitter may want to make sure that he hits the ball on the ground to the right side of the infield. Whether he is a left-handed or a right-handed hitter, this task requires that he be able to exercise enough control in his hitting stroke to effectively complete this particular hitting task. The only way to achieve this kind of bat control is to allow for practice time in which these techniques can be learned. Periodically, during batting practice, the coach should designate the area of the field to which he wants the hitters to hit the ball. He may suggest that they attempt to hit every pitch through the middle of the diamond, for instance, or he may require them to hit the ball on the ground to the right side of the infield. By defining carefully the place where the hit should go, the coach sets the stage for effective practice in the important technique of bat control.

The successful hitter learns what pitches he should attempt to hit. It was suggested in Chapter 3 (see principle eighteen) that a knowledge of the strike zone is fundamental to successful hitting. An accurate knowledge of the strike zone also helps the hitter to learn what are the best pitches for him to hit. Good pitches to hit are not necessarily pitches that are within the boundaries of the strike zone. Indeed — and this point is an important one for coaches to recognize — a fast ball that is chest high and just off the inside of the strike zone may be an excellent pitch for most hitters to swing at. Likewise, a curve ball that is in the low-outside part of the strike zone is a poor pitch to swing at, even though it is technically a strike. Each hitter must analyze his own strengths and weaknesses in terms of hitting pitches that are in certain areas. The coach can also offer valuable assistance by carefully watching each hitter during both batting practice and game situations. Together, they may find that the hitter is a high-ball hitter who likes to pull the inside pitch, or they may discover that the hitter likes to go to the opposite field. The first of these hitters will want to lay off the outside pitch and look for the inside pitch. The latter should lay off the pitch that "jams" him, and look for the pitch that is on the outside half of the plate. When pitchers, too, possess this kind of knowledge about each hitter, the battle between pitcher and hitter becomes a matter of who will make the first mistake.

5. Good hitters compensate for different pitchers, game situations, field type and conditions, and weather elements. The successful hitter learns to adopt different strategies to meet the requirements of each particular situation. Earlier (see Chapter 3), it was suggested that the successful hitter may slightly modify his stance and stride to accomplish different tasks. To exhaust all the possible situations that might call for different hitting strategies would require a book in itself. Several will be suggested here, and each coach will be able to create his own list of additional situations. The hitter should choke-up and initiate his stride more quickly against an overpowering fast ball pitcher. Against the "junk" pitcher, the hitter should wait as long as possible before initiating his hitting stroke. Putting the weight on the front foot in the stance is one technique thought to be successful in helping the hitter to wait. When his team is behind in a game, the hitter must attempt to get on base in any way he can. This will cause a modification in his hitting strategy. With a man on second base and nobody out, the hitter should attempt to hit the ball on the ground toward right field. For the

A line-drive hitter tends to lean forward during the hitting motion.

right-handed hitter, this means moving his front shoulder toward the outside part of the plate and modifying the direction of his stride. It also
means using a shorter hitting stroke in which the downward movement of
the bat is emphasized; this will insure that the hit is a ground ball. The type
and condition of field can also affect hitting strategy. If the infield is hard
and the grass is cut short, the hitter should try to hit the ball on the ground.
The hard grounder on this type of infield has an excellent chance of getting
through to the outfield for a base hit. If the outfield fences are short, the
hitter may want to hit the ball in the air with more force than usual. To do
this, he might grip the bat near the knob and use a hitting stroke that is
slightly upward in direction.

Many coaches disagree with the idea of using modified hitting strategies
that is proposed in this chapter. They argue that hitters should swing with
the same stroke at all times. Even when there is a short outfield fence,
these coaches believe the hitter should just use his regular stroke, and the
home runs will take care of themselves. This position has some merit. Hitters should never be so conscious of a particular goal that it upsets their
hitting concentration, as sometimes happens when hitters attempt "to go
for the fences." Nevertheless, this problem does not refute the wisdom of
adopting different hitting strategies for different situations. There are times
when the hitter should attempt to hit the ball to right field, keep the ball on
the ground, or even go for a short fence. The important thing is that the
coach must learn how hitting strategies can be modified to achieve different
goals. Moreover, the coach cannot merely ask a player to hit the ball to the
opposite field. He must be able to *show* the player *how* to hit the ball to

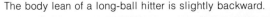

The body lean of a long-ball hitter is slightly backward.

that field. To do this he must have a thorough understanding of the techniques of the various hitting strategies.

6. Hitting power may be increased in at least three ways. Whenever an implement (such as a bat) is used to impart force to a projectile (such as a baseball), principles of leverage may be applied to the situation. The body and the implement, as an extension of the body, act as a lever in the application of force. This force may be increased through efficient application of leverage principles in three important ways. First, the length of the lever may be increased. That is, a longer bat will impart greater force to the ball – other factors being equal – than will a shorter bat. Second, the distance through which the lever moves in the application of force may be increased. This principle comes into play in the use of the body in the hitting stroke. The backward rotation of the hips and shoulders allows the hitter to increase the distance through which his bat moves in the hitting stroke. The closed stance (see Chapter 3) is a definite aid in utilization of this principle. Third, the amount of leverage exerted may be increased by increasing the speed of the lever. Thus, the faster the bat is moving, the more force is being applied. It has already been suggested that the speed of the bat is the most important component in the generation of hitting power. Leverage, in hitting, therefore, can be increased by quickly moving a long bat through a wide arc. It should be noted here that these principles are not universally applicable to all hitters. Singles hitters, for instance, are not primarily concerned with the generation of more force. But to the young hitter attempting to increase his range and flexibility, they can be of great value.

7. Hitting the ball where it is pitched requires moving the front shoulder in the direction of the pitch during the hitting stroke. It has long been suggested that to meet the ball where it is pitched, the hitter should move his stride foot in the direction of the pitch. Thus, a right-handed hitter would have to stride toward right field in order to hit an outside pitch to the right side of the diamond. This is impossible to do unless the hitter has decided before the pitch is thrown to stride in that particular direction. He simply does not have enough time to decide where to move his stride foot after seeing where the pitch is going. The average high-school hitter probably has less than three-quarters of a second to react to a pitched baseball. From one-fifth to one-third of this time is taken up in the physical transmission of the nerve impulses that combine to make the reaction time. The time necessary to complete the stride far surpasses the less than one-half of a second that remains in this situation. The obvious truth is that the hitter begins his stride early in the total pitching movement, often before the pitcher releases the ball. High-speed movies have clearly shown that most hitters stride to exactly the same spot on each pitch. They do not make adjustments in their stride according to where the ball is pitched. What then makes a hitter able to hit the ball where it is pitched? Movement of the front shoulder during the hitting stroke is responsible for this. The pull-hitter will "open up" the front shoulder regardless of where the pitch is going. The hit-the-ball-where-it-is-pitched hitter will move his front shoul-

der toward the outside pitch, and open up the front shoulder only for the inside pitch. Thus, the ability to hit the ball to all fields can be developed by advantageous use of the front shoulder in the hitting stroke.

8. Many young hitters have a great deal of trouble hitting the curve ball. In fact, many major-league hitters have the same difficulty. It is rare to find a hitter who hits the curve ball better than he hits the fast ball ("curve ball" being broadly defined here to include other breaking pitches such as the slider and the screw ball). There are several methods by which the coach can help his hitters have better success in hitting the curve ball. First and perhaps most important, he can schedule adequate practice against curve ball pitching. Many young hitters simply do not get enough of this type of practice—primarily because coaches often do not allow their regular pitchers to pitch batting practice. Other squad members or second-line pitchers handle the batting practice chores. These batting practice pitchers usually do not have even average curve balls, let alone sharply breaking curves. This means that in a game situation, the hitter is attempting to hit a curve ball that is very different from those he has been hitting in batting practice sessions. For professional players who play daily in game situations, this is not a serious problem, but high-school and college players often have only two games a week. It is important, therefore, that these hitters see reasonably good curve balls during the practice session.

A second method for helping batters to hit the curve ball more effectively is to have them put the bulk of their weight on their front foot in the hitting stance. In this way the hitter will be less inclined to pull away from the curve ball, and he will tend to curb the premature shifting of weight that makes that pitch difficult to hit with any appreciable force.

A third method that has recently been used (Ken Harrelson used this techniques will reveal that they accomplish similar purposes. In each case, the purpose is to help the hitter wait as long as possible before committing ground. In the hitting stance, this technique allows the hitter to maintain the stance for the longest possible time before initiating his stride, thus giving him the best chance to successfully wait for the curve ball. While the last two methods seem to be directly opposite, careful inspection of the two techniques will reveal that they accomplish similar purposes. In each case, the purpose is to help the hitter wait as long as possible before committing himself in his hitting stroke. This allows him the best possible look at the curve ball.

9. The successful hitter picks up information about the incoming pitch at the earliest possible moment. In psychological terms, the pitcher and the pitch represent a total stimulus situation to which the hitter must respond. It has been previously noted that the pitch takes only about one-half second to reach home plate after it is released. Most hitters glean their information concerning the pitch from the actual flight of the ball and the path that it follows. However, it is extremely helpful if the hitter can pick up pertinent information about the pitch before the ball is released. What the hitters want to determine is what kind of pitch is being thrown and whether it is a good pitch to swing at. These are really two separate pieces of infor-

mation. If one of those things (the type of pitch) can be determined early, the hitter has a much simpler reaction response to make because he only has to decide whether or not the pitch is a good one to swing at. He may notice, for example, that the pitcher throws the curve ball from a higher position than he does the fast ball. Naturally, this kind of early information gives the hitter much more time to make the necessary adjustments so that his response can be successful. For this reason, coaches should carefully study both the opposing pitchers and their own for any mannerisms or changes in delivery that might act as tip-offs to what kind of pitch is planned.

10. Guess hitting, or attempting to outguess the pitcher, is a controversial practice. Some coaches believe that the hitter should almost always be set for the fast ball and take his chances with the other pitches. We feel that guess hitting is acceptable for all hitters in certain situations. To explain, a pitcher may throw an average of 110 pitches in a nine-inning game. If a certain pitcher normally throws 90 fast balls and 20 curve balls in such a game, it is a good policy for all hitters who face him to guess that in most situations a fast ball will be thrown. Likewise, if observation of a certain pitcher indicates that he relies on the fast ball with a 2 – 0 count on the batter, it is a good guess that a fast ball will be thrown in this situation. Many other like examples could be cited. What becomes obvious is that, in this sense, guessing, or guess hitting, does not mean that the hitter is relying on pure chance. Rather, it means that he uses observed information to make intelligent estimates about the probability that a certain type of pitch will be thrown in a certain situation. He is employing "educated" guesses. To do this successfully, hitters and coaches must closely observe opposing pitchers to determine patterns of pitching and frequency of use of pitches. This means that pitching charts must be kept so that this information can be accurately gathered and used. The hitter who has made careful observations and has made an intelligent guess on the basis of this information may be fooled on occasion, but more often he will have a definite advantage in that he will have prior knowledge about what is being thrown to him. Naturally, the pitcher who has an assortment of pitches and mixes them up well presents a formidable problem to the hitter. Here, the probability of guessing correctly is not high enough to warrant the use of this hitting strategy.

11. Coaches differ on what they consider to be major batting faults. The present authors consider these seven problems in hitting to be of major concern:

1. Use of a bat or style that does not fit the capabilities of player.
2. Fear of the ball.
3. Early stride.
4. Overly long stride.
5. Holding the bat too loosely.
6. Overswinging.
7. Pulling the head away.

Several of these errors have already been discussed in this chapter or in Chapter 3. It has already been suggested that each hitter must use a bat and develop a style that fits his abilities and goals as a hitter. It has also been suggested that fear of being hit by a pitched ball can be overcome, and several methods for doing this have been discussed.

Turning to the third batting error, it is a fact that many young hitters stride too soon; that is, they initiate their stride too early. The early or premature stride causes inefficient use of generated force, and it makes the hitter susceptible to off-speed pitches. The legs, hips, shoulders, arms, and wrists of the successful hitter all build up force during the hitting stroke. In biomechanical language, this refers to the efficient summation of forces. To achieve maximum efficiency, each new force must come into play at the height of the build-up of the previous part of the movement. The efficiency of the total movement is heavily dependent upon the initiation of the buildup of force in the first part of the movement, which in the hitting stroke is the stride movement. If the stride starts too soon, the generated force will have been expended before the actual swing takes place. The early stride is also a serious error because it makes the hitter susceptible to the off-speed pitch — again because the generated force is used up. Thus, the hitter may lean way out on his front foot trying to hit the change-up. But, he has no force left in his hitting stroke, and even if he contacts the ball with the "fat" part of the bat, it is unlikely that the resulting hit will have enough force to be a base hit.

In addition, hitters often use too long a stride. The stride may not be too early, but because it is too long it does not allow the hitter to make the most efficient use of the force generated in his hitting stroke. Most major league hitters have short strides, six to twelve inches in length. The coach should have each hitter check the length of his stride during batting practice. This can be accomplished easily if the hitter will draw a line to indicate where his front foot is in his hitting stance and measure how far from this line his foot is after he has made his stride.

Holding the bat too loosely is another serious hitting error. A ball traveling 70–90 miles per hour has a great deal of force; a 34-ounce bat swung by a 180-pound hitter generates even more force. Newton's third law suggests that for every action there is an equal and opposite reaction. This means that, other things being equal, a faster pitched ball can be hit farther than a slower pitched ball. This, however, is dependent upon the force of the ball not being dissipated when it contacts the bat. A loosely held bat tends to dissipate the force and weaken the resulting hit. The bat must be held as firmly as possible upon contact so that the force can be fully employed to give impetus to the ball.

12. Research studies have detected certain consistencies in the hitting strategies of successful baseball players. Breen[1] took high-speed films of six outstanding major league hitters (Ernie Banks, Ted Williams, Stan Musial, Henry Aaron, Willie Mays, and Mickey Mantle). Analyzing these films, he found five consistencies in hitting style. First, the center of gravity followed a relatively level plane throughout the swing. This suggested two

[1]James L. Breen, *Journal of the American Association for Health, Physical Education, and Recreation* Vol. 38 (April 1967): 36.

things: 1) that the stride was fairly short because a long stride would lower the center of gravity, and 2) that the knees were slightly flexed in the stance so that the resulting extension of the knees during the stride could keep the center of gravity on a level plane. Second, Breen found that the head was adjusted for each pitch so that the hitter could get the best possible look at the ball. Third, it was found that the lead forearm was straightened immediately at the onset of the hitting stroke. This resulted in a greater velocity in the hitting implement. Fourth, it was seen, as has been seen in many other studies, that the length of the hitting stride was generally the same for all pitches. Fifth, it was found that after the ball was contacted, the upper body was pointed in the same direction as the flight of the ball, thus necessarily placing the hitter's weight on his front foot. This lends credence to the idea that the front shoulder should move in the direction of the ball in successful hitting styles.

Chapter 10
Coaching the Pitchers

Baseball experts agree that a strong pitching staff is the single most important factor in building a successful baseball team. The experts feel that pitching strength is responsible for more than 50 percent of the total team effectiveness, and some have even gone so far as to suggest that pitching is 90 percent of the game. The disagreement over the degree of importance attached to pitching is superfluous to successful coaching if the coach recognizes the basic importance of pitching strength in the make-up of his team. A glance through the record books lends credibility to the statement that "good pitching will always beat good hitting." In recent years, World Series games and All-Star games have been dominated by good pitching. Pitting strength against strength, it seems that the hitter is at a disadvantage when facing a good pitcher. A basic understanding of the fundamentals underlying successful performance as a pitcher, then, is of great importance in successful baseball coaching. Some basic consideration has already been given to throwing the baseball (see Chapter 1), and principles pertaining to that skill should be reviewed before reading of this chapter. Pitching strategy and the more sophisticated aspects of coaching pitchers will appear in Chapter 14.

Principles of Pitching

1. In the preparatory pitching stance, the ball of the pivot foot should be on the front edge of the rubber, with all of the front spikes in front of the rubber.
2. The toe of the pivot foot should be angled toward the baseline.
3. The pivot foot should be positioned on the end of the rubber.
4. The pitcher should be in a relaxed position when he receives the signal.
5. The baseball should be kept hidden so that the desired grip may be established undetected.
6. The various styles of winding-up have more to do with establishing rhythm than with adding force to the pitch.
7. The weight shift in the full wind-up is forward-backward-forward, while in the no-wind style it is backward-forward.
8. The degree of leg lift and kick is largely a matter of personal preference.
9. The pivot should be made when the weight is toward the rear foot.
10. The type of delivery is determined by the degree of body lean, not by the position of the pitching arm in relation to the body.
11. Regardless of the style of delivery used, the pitcher should fully extend his arm to the rear in order to lengthen the arm lever as much as possible.
12. Bending to the rear or turning the hips increases the distance through which the arm lever moves, thus adding force to the pitch.
13. The push-off from the rubber should be vigorous without throwing the pitcher off balance.

14. The stride should be taken in a straight line from the point of pivot to home plate.
15. The stride should be vigorous and long without overextending the pitcher.
16. The stride foot should land on the toe, and the toe should point directly toward home plate.
17. The follow-through should be smooth and complete with the pitcher ending in a "squared-out" stance.
18. The baseball should be gripped securely in the fingers such that most of the undersurface of the first two fingers is in contact with the ball.
19. The two basic grips are the cross-seams grip and the with-seams grip.
20. The four basic pitches are the fast ball, the curve ball, the slider, and the change-up.
21. Holding the fingers closer together in the grip usually allows the pitcher to have more "stuff."
22. Factors contributing to the force behind the pitch include leg extension, hip rotation, shoulder medial rotation, wrist flexion, and wrist and forearm pronation.
23. Successful pitching technique employs the stretch reflex and the cross-extensor reflex.
24. In throwing all pitches, the pitcher should concentrate on achieving a sharp, downward break of the wrist.
25. For breaking pitches, the grip is moved slightly off-center and the axis of the ball is slightly turned.
26. While there are many techniques for throwing change-ups, most pitchers will achieve the desired effect by merely using the same motion and technique they use for other pitches, but throwing the ball more slowly.

Discussing the Principles

1. In the preparatory pitching position, the ball of the pivot foot should be on the front edge of the rubber, with all of the front spikes in front of the rubber. This will make the pivot movement as easy as possible and lessen the chances of the pitcher's being thrown off balance by catching his front spikes on the rubber as he pivots. The young pitcher sometimes puts his entire foot on top of the pitching rubber and thereby loses his balance during his pitching motion. This threat is especially serious if the pitching mound has not been adequately cared for and a hole has been worn in front of the pitching rubber.

2. The toe of the pivot foot should be angled toward the baseline. The right-handed pitcher should angle his toe toward the third-base line, and the left-handed pitcher should angle it toward the first-base line. This slight angling of the pivot foot enables the pitcher to make his pivot movement without strain. If the pivot foot is pointed directly toward home plate in the preparatory pitching stance, the resulting pivot will be a full 90-degree

movement. By slightly angling his pivot foot, the pitcher can cut this down to an approximately 45-degree movement. The pivot can then be accomplished with less strain and less chance of losing the pitching rhythm. The preliminary angling of the pivot foot in no way lessens either the force generated in the motion or the accuracy of the pitch.

3. The pivot foot should be positioned on the end of the rubber. For example, the right-handed pitcher should position his pivot foot so that it is at the third-base end of the pitching rubber. Although this need not be viewed as a hard and fast rule, it is a good principle to follow because it allows the pitcher to make the most of all his pitches, especially his breaking pitches. By pitching from this position, he interferes with the angle of the hitter's vision. It will be particularly hard for the hitter to follow the breaking pitches. Again, this technique in no way hinders either the generation of force in the pitching motion or the resulting accuracy of the pitch.

4. The pitcher should be in a relaxed position when he receives the signal from his battery mate. The preparatory stance of the pitcher should be, above all else, one in which the pitcher feels comfortable and relaxed. Relaxation of the neuromuscular system between pitches is essential to successful performance over a seven- or nine-inning stretch. This might be an upright standing position, or it may be a position in which the pitcher bends at the waist, placing his hands against his legs for support. The important point is that the stance is comfortable.

The proper foot position on the pitching rubber for a left-handed pitcher.

5. The ball should be kept hidden so that the desired grip may be established undetected. Most pitchers modify their grips slightly for each pitch in their repertoire. This means that a different grip must be established for each pitch thrown. This should be done before the pitcher goes into his pitching motion; otherwise the pitcher may not be able to get exactly the grip he wants before he throws the pitch. The establishment of the grip, however, must go undetected. The opposition must not be able to see what pitch is being planned. There are two preferred methods for hiding the ball during the preparatory stance. Pitchers who stand upright can hide the ball by bringing their hands together in front of their body so that the glove-hand hides the pitching hand while the grip is being established. Pitchers who bend at the waist can also use this method, or they can hide their grip by putting the ball behind their legs and hiding it in back of the knee of their pivot leg. The important point is not what method is used, but that the coach and pitcher recognize that the ball needs to be hidden during the grip-changing movements.

6. The various styles of winding-up have more to do with establishing rhythm in the pitching motion than with adding force to the pitch. Rhythm in the pitching motion is essential. Different pitchers find it necessary to use different body movements to establish a successful rhythm. Some need the full wind-up motion with all the accompanying arm and trunk move-

With a runner on base, the pitcher must both relax and concentrate when taking his set position.

ments. Others seem to just rear back and throw the ball. The coach should not be deceived, however. The successful pitcher who uses the no wind-up motion has established a rhythm that is just as beneficial to him as the pitcher who uses the full wind-up motion. The difference seems to lie merely in the amount of movement needed to establish this rhythm. For years, it was thought that the full wind-up motion allowed the pitcher to generate more force. This, however, does not seem to be the case.

7. The primary difference between the two styles of winding-up is in the shifting of weight, or, more precisely, in the number of times the weight is shifted. In the full wind-up style, the weight first goes well forward on the pivot foot, then back to the stride foot behind the pitching rubber, and then forward again during the actual throwing motion. In the no wind-up style, the first forward weight shift is eliminated. From the preparatory stance, the pitcher merely shifts his weight back to the stride foot behind the pitching rubber, and then forward during the actual throwing motion. It is the first forward shifting of the weight that distinguishes the full wind-up style from the no wind-up style. Once that movement has been accomplished, the styles are basically the same. All pitchers must shift their weight backward at some time in the pitching motion so that they can then move forcefully forward again to throw the ball.

8. The degree of leg lift and kick is largely a matter of personal preference and pitching style. For reasons that will be explained later (see principle 12 below), overhand pitching requires a higher leg lift than three-quarters or sidearm pitching. Pitchers who use the three-quarters style of delivery, however, may vary widely in the degree of leg lift and kick in their pitching motions. This is largely a matter of personal preference. The higher leg kick does aid the pitcher in bending backwards, which is to his advantage, but it also makes the maintenance of balance more difficult.

9. The pivot should be made when the weight is toward the rear foot. This is basic to the maintenance of rhythm and balance in the pitching motion. Some pitchers attempt to make the pivot (the shifting of the foot on the pitching rubber to a position that is parallel to and along the front edge of the rubber) when their weight is directly over the pivot foot. This makes the pivoting very difficult and may hinder the balance and rhythm of the pitching motion. The time to pivot is when the weight has just been shifted back to the stride foot behind the pitching rubber. At that point, the pivot foot is not supporting the weight of the body and can therefore be moved with great ease. Thus the proper pivot can be made easily and comfortably without any loss of balance or rhythm. The rules of baseball say that the pivot foot cannot be lifted from the rubber during the pivot movement. Therefore, the pivot should be made by plantar flexing the ankle of the pivot foot so that the heel of that foot remains in contact with the rubber at all times. The toe, however, can be moved to the proper position parallel to and along the front edge of the pitching rubber, so that when the forward weight shift is initiated, the pivot has already been made and the pitcher can begin to push off the rubber with the pivot foot. There are two important reasons for keeping the pivot foot parallel to and along the front edge

of the pitching rubber. First, this allows for a greater backward bend of the body and rotation of the hips, which in turn makes for the generation of greater force in the pitching motion. Second, it creates a greater area of contact with the pitching rubber. This provides better balance for the pitcher during the push-off from the rubber.

10. The type of delivery—sidearm, three-quarters, or overhand—used by the pitcher is determined by the degree of body lean, not by the position of the pitching arm in relation to the body. (See Chapter 1 for a detailed explanation of this principle.) To throw overhand, for example, does not mean that the pitcher has to have his arm in a different position relative to his trunk. It means, rather, that the trunk itself is in a different position, and this fact should be recognized by coaches who wish to teach their pitchers to throw better overhand curve balls.

11. Regardless of the style of delivery he uses, the pitcher should fully extend his arm to the rear in order to lengthen the arm lever as much as possible and use all the natural leverage that he has. A long lever (the pitching arm) will generate more force than a short lever. Pitchers have long been admonished to "reach back" for something extra on their pitches. This "reaching back" means lengthening the arm lever to its fullest ex-

Pitchers need both arms to gain leverage in the pitching motion.

tent and providing for a greater distance over which force can be applied to the ball. As the pitcher begins to bring his arm through for the actual throwing motion, he flexes that arm at the elbow. This adds speed to the arm's movement. In mechanical terms, the radius of rotation is shortened momentarily which results in greater speed of the arm. Just before the position for release of the ball is reached, however, the elbow of the throwing arm is again extended so that at release the arm lever is as long as is possible. All pitches and throws should be made with the arm fully extended. Some baseball texts picture the curve ball as being thrown with a flexed elbow, but this does not happen.

12. Bending to the rear or turning the hips in a backward rotation increases the distance through which the arm lever moves, thus adding force to the pitch. In effect, the pitcher is "turning his back on the hitter" so that the batter can actually see the numbers on the back of his uniform. All successful pitchers adhere to this principle. One can readily picture a Juan Marichal, Warren Spahn, or Sandy Koufax with his stride leg extended in a high kick and his throwing arm thrust back so that the ball nearly touches the dirt in back of the pitching rubber. The pitcher who uses the overhand delivery leans backward to increase the distance through which the arm lever can move; the man who uses the three-quarters delivery will not lean backward so much as he will rotate his hips in that direction. Both styles

The entire body of the pitcher is involved in building the force used in the pitching motion.

accomplish the same purpose: to increase the force generated in the throwing motion through the increased leverage that results from having the arm lever move through a greater distance in the application of the force to the ball.

13. The push-off from the pitching rubber should be vigorous without throwing the pitcher off balance. The push-off is an important factor in the generation of force in the pitching motion, and the rubber plays a significant role in the creation of this force. Watch a pitcher stand on a gymnasium floor or on the dirt part of an infield, and throw. The lack of traction in these two instances prevents him from generating nearly as much force as he can by pushing off from a pitching rubber. The push-off from the rubber should not, however, be so forceful and vigorous that it breaks up the rhythm of the pitching motion and throws the pitcher off balance. Even and sustained strength, rather than explosive strength, characterizes the proper push-off technique. If a pitcher is having difficulty maintaining rhythm and balance in his pitching motion, the coach should examine the pitcher's push-off motion. He may find that it is either too weak or too strong. Correction of this fault could prove highly beneficial to the pitcher.

14. The stride should be taken in a straight line from the point of the pivot to home plate. Making the stride leg move directly toward home plate insures that the force generated in the pitching motion will be used in the most efficient manner. This is true because force is most effectively applied at a 90-degree angle to the intended target. Failing to achieve the proper direction with the stride foot results in an angle that is usually less than 90 degrees. Using the proper stride also has another advantage: it allows the pitcher to end up in a "squared-out" position that is beneficial for successful fielding. There is convincing proof that the pitcher can act as a "fifth infielder," and help his team and himself greatly, by doing a good fielding job.[1] There is an easy way for coaches to check their pitchers on this fundamental. A line can be drawn in the dirt on the pitching mound that will run from the pivot foot to home plate. The right-handed pitcher can check to see that his left leg (stride leg) is crossing over and landing just to the left of this line. The opposite goes for the left-handed pitcher. The same thing can be accomplished indoors by using tape on the gymnasium floor. By checking his landing spot after each pitch, the pitcher can quickly and easily get into the habit of making the correct stride.

15. The stride should be vigorous and long without overextending the pitcher. The fact that with many pitchers the thigh of the stride leg often comes very close to the ground indicates the length of the stride that can be used. To achieve an adequately long stride, the pitcher must forcefully project his stride leg both via his kick and by using the push-off from the rubber to good advantage. The long stride will enable him to generate greater force with the movements of the lower body. If the stride is too short, the

---

[1]Note: Co-author Jim Kaat provides a prime example of the value of an excellent defensive pitcher. On numerous occasions his fielding ability has helped his team out of jams and thus given him a better chance to win games.

rhythm of the pitching motion will be disrupted, which in turn will dissipate the force that otherwise would go toward throwing the ball with significant velocity.

16. The stride foot should land on the toe, and the toe should point directly toward home plate. The latter point will aid control; it will also help the pitcher achieve an efficient application of force, because it will ensure that the force is applied at an approximately 90-degree angle from the target. Landing on the toe will allow for the smoothest transition of the body weight from the pivot foot to the stride foot. Warren Spahn has long been an advocate of what he calls the "toe-to-toe" method of pitching. By this he means that the toe of the pivot foot is the last part of that foot to be in contact with the pitching rubber, and the toe of the stride foot is the first part of that foot in contact with the ground. The "toe-to-toe" method prevents the jarring that occurs when the heel of the stride foot contacts the ground first. This method also helps the pitcher to achieve a long stride and to point his toe directly toward the plate. While many baseball coaches teach pitchers to land on the ball of the stride foot, the authors feel that the "toe-to-toe" method has real merit and warrants the coaches' consideration.

17. The follow-through of the pitching motion should be smooth and complete with the pitcher ending in a "squared-out" position. The fact that

Concentration and mastery of technical skills—such as stepping directly toward the target—are important to good pitching.

the squared-out stance helps the pitcher to be a better fielder has already been mentioned, as has the importance of the pitcher's fielding. Coaches should be especially concerned with helping their pitchers — particularly the younger ones — to establish the squared-out finishing position. It is doubtful, however, that the coach should try to alter the pitching motion of an established successful pitcher. Pitchers such as Jim Bunning or Bob Gibson fall off to the left side of the mound as they complete their pitching motions. No coach would attempt to alter the established patterns of such players. It is primarily the young player who should be corrected so that he will better adhere to this principle.

18. The baseball should be gripped securely in the fingers such that the undersurface of the pitcher's first two fingers is in contact with the ball. The ball should not be smothered, however, as it is in the change-of-pace pitch. This technique places as much of the surface area of the fingers as possible in contact with the ball. For all pitches, except the knuckle ball, the ball rolls off the fingers. Therefore, the more surface area that is in contact with the ball, the more spin that can be imparted to it. And it is the spin or rotation of the ball that makes it curve, both in the fast ball and in all breaking pitches. A faster spin will produce a sharper break on the ball. It should be a goal of all pitchers to develop more spin on the ball as they throw it, as this will make their pitches more difficult to hit successfully. If a pitcher is having difficulty getting his fast ball to "move" and his curve

Some pitchers use the "toe-to-toe" method of striding.

ball to break sharply, one of the first things that the coach should check is the grip to see if the ball is being held properly, not too far out, in the fingers.

19. There are two basic grips used by pitchers: the cross-seams grip and the with-seams grip. Which grip a pitcher uses is almost entirely a matter of personal preference. Coaches should encourage their pitchers to experiment to see which grip enables them to put more spin on the ball, thus giving them better "stuff" on their pitches. Some pitchers find that gripping the ball across the seams helps them to get more spin on their fast ball. The reason for this is that the cross-seams grip provides more friction when the ball rolls off the fingers, and the increased friction helps the downward snap of the wrist and fingers to impart more spin to the ball. On the other hand, pitchers often find that they can throw better curve balls by gripping the ball with the seams. The reason is similar. The fast ball is released mostly off the ends of the fingers; thus the cross-seams grip yields more spin on this pitch. The curve ball, however, is released more off the sides of the fingers; thus the with-seams grip is more likely to produce spin in that case. Almost all baseball texts suggest that regardless which grip is preferred by a pitcher, he should use the same grip for all pitches. This is good advice. It is to the pitcher's advantage to be able to use the same grip for all pitches, since a change in grip can sometimes be detected by the opposition. It is not, however, a hard and fast rule. It is far more important for pitchers to

Squaring around after the follow-through allows the pitcher to maintain good fielding position.

throw the best pitch possible than to always use the same grip. If a pitcher can throw a better curve ball by slightly modifying his grip on the ball, the coach should encourage him to do so. Methods for hiding such modifications of grip have been suggested earlier in this chapter. What is most important is that the coach and the pitcher understand what each grip can do in terms of applying spin to the baseball.

20. For the vast majority of pitchers, the four basic pitches are the fast ball, the curve ball, the slider, and the change-up. Younger pitchers may want to postpone the development of a slider until they have fully mastered the other three pitches. Pitches such as the screw ball and the knuckle ball are also useful pitches, but are used regularly by so few pitchers that they will not be considered here. The most basic pitch in baseball continues to be, as it has been in the past, the fast ball. This is the "bread-and-butter" pitch for at least nine out of every ten pitchers. The fast ball is, literally, the fastest pitch the pitcher can throw. It is not, of course, a straight ball. In fact, pitchers must experiment to find ways to make their fast balls move more. The fast ball delivered from the overhand position tends to rise. Delivered from the three-quarters position, it tends to move like a screwball (in-curve), and it may also sink. The movement on the fast ball is determined by the grip used on the ball. Some fast ball pitchers have developed their

A pitcher should grip the ball firmly with four fingers—without using his thumb.

abilities to such a high level that they can, by gripping the ball slightly off center to either the left or right, make their fast balls break in different directions. The movement of the arm that creates the spin that enables the fast ball to move is called pronation of the wrist and forearm (pronation means inward or medial rotation of the wrist and forearm). Physical educators who specialize in biomechanics have for some time recognized that wrist and forearm pronation is the primary characteristic of all forceful throwing motions. This is true for a football pass, a discus throw, a javelin toss, a shot put, and all baseball pitches. The pronation movement causes the fast ball to spin on a slightly tilted axis, which in turn causes the pitch to move in a plane that is somewhere between horizontal and vertical. The downward movement caused by the flexion of the wrist produces the backspin. Thus the in-curve, sinker, and hop of the fast ball are created.

Exactly how the curve ball is thrown remains something of a mystery. The authors have examined high-speed films and stroboscopic photographs of pitchers in an attempt to determine exactly how the spin is imparted to the curve ball. Unfortunately, the results have not revealed detailed information that can be fully documented at this time. Several things, however, can be stated with reasonable assurance. Most texts on baseball and journal articles on pitching suggest that the curve ball is delivered with a supinated movement of the wrist and forearm, with the fingers actually moving over the top of the ball during the release. A careful examination of films and photographs will reveal that this is not correct. Note these facts about throwing the curve ball, which are readily apparent. First, the axis of the ball is tilted. For example, the right-handed pitcher tilts the axis to the right of vertical. This will move the ball 45 to 90 degrees. (In terms of reference to the planes of the body, the ball is tilted from the sagital plane almost to the frontal plane.) Second, most pitchers hold the ball slightly off center. Again, the right-handed pitcher grips the curve ball slightly to the right of the center of the ball. Third, the curve ball is released with the arm fully extended. Many baseball texts are in error on this point. Illustrations sometimes appear to indicate that the curve ball is released with a flexed elbow. This is not correct. The curve ball, like all other pitches, is released with the arm fully extended. Fourth, wrist and forearm pronation is evident in throwing the curve ball just as it is in throwing all other pitches. Pronation, of course, is the direct opposite to supination, in terms of body movement. The right-hander who supinates his wrist and forearm turns them outward, while the pronation movement involves turning them inward. Most texts indicate that the wrist and forearm supinate during the curve ball motion. In films or photographs of pitchers in action we have been unable to detect a single instance where this may be shown to be true. What is obvious, and easily documented, is that extreme *pronation* of the wrist and forearm occurs. It is doubtful that the arm could move from a supinated to a pronated position in the space of time during which the ball is released. It therefore seems reasonable to assume that the supination movement does not play a role in the throwing of the curve ball. However, in order for the baseball to curve, it must have a spin that is almost directly opposite to that of the fast

Sequence of arm action during the pitching of a curve ball. Note that the axis of the ball is tilted and that pronation is evident even after the ball has been released.

ball. On the basis of the information at hand, therefore, it seems reasonable to hypothesize that the curve ball has to be released with a sharp downward flexion of the wrist and wrist-forearm pronation. With the ball held off-center and the axis tilted, this means that the curve ball should be released off the top inside surface of the first finger, with the fingers moving under the ball as the wrist is pronated—rather than over the top of the ball, as would be the case if the wrist were supinated.

The slider is a fast, flat curve ball. It has also recently been called the "slurve." The mechanics of the slider are similar to those of the curve ball. The ball is merely held less off-center than for the curve (but further off-center than for the fast ball). The axis of the ball is turned slightly. The slider is thrown hard, with the pitcher's conscious attention given primarily to imparting force or speed, rather than to imparting enough spin to make the ball break sharply. The slider has become a popular pitch in recent years. It gives the pitcher a breaking pitch that he can throw confidently in situations where the difficulty in controlling the curve ball renders that pitch impractical. Once a coach and pitcher understand how a ball spins for various pitches, and how holding the ball off-center and tilting the axis contribute to the different spins, the slider becomes an easy pitch for the coach to teach and for the pitcher to learn.

The change-up is, as its name implies, a pitch that has a different speed (almost always slower) than the other pitches in the pitcher's repertoire. The change-up is a necessary and effective pitch because it throws the hitter off balance and forces him to hit after the momentum of his swing has already been dissipated. The change-up may be a slow curve ball, but more often it is a slow fast ball. Technically, the change-up should be thrown with a motion that is as similar to the normal throwing motion as the pitcher can make it. This causes the hitter to "swing at the motion." There are many suggested ways to throw the change-up, but the most important aspect of the technique is to grip the ball farther back in the fingers than is done with the other pitches, so that the pitch is "smothered."

21. Holding the fingers together in the grip usually allows the pitcher to have more "stuff." With the fingers closer together, more spin can be imparted to the ball, and the more spin the ball has as it is delivered, the better it will break. This is true for the fast ball (this is what is meant by the term "live" fast ball) as well as for the curve ball. The coach should be careful, however, to have his pitchers experiment with this technique in practice before they use it in a game situation. Holding the fingers together, while helping a pitcher put more spin on the ball, will also make the pitch more difficult to control. The coach must help each pitcher find the grip which will produce the best combination of spin and control.

22. Factors contributing to the force behind the pitch are plantar flexion of the ankle, leg extension, hip rotation, shoulder medial rotation, wrist flexion, and wrist-forearm pronation. The successful fast ball pitcher is often described as throwing "right from the toes." This description is literally correct. Many muscle groups contribute to the effective summation of forces necessary for generating force in the pitching motion (see princi-

ple 12 in Chapter One). The push-off from the pitching rubber, for example, is accomplished by plantar flexion of the pivot foot, knee extension of the pivot leg, and the thrust forward of the stride leg. Hip rotation comes into play as the pitcher "opens up" in his motion. Shoulder medial rotation, characteristic of all throwing motions, may be observed as the throwing arm comes through with the elbow flexed. A very vigorous flexion of the wrist, accompanied by wrist-forearm pronation, is the last major contributor to the force generated in the pitching motion. The faster the pitch, the greater the contribution of the wrist-forearm pronation. Effective summation of the forces generated in these muscle groups enables a pitcher to throw the baseball at speeds upward of 90 miles per hour.

23. Two reflex actions contribute to the generation of force in the pitching motion. The stretch reflex occurs whenever a muscle group is lengthened or "put on stretch." This reflex is a protective device that causes the muscle group being stretched to respond with a more forceful contraction than it otherwise would. When the pitcher brings his throwing arm back, he stretches the muscle groups in the front part of the shoulder area. When he brings his arm through to throw, the stretch reflex helps these important muscle groups to contract forcefully. The cross-extensor reflex is primarily a built-in balance device. In pitching, however, it helps to generate force. Left-handed pitchers, for example, often bring their glove-hand forcefully around to the right as they start the forward movement in the throwing motion. The extended right arm causes a reflex action that tends to help the left leg extend forcefully. For the left-handed pitcher, the left leg is the pivot leg that pushes off from the pitching rubber. The cross-extensor reflex also helps make this push-off more vigorous. Even at the subconscious reflex

All the elements of good pitching form are evident here. Can you identify them?

level, then, the pitcher finds ways to use the built-in devices of the body to aid him in his pitching motion.

24.. In throwing all pitches, the pitcher should concentrate on achieving a sharp, downward break of the wrist. Note that this should be a primary area of concern in the coaching and development of a pitcher. It is not suggested that the pitcher think about his wrist movement as he throws the pitch. By that time, his full concentration should be on his target. The important point is that the downward break of the wrist should be the same for all pitches, and should not differ whether the pitcher is throwing a fast ball or a curve ball.

25. For breaking pitches, the grip is moved slightly off-center and the axis of the ball is slightly turned. Since every pitcher should strive to have each pitch he throws move in some direction other than straight, it seems reasonable to suggest that every pitch should be held off-center. The good fast ball actually curves. It may hop, sink, in-curve, or slide, but if it travels in a straight line, it is not a good fast ball. The fast ball should be held just slightly off-center, the slider a little more off-center, and the curve ball well off-center. The center, of course, refers to that line which divides the ball into two equal parts.

The axis of the ball should be turned for breaking pitches. For the fast ball, thrown with the grip slightly off-center, the axis of the ball should be straight, that is, parallel to the sagittal plane of the body. (The sagittal plane is that plane which divides the body into right and left sides.) For breaking pitches, however, the axis of the ball should be turned. For the slider it should be turned only slightly, perhaps no more than 20 degrees from the sagittal plane. For the curve ball, the axis may be turned a great deal more.

Some pitchers turn the axis a full 90 degrees, so that it reaches a line parallel to the frontal plane of the body (that plane which divides the body into front and rear sections). It is the off-center grip and the turned axis that produce the spin which enables the ball to "curve." Coaches and pitchers should experiment with various degrees of grip and axis. The knowledge gained from such experimentation will enable the pitcher to fully understand his skill, and help him to become a better pitcher.

26. While there are many techniques for throwing change-ups, most pitchers will achieve the desired effect by merely using the same motion and technique they use for other pitches, but throwing the ball more slowly. It has already been suggested that throwing a good change-of-pace pitch requires gripping the ball more deeply in the fingers and hand than would be done for a fast ball or a curve. Other than that, most pitchers will have acceptable change-ups merely by throwing the ball more slowly than they normally do. Many experts suggest that the ball should be released sooner, thrown with a stiff wrist, etc. These techniques are extremely difficult to master and control, and the average pitcher would probably be better advised to merely throw his pitch more slowly than normal. This will probably assure him good control of his change-up and thus help him accomplish the purposes for which the pitch is designed. Further aid in developing a good change-up pitch can also be sought in the mechanics of pushing off from the rubber. By slightly relaxing the push-off leg just prior to release, the pitcher can slow his momentum considerably and thus take away some of the force that might otherwise have gone into the pitch. In addition, it should be remembered that the change-of-pace pitch must be accurately thrown. If it is thrown above the waist, it is a good pitch for the hitter to hit.

The Sain Theory

John Sain was a great pitcher for the old Boston Braves in the National League. His most recent baseball jobs have been as a pitching coach for the New York Yankees, Minnesota Twins, Detroit Tigers, and Chicago White Sox. Interestingly, each of these teams won a pennant when Sain was on the coaching staff; the Yankees and Twins have not won pennants since he left them. Sain is generally acknowledged to be the premier pitching coach in organized baseball. Many fine pitchers have had their greatest seasons under his tutelage, and their testimonials to his knowledge and coaching ability are reason enough for taking his pitching theory seriously. This chapter has been greatly influenced by Sain's theory. In acknowledgment of the debt that we owe to Sain, and in respect for his knowledge about pitching, the basics of his theory are included intact here. The reader will be immediately aware of the similarities between the Sain theory and the principles advocated in this chapter.

PRINCIPLES OF PITCHING

1. The pitcher must understand what type of spin he wants to impart to the ball. Once he understands what spin is required to reach his goal, he should practice achieving it by throwing slowly, always maintaining the desired spin. He should gradually throw faster and faster, all the time making sure that the desired spin is still being imparted to the ball.
2. The ball should be gripped securely in the fingers. It should not be smothered, nor should it be held loosely. The thumb should not be too tight on the ball.
3. The pitcher must work to develop a fast, loose, wrist action. He must seek to maintain this action in all of his pitching.
4. The pitcher must concentrate on finger action. The fingers are the last part of the body in contact with the pitch, and finger action can aid the pitcher in imparting the desired spin to the ball.
5. Use of the with-seams or the cross-seams grip is largely a matter of personal preference.
6. The degree of leg lift and stride are also largely matters of personal preference.
7. The middle finger plays the most important role in throwing the curve ball.
8. The pitcher may change the type of spin that he is imparting to the ball by moving his grip on the ball in either direction from the center and by tilting the axis of the ball.
9. An organized plan of pitching and conditioning is essential to a successful pitcher. The pitcher must know his own strengths and weaknesses, and he must plan his program for every day of the season.

Chapter 11
Preparing for the Game

Preparing for a game means different things to different coaches. Some, at smaller schools, must act as equipment manager, athletic director, and groundskeeper in addition to coach. Coaches at large universities may have some administrative detail to handle, but their pre-game attention can be devoted primarily to thoughts about how to win the game. Whatever situation a particular coach is in, there are certain items of business that must be tended to, and coaches would do well to see that each is properly taken care of well before the game time. These duties fall into two main categories: 1) administrative duties concerning game preparation, and 2) getting the team ready to play its best brand of baseball. Listed below are principles which can guide successful planning in these important areas.

Principles for Game Preparation

1. Competent umpires must be hired for each home game.
2. Visiting teams must be provided with adequate facilities and given hospitable treatment.
3. The baseball field must be as well prepared as possible.
4. Accommodations must be made for spectatotors so they can enjoy the games to the fullest.
5. Game equipment must be organized and in good condition in terms of both quality and quantity.
6. Practice the day before the game should be spirited and purposeful.
7. Preparing the team psychologically may include watching such things as players' eating and sleeping habits, providing clean equipment, and scheduling team meetings.
8. The warm-up period before the game should serve the dual purpose of preparing the team physically and psychologically.
9. Home baseball games need not be small-time affairs, even if the home team's school is a small one.

    1. Competent umpires must be hired, usually on contract, for each home game. This detail should be taken care of during the fall months preceding the baseball season. Only umpires officially sanctioned by state organizations should be used. If the home team is in an athletic conference, it is good policy for the conference athletic directors or baseball coaches to draw up a list of approved umpires. Game umpires can then be selected from this approved list. The standard fee should be paid; schools should not attempt to save money by hiring less expensive officials. Two weeks before each home game, the umpires should be contacted by mail concerning the date, the time, and the place of the game. It is the responsibility of the home team to provide dressing facilities for the umpires. These facilities should be heated and should include comfortable chairs, provisions for changing and hanging up dress clothes, and showers, towels, and soap. They should be checked the morning of the game, so that when the umpires arrive everything will be in order. In return, the home team has the right to expect that the contracted umpires have proper and official dress

uniforms and conduct themselves as befitting their position. It is imperative that these men be under contract. That contract should contain provisions regarding rained-out games. The coach should carry the payment for the umpires — usually a check drawn on the school account — with him when he goes to the game. If all these matters are adequately transacted, umpires will look forward to working games for the home team, and the best possible relationship between coach and umpire will be established.

2. Convenient and comfortable accommodations should be made available to visiting teams. Many schools appoint a varsity club member to act as a host for the visiting team. This student meets the team when it arrives, and serves as liaison in case the visitors need assistance with equipment or other matters. At least one week prior to the game the visitors should be sent a final confirmation of the game with information concerning starting times, sites of dressing facilities, and other pertinent facts. Making this standard practice can eliminate the frustrating mix-ups that sometimes occur on the day of the game.

The facilities for the visitors should be the best available. The guest team should have ample room in a clean, well-lighted building to change into their game uniforms. Hangers and hooks should be readily available for hanging up suits and slacks. The shower facilities should be close to the dressing room and there should be enough shower heads for the team to shower in a short time. Towels should be in the locker room when the visitors arrive. It is good policy for the manager to provide a towel and a bar of soap at every locker or cubicle. The home-team training facilities should be made available in case any member of the visiting team has need of them. The home coach should make very clear to the visiting coach just what the policy is concerning storage of valuables. Regardless of how this problem is handled, clarifying the policy at the outset will prevent unnecessary controversy. The coach must never forget that his own reputation and that of his school depends, at least in part, on the care he takes in planning for the provisions and treatment of visiting teams.

3. The coach must see that his baseball field is as well prepared as possible for each game. At small schools, this might mean that he will have to act as a groundskeeper, but in most school situations it means that the coach bears the responsibility for administering the preparation of the playing field. The grass area of the field should be cut no more than two days before each game. The skinned part of the infield should be dragged and "manicured" the morning before the game. A steel drag towed behind a jeep or other school vehicle can be used for this purpose. The hard-to-get-at parts of the infield can be manicured with a hand rake. This treatment can also be used for the pitching mound and the batter's box. Since most teams have to use their game field for practice, holes are often worn in the mound and batting areas during practice sessions. Therefore, the night before the game the coach should make sure that the pitcher's mound and batter's box are filled in with wet dirt and clay wherever necessary. By the next morning they will have hardened sufficiently to allow for the last-minute manicuring of the field.

Once the field has been dragged and cut, it must be marked. The coach should supply the school groundskeeper with a detailed drawing indicating how the lines are to be placed on the field. Either dry lime, wet lime, or the newer special marking paint can be used to mark lines on a baseball field. The foul lines should be marked from home plate all the way to the outfield fence. All lines should be wide and heavy enough that they can easily be seen from the plate. The forty-five feet restraining line down the first-base line should be marked next. After this is completed the coaches' lines and batters' boxes may be marked. Many coaches also like to dress up the field by marking in on-deck boxes, outlining the semi-circle behind home plate, and chalking a walkway from the bench or dugout to the home-plate area.

Next, the groundskeeper should make a routine check of the field to see if any last-minute repairs have to be made. He should check the outfield fence for holes and breakage, the foul poles for straightness and security, the dugouts for cleanliness, and the backstop for possible curling of the chain-link fence. Once this has been done, the field can be considered ready except for the last-minute game preparations. These last-minute preparations should consist of installing and securing clean bases, checking warm-up mounds and plates, and seeing that extra equipment such as batting cages are in the proper places. The coach should set up a checklist to make sure that each of these tasks is accomplished. One such list appears at the end of this chapter.

4. Accommodations must be made for spectators so they can enjoy the games to the fullest. This moves the coach into the crucial area of public relations. First, the game must be well publicized. Baseball schedules should be displayed in prominent places in the school and community. Local and school newspapers and radio-TV stations should be notified concerning each home contest. Portable posters can be made publicizing the home games. The coach must make sure that adequate seating is available for the games, and the groundskeeper must make sure that the seats are clean and the area is clear of unsightly papers and other trash. It is helpful if the coach will prepare programs for each home game. These can usually be made inexpensively and quickly by using the school's duplicating service and can be distributed to spectators as they arrive for the game. The programs should list the line-ups for each team and include other pertinent information such as hitting and pitching data on team leaders and conference standings. A public-address system is another helpful aid for the spectators. The coach can usually enlist the aid of an interested student to act as announcer. This feature can add considerable spectator interest to the game, and it fosters community interest in the baseball program as well.

For the convenience of both the spectators and the players, a drinking fountain and public restrooms should be located near the playing field. Finally, the coach may want to arrange for some refreshments for the spectators and the visiting team. During cold spring days, a cup of warm coffee can do much to help the spectator enjoy the game, and on warm days a bottle of pop can accomplish the same task. The coach who is willing to investigate this possibility will find that the small investment required to provide refreshments will result in increasing school and community attendance at home baseball games.

5. Game equipment must be organized and in good condition for each home game. This equipment must be acceptable in terms of both quantity and quality. The coach should buy his game baseballs in bulk before the season begins; he will need an average of six for every nine-inning game. If fewer than six balls are allotted per game, the teams will usually have to play with old baseballs by the time the sixth inning begins. The coach should also have the manager prepare the game equipment the night before each home game. He should have pitcher's resin, batter's resin, extra bases, an extra set of catching gear, towels for the on-deck circle, clean bats, bat bags for transportation to the field, and any other equipment that might be necessary due to local conditions. If these tasks are accomplished at this time, the coach can use the time on the day of the game to prepare his team psychologically and physically for the upcoming contest. There is nothing more frustrating for a coach and team than to have to see to these chores just minutes before game time.

It is the firm opinion of the authors that quality equipment should be purchased in almost every instance. A good quality game ball and good quality bats will save money in the long run, and they will also help to increase the skill of the team and the enjoyment that the players get from the game. Schools do not have to purchase major league quality items, but they should not purchase low-priced bargains when the bargains are actually faulty and inefficient equipment.

6. Practice on the day before a game should be both spirited and purposeful. It should be somewhat shorter than normal, and should be fast-paced and highly motivated. During batting practice, the coach should make every effort to have his first string hitters face a batting practice pitcher whose style resembles that of the opposing pitcher they will face that day. A spirited infield practice should come next in the pre-game workout. Last-minute strategy techniques should be reviewed. In anticipation of a close game, for example, the coach may want to review the technique for the squeeze bunt. Should he expect his opponents to have a weak throwing catcher, lead-off and stealing techniques might be reviewed. These reviews should be accomplished quickly and should be reviews rather than actual learning sessions. A last-minute pep talk to stress the importance of the upcoming game, and a quick run to the showers should end the practice session on a high note and leave the players eager with anticipation.

7. The coach must plan well to prepare his team psychologically for an upcoming game. In baseball, emotions do not normally run high. Unlike with basketball and football, baseball players normally approach games with a calm, determined mind-set, and last-minute pep talks designed to raise the emotional feeling to a high pitch may fall flat. This is not, however, to suggest that the coach should neglect the psychological preparation of his players. The preceding suggestions concerning the organization of the practice session on the day before the game are an example of psychological as well as physical preparation. The coach should also take into

consideration such things as his players' eating and sleeping habits, clean equipment, and team meetings. The authors feel that baseball players can perform well on normal eating schedules. They do not need special pre-game meals to prepare them physiologically. There is abundant research evidence to suggest that eating has little physiological effect on exercise if the food is consumed an hour or more before the performance. Due to the time of the game, or for psychological reasons, the coach may want to have his team eat together before a game. Regardless, there is no need for the players to have any special food. It is far better for them to have the kinds of food that they normally eat.

If a coach insists on or advises his team to get a normal amount of sleep, there is little reason to require players to get extra sleep on the night before a game. In fact, as with eating, it is probably wiser to have them continue to follow their normal routine.

There is nothing more discouraging to a baseball player than to have to put on dirty equipment and a dirty uniform to play a game in front of spectators. The coach should make absolutely sure that the team gets a complete set of clean equipment before each game and that the game uniforms are clean and neatly pressed. The player can then go out onto the field proud of his appearance. Additional information concerning equipment and uniforms can be found in Chapter 19.

The coach may want to schedule a team meeting the evening before, or the morning of, a game. This meeting can be used to kindle enthusiasm and to review strategy and signals. The meeting should be short and team members should have an opportunity to ask questions and voice their opinions. Clean equipment can be issued at this meeting if the coach so desires. The pre-game time can then be less encumbered with such details and the coach and players can devote their full attention to preparing to play well.

8. The warm-up period before the game should serve the dual purpose of preparing the team physically and psychologically. This pre-game warm-up time must be highly organized and carefully planned so that maximum use can be made of the available minutes. The coach should prepare a list that can be posted on a bulletin board the day of the game. This list should include all assignments for the pre-game activity — such as batting practice pitchers and catchers, fungo hitters, infield assignments, and other necessary information. (An example of such a list may be found at the end of this chapter.) Specific times for each activity should be indicated on the assignment sheet and the coach should see that each activity gets its allotted amount of time and no more. During batting practice, the coach must see that his first string players get adequate preparation. Any time that is left over can be allotted to other players. The infield and outfield drills should be snappy and high spirited. Their purpose is to give the players a last-minute review of skills, a knowledge of how the field "plays" according to bounce and weather elements, and a psychological boost before the game begins. For these reasons the coach should not make these drills too difficult. The balls hit to the infielders and outfielders should be easily play-

able so that the above goals may be achieved. Little else can be as psychologically devastating to the team as sloppy and misplayed infield and outfield drills. These drills usually provide a grand opportunity for the opponents to mock the players for their ineptness. The authors are not advocating that the person conducting this aspect of pre-game practice hit ground balls that barely have enough force to reach the infielders. The person hitting the fungos should hit them firmly, but with no intent of foiling or handcuffing the infielders.

9. Much of what has been said in this chapter may seem routine to the coach at a university or a large high school, but the suggestions may seem out of reach for the coach at the small college or the smaller high school. It should be remembered, however, that a baseball program need not be "small time" even if the school is a small one. If the coach has a little imagination, a little ambition, and is willing to try to make use of the school resources, much can be accomplished. Nothing that has been suggested in this chapter requires a great deal of money. Indeed, for every item discussed there are probably shortcuts that can result in a minimal expenditure of money. A drag for the infield, for example, can cost as much as $50 but an old section of chain-link fence or even an old steel doormat will do the job nearly as well. Shop and woodworking classes can be enlisted to make bleachers and dugouts for the field. The audio-visual department can be contacted to help with a public-address system. Game programs can be mimeographed from a ditto on inexpensive paper. The total baseball program should serve the players, the student body, and the community. With a little imagination and a small amount of old-fashioned effort, the baseball coach can make sure that his program is running at optimum efficiency and effectiveness.

BASEBALL ASSIGNMENTS FOR PRE-GAME WARM-UP

Opponent	Spring Arbor College	Date: May 4
1:00–1:15	Batting Practice for Starters	Pitcher: Farmer Catcher: Piersma Retriever: Jones Infield Fungo: Bosworth Outfield Fungo: Van Wieren
1:15–1:25	Batting Practice for Other Squad Members	Pitcher: Pluister Catcher: Kroodsma Retriever: Pelon Infield Fungo: Van Til Outfield Fungo: Cotts
1:25–1:40	Rest and Fully Warm up Throwing Arms	
1:40–1:45	Outfield Throwing Practice	Hitter: Coach Retriever: Troost
1:45–1:55	Infield Practice for Starters	Hitter: Coach Outfield Fungo: Farmer
1:55–2:00	Prepare for Game	
2:00	Play Ball!!!	

A CHRONOLOGICAL CHECKLIST FOR GAME PREPARATION

Item	Date Completed	Initials
1. Opponent scheduled and duplicate contracts signed by proper school officials.	_____	____
2. Game officials hired and under contract.	_____	____
3. Balls for game ordered.	_____	____
4. Visiting team contacted two weeks prior to game.	_____	____
5. Umpires contacted for game verification.	_____	____
6. Publicity for game distributed one week prior to contest.	_____	____
7. Field dragged and limed.	_____	____
8. Spectators' seats cleaned and ready.	_____	____
9. Game equipment prepared: extra catching gear batter's resin pitcher's resin extra bases towels	_____ — — — — —	
10. Visitors dressing facilities ready.	_____	____
11. Umpires dressing facilities ready.	_____	____
12. Clean equipment and game uniforms ready.	_____	____
13. Eating arrangements for team made.	_____	____
14. Pre-game practice schedule prepared.	_____	____
15. Public address system and programs ready.	_____	____
16. Time and location for departure of away game posted.	_____	____

Chapter 12
Offensive Strategy

Offensive strategy is an important aspect of baseball coaching, but good strategy alone will not result in a winning team. A coach must also be a good teacher of the fundamental skills of baseball. The fundamentals of hitting, bunting, and running are the basis of what can become offensive strategy in the game situation, and recognition of this fact must underlie all discussion of offensive strategy. Too many young coaches approach their jobs with the impression that they can be successful by becoming outstanding strategists. This can only happen if someone else has done the previous work on fundamentals that is necessary to produce winning baseball teams.

The degree to which a baseball coach will use offensive strategy will depend on his personnel. A coach who has six or seven good line-drive hitters in his lineup need not be greatly concerned about the fine points of offensive strategy. For this kind of team, the sacrifice bunt, the squeeze bunt, and the hit-and-run play are not strategies that will be employed often. This type of team has only one primary offensive strategy: hitting line drives. Most coaches, however, are not fortunate enough to be able to field a lineup that includes this kind of hitting ability. Therefore, they are necessarily dependent upon the use of offensive strategy to score runs. This chapter is designed to provide the coach with guidelines for using such strategy. No attempt will be made to suggest that one particular strategy is the *only* way to approach offensive baseball. Such absolute statements could never cover the range of possibilities in terms of personnel and game situations. Instead, this chapter will consider areas of offensive concern, rather than specific principles.

Areas of Offensive Concern

1. Batting order
2. Hitting philosophy
3. The sacrifice bunt
4. The squeeze bunt
5. Hit and run
6. Run and hit
7. Steal situations
8. Hitting to the right side
9. Base coaching
10. Pinch hitting
11. Base running

Discussing the Areas of Concern

1. No doubt the first area of offensive concern to a coach when he is preparing for a game is the batting order that he will use. The purpose of any particular batting order is to line up the hitters so as to maximize the probability of scoring runs. There are many views on batting-order strategy,

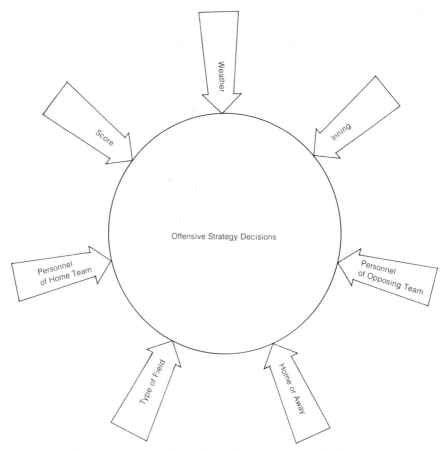

There are many factors which contribute to the development of an offensive strategy in baseball.

and there is *no one best strategy* for placing hitters in the batting order. There are, however, certain factors that each coach should consider in determining his batting order for each game.

The coach should attempt to give his better hitters more times at bat. In high-school or college baseball, therefore, he should not put one of his better hitters in the 6th, 7th, or 8th spots in the batting order. These hitters simply do not get to bat as often as those placed in the upper part of the order. There is a school of thought which says that the best hitter should be first in the batting order, the second-best hitter number two in the order, and so on. This would adhere to the guideline of giving the better hitters the most chances to hit. However, it does not necessarily adhere to the even more important guideline of arranging the batting order so that the possibility of scoring runs is maximized. Often, skills other than hitting ability are necessary to score runs. The coach may feel a sacrifice bunt is needed, and in this situation a good bunter maximizes the probability of scoring. Or, a team may need to stay alive in an inning by avoiding a strikeout; in this case a hitter whose average is low but who gets wood on the ball consistently is probably more likely to get the job done. It is important for the baseball coach to remember that *the team which gets the most runs wins the game.* This may or may not be the team which gets the most hits.

Generally, the first hitter in the batting order should be able to get on base in many different ways. This player should be one who does not strike out often, who can get the base on balls, who can bunt, and who can hit fairly well. The second hitter in the order should have speed and bat control. These essential qualities have characterized all the great second hitters in the major leagues. In most cases, a team's three best hitters should occupy the next three places in the batting order. (By "best hitter," we mean the player who gets the most base hits.) Most coaches would have optimum success if they followed this practice instead of attempting to emulate major-league strategy by looking for a line-drive hitter for the third spot, a powerful pull-hitter for the fourth spot, and a good RBI man for the fifth spot. Below the fifth spot in the batting order, the coach has more latitude in placing his players. Some coaches like to think of the sixth batter as a second lead-off hitter. Other coaches prefer to place a potential long-ball hitter in this spot. How the seventh spot is filled will depend on whom the coach has chosen to hit in the sixth spot. Most coaches try to have a fairly good hitter in the eighth spot in the batting order. The reason for this is that the ninth hitter is always the weakest hitter in the lineup, and it is a great disadvantage to have two such hitters batting back-to-back. For most high-school and college teams, the question as to whether the ninth hitter should be the pitcher or not is irrelevant. If the pitcher is the weakest hitter, he should be in the ninth spot. If he is not, he should be placed where his hitting abilities will be of most use to the team.

2. The question of hitting philosophy is basic to any discussion of offensive strategy. To gain insight into an individual coach's philosophy, one need only observe when he flashes the take sign to his hitters. Some coaches prefer their hitters to take up to one strike early in the game. Others will flash the take sign to many hitters on the 2–0 pitch, and even on the 3–1 pitch to some hitters. Some coaches like to have each hitter take up to one strike when the opposing pitcher is wild or when their team is behind in the late innings and needs to get men on base. We believe that to hit well a hitter must hit aggressively. Translated into game strategy, this means that the coach should use the take sign very infrequently as it tends to hinder aggressive hitting and is defensive in nature. The 2–0 pitch and the 3–1 pitch are often excellent pitches to hit. The take sign should be used with individual hitters who tend to become overly aggressive in their hitting, swinging at bad pitches and so forth. Use of the take sign can curb this kind of over-aggressiveness.

3. Sacrifice-bunt situations require the coach to develop a specific strategy or strategies. The first decisions to be made concern how often to use the sacrifice bunt, in what situations, and with what players. There are three basic reasons for using the sacrifice bunt. First, the sacrifice advances a runner or runners into scoring position; second, it tends to prevent the

double play; third, the sacrifice that is successful puts a great deal of pressure on the pitcher. The sacrifice is often avoided, of course, because the batter might be able to get a hit instead of bunting into an almost sure out.

Some coaches will call for a sacrifice with certain players at bat, but not with others. The slower player who tends to hit the ball on the ground is often called upon to sacrifice because when he swings away he is prone to hitting into double plays. Other coaches will seldom call upon any hitter below the number five spot in the batting order to sacrifice. These coaches reason that the hitters coming up next are not good enough to warrant the giving up of an out to move a runner into scoring position. Some coaches will signal the first two hitters in their batting order to sacrifice, while other coaches will almost never call upon these hitters to sacrifice. Sometimes, coaches will not sacrifice when there is one out in an inning if the team is more than two runs behind in the game. The coach must examine all of these alternatives for himself, but he can have certain guidelines to help him choose among them.

It is our contention that the use of the sacrifice bunt depends primarily upon the personnel involved. The coach must, above all, know his players and their abilities. In addition, the expectations and abilities of the opponents must be considered. There is great merit in being unpredictable in terms of sacrifice-bunt strategy. If the opponents are good defensively and are fully expecting a sacrifice, the coach should consider alternatives other than the sacrifice in obvious situations such as exist when there are men on first and second with no outs in an inning. The third factor that must be weighed carefully is how the coach expects the game to go. If both pitchers are in good form and the coach expects a tight, low-scoring game, the sacrifice bunt becomes a much more attractive and needed strategy.

The situation in which a team has a man on first is common in baseball. Generally speaking, the sacrifice should be used in this situation only when there are no outs in an inning. A bunt at this point should be either down the first-base line or down the third-base line, not directly toward the pitcher. This bunt should not be a hard bunt. If the coach is familiar with the defensive abilities of the opponents, he should instruct his hitter to bunt to the poorest three opposing infielders (third baseman, pitcher, and first baseman) who will be most likely to field the ball. In high-school and college baseball particularly, the first baseman quite often is playing that position because he is a good hitter but is not good enough defensively to play anywhere else. If this is the case, the offensive team will maximize its chances of sacrificing successfully by bunting the ball to that fielder.

The situation with men on first and second is, perhaps, the most likely bunting situation in baseball. Almost all coaches agree that this situation generally calls for the sacrifice bunt, sometimes even when there is one out (so as to avoid the double play). The coach should find out as quickly as possible how his opponents defend against the sacrifice in this situation. If they use the normal defense (with the pitcher covering the third-base line and the third baseman holding back), the bunt should be made hard down the third-base line. The coach might also make a judgment as to how good the opposing pitcher and first baseman are as fielders. If they are not quick and agile, the sacrifice bunt in this situation can be aimed directly back at the pitcher's mound. This often results in all runners being safe and the bunter being credited with a base hit.

Using the sacrifice bunt with a man on second base is frequently not wise regardless of the number of outs in the inning. One occasion when this strategy might be valuable is when the hitter is very poor—the pitcher, for example. Another occasion might be when the runner on second represents the tying or winning run in the late innings. With no one out, for example, the coach might want to sacrifice the runner to third base and then try for a squeeze play or a fly ball. This would be acceptable strategy. Normally, however, other strategies are much more useful. In this situation, major league players often attempt to hit the ball on the ground to the right side of the infield. (This strategy will be discussed later in this chapter.)

4. As one moves from the lower to the higher levels of competition in baseball, one finds that the squeeze bunt is used less and less. For most high-school teams, the squeeze bunt is a regular aspect of offensive strategy; in the major leagues, one can go for weeks without seeing it used in a game. The reason for this is that as one moves up the competitive ladder, defensive abilities in baseball become progressively better. High-school teams have a difficult time defending against the squeeze bunt no matter how poor the bunt may be. Professional teams, on the other hand, tend to defend against this play quite successfully unless the bunt is nearly perfectly executed.

We believe, however, that more teams could profit from the squeeze-bunt strategy than ordinarily do. As with the sacrifice, the decision to use the squeeze bunt should hinge upon the personnel involved and how much the run means to the offensive team. If the personnel are reasonably capable and the run means a great deal, the squeeze-bunt strategy is worthwhile.

In the "safety" squeeze bunt, the runner on third base does not break for the plate until he is sure that the hitter is going to successfully bunt the ball on the ground. If the bunter pops the ball up or misses it entirely, no damage has been done. It is from this safety element that this bunt takes its name. In the "suicide" bunt, the runner breaks for the plate as soon as he can. He commits himself very quickly and is dependent upon the hitter's bunting the ball successfully. The pop-up bunt in this situation almost always means a double play for the defensive team. The safety squeeze should be used primarily in the early or middle innings of a game, when there is really no need to take the extra risk that is associated with the suicide squeeze. In the late innings, however, the opposite is true, and the suicide squeeze becomes a much better strategy. The element of surprise can be very crucial to the success of the suicide squeeze. If the defenders have an inkling that the suicide is going to be attempted, they have a very good chance of preventing its successful execution. The pitcher can throw a pitch that is almost impossible to bunt, and the catcher can move down the line to tag the incoming runner. If, however, the opponents are not expecting the suicide, it can be quite easily accomplished by a reasonably good bunter. Because the element of surprise is so important, we believe that it is good strategy to occasionally call for the suicide squeeze bunt when there are two strikes on the hitter. A bunt that goes foul in this situation will mean a strikeout for the hitter, but the risk is worth taking in view of the surprise that would exist in this situation.

Regardless of which squeeze-bunt strategy is used, the techniques should be fundamentally sound. The batter, in both instances, should not attempt to fool the defense for too long a time. He should assume the bunting stance in plenty of time to execute a good bunt. The success of a squeeze bunt is dependent not only on fooling the defense, but also on making a good bunt. The runner should be alert at all times. In the safety squeeze bunt, the runner should take a good secondary lead-off and be ready to break for the plate the instant he knows that the bunt is going to be on the ground. In the suicide squeeze, the runner should make his break for the plate the moment the pitcher has committed himself to his pitch. Naturally this is more difficult to discern when the pitcher has taken a stretch position; in fact, the suicide squeeze is not a good strategy to use when the pitcher is taking a stretch instead of using a wind-up. In either case, however, the runner must break for the plate at the earliest sign in the pitcher's delivery movement that indicates that he is going to throw to home plate.

Any coach who wants to incorporate the sacrifice-bunt strategy or the squeeze-bunt strategy into his total offensive capability must schedule specific practice of these skills. No player should be expected to perform adequately in these situations unless he has had ample time in practice to develop the skills necessary for successful completion of the various types of bunts.

5. The hit-and-run play is widely used at the major league level, but it is used less often in college and high-school competition. The reason for this is that a high level of skill is required to execute the hit-and-run play successfully. The "picture-book" hit and run occurs when there is a man on first base and a right-handed hitter at bat. The runner on first breaks for second with the pitch, and the hitter sends the ball behind the runner into right field. The result is men on first and third. This play is designed to take advantage of the fact that when the runner on first base breaks for second, the second baseman tends to break with him to cover the base for the attempted steal. This move by the second baseman actually leaves the entire right side of the infield open because the first baseman is close to his base, having been trying to hold the runner there. Thus, a ground ball hit almost anywhere between first and second will usually get through to right field for the base hit needed to send the runner to third base. This play is classic, but it is difficult to execute. The hitter must have a high degree of bat control to be able to hit the ball behind the runner. This skill can be developed if the coach will emphasize it in practice and give his players ample instruction and opportunity to learn it. The difficulty, of course, is that the hitter must hit the pitch no matter where it is thrown. The runner may be able to

return to first base if the ball is hit in the air. But if the hitter lets the ball go by or misses it, the runner will almost always be thrown out at second base. In short, a great deal of pressure is placed on the hitter in this play.

We believe that the hit-and-run strategy should be used much more often than it is at every level of competition. One advantage of the hit-and-run play is that it tends to make the double play very difficult to execute. Moreover, this play can create situations in which the defense might make errors; thus, its use should be more fully explored, especially at the high-school level.

6. The run-and-hit strategy is very similar to the hit-and-run except that in the former the hitter does not *have to* hit the ball. If the pitch is not a good one to hit, the hitter can simply let it go by. The runner also adopts a slightly different strategy. He is actually attempting to steal second base when he breaks from first. The run-and-hit can be best characterized as a steal situation in which the hitter does not have the take sign. This play is especially useful when the runner is fairly quick and the hitter is a natural right-field hitter. The coach should have both of these strategies in the

In the hit-and-run play, the runner breaks for second base and the second baseman moves to cover the base. The hitter then attempts to hit the ball to the right side of the infield which is almost completely vacated.

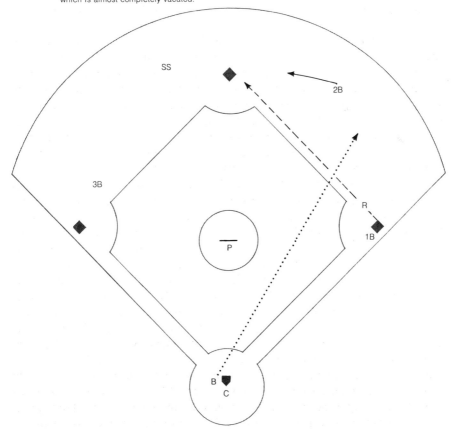

offensive repertoire of his team. By using each of them on occasion, he can keep the defense off balance and thus prone to committing errors in the field. Perhaps the most important factor for the coach to consider in deciding whether to use the run-and-hit or the hit-and-run is the ability of the hitter. If a hitter does not produce effectively under the added pressure of having to hit the ball no matter where it is pitched, then the run-and-hit is the better strategy. If, however, the hitter likes to accept this kind of challenge, the hit-and-run will yield the greatest benefit.

7. The steal is another offensive strategy that is often used at all levels of baseball. Such fleet runners as Maury Wills, Lou Brock, and Bert Campeneris, have given the steal a big boost as an offensive weapon in baseball. In recent years, the emphasis has been on speed on the basepaths, with the steal playing the major role in offensive strategy. Like all other offensive strategies, the success of the steal depends primarily on the situation and the personnel involved. When to call for the steal and when not to do so is the first question the coach must answer. Generally speaking, the steal should be avoided when the team is more than two runs behind—especially in the later innings of a game. It is also poor strategy to attempt to steal third base when there are two out in any inning. Some coaches will not signal for a steal when their best hitters are at the plate because the steal attempt might lessen the chance of scoring runs on the long base hit by the good hitter.

Who should steal is another question. The coach must find out which of his players are most capable of stealing bases. This ability depends upon speed, quickness, alertness, and aggressiveness. (For a detailed account of the mechanics of base stealing, consult Chapter 5.) Some coaches prefer to select one or two good stealers and put these players on their own, allowing them to attempt to steal whenever they wish. The great advantage of this is that the runner can decide to steal on the spur of the moment if he happens to notice something favorable in the movement of the pitcher or if he thinks he can get a big jump on a particular pitch. One disadvantage to this, from the coach's point of view, is that it takes the responsibility for strategy out of his hands and puts it into the hands of the player. Another disadvantage is that this practice makes coordination with the hitter more difficult. Second base is the one that players at all levels of baseball most often attempt to steal. The stealing of third base is less often tried. Most good runners consider stealing third to be the easier task, but there is considerably less to gain by using that strategy. Most base hits will score a runner from second base, so that stealing third is frequently not worth the risk involved. The double steal with men on first and second is slightly more advantageous; it tends to take away the possibility of the double play. With runners on first and third bases, however, the double steal is often used by high-school and college teams because defense against it is difficult. Against more experienced players, though, the play should be used with caution. In this particular double steal, the runner on third base usually waits until he sees the throw go past the pitcher's mound before he breaks for home plate. Often the runner on third can bluff so that the runner on first base, with the opponents' attention diverted, can attempt to steal. Many teams at lower levels of competition do not even attempt to throw the runner out at second base in this situation. In this case, the coach would do well to employ this strategy at every opportunity.

8. Hitting to the right side of the infield is an offensive strategy that is not used sufficiently below the professional level in baseball. Yet this type of hitting is very helpful to the offense, and the skills involved are not overly difficult to master if the hitters are given a minimum of instruction and ample opportunity to practice. The ground ball to the right side of the infield gets the runner to third base so that he can score on a fly ball to the outfield. The Los Angeles Dodgers just a few years ago won several National League pennants by taking advantage of this type of strategy. This strategy should be employed whenever there is a runner on second base with nobody out. An exception may be made, however, if a good right-handed pull-hitter is at bat. Hitting to the right side of the infield at particular moments is not officially called sacrificing, but this is often what it amounts to. However, this strategy — as opposed to the sacrifice — may also result in a line drive base hit. The coach should emphasize the development of the skill of hitting the ball to the right side of the infield, and he should then use this strategy in game situations. As with any learning effort, he should also make sure that when the strategy is properly executed, the hitter receives recognition for carrying out his assignment.

9. Base coaching must be considered an important aspect of offensive strategy. The base coaches guide runners, make important split-second decisions, and usually flash signs to both hitters and runners. Thus, these coaches have a great deal of responsibility, and proper execution of this responsibility should not go unrewarded. Below the professional level of

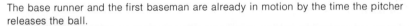

The base runner and the first baseman are already in motion by the time the pitcher releases the ball.

baseball, the job of base coaching will fall, at least in part, to members of the team. In some cases, the team coach may want to coach third base; in others he may want to remain in the dugout and leave the base coaching to his players. Two qualifications are essential for successful performance as a base coach: decisiveness and the ability to maintain poise under pressure. This is what a team coach should look for when he attempts to pick a base coach from among his players. Taking another tack, many coaches will pick a boy who is not necessarily a baseball player and train him for the coaching job. This, too, is an idea worth exploring.

Since he is in a position where he can be easily seen, the third-base coach should flash the signs to the hitter and the base runners. If the team coach prefers to remain in the dugout, he will have to develop a relay system whereby he can flash the signs to the third-base coach who in turn can relay them to the hitter and the runners. This relay system should be simple and different from the regular system of signs employed by the team so that the hitter and the runners will not be looking into the dugout to try and see the signs as the coach flashes them.

The sign system used by the team should also be easily understandable so as not to create confusion on the field. It is highly desirable to include a "key" in the system which can be used to indicate which signs are legitimate. For instance, a player should know that he must take the first sign *after* the key is flashed and that he must not take any sign unless he first sees the key. If "skin-on-skin" is the sign for the sacrifice bunt, and the brim of the hat is the key, the hitter will not sacrifice if he does not first see the brim sign even though he may see the skin-on-skin sign several times. Several examples of sign systems are provided here.

SIGNALS: Typical Offensive Signs and Examples of Their Uses

Key: either hand touching the brim of the cap

Sacrifice bunt: either hand touching the letters

Hit and run: either hand hitching the belt

Take: Either hand holding the opposite arm

Steal: skin on skin

Safety squeeze: either hand wiping pants

Suicide squeeze: both hands wiping pants

Examples: the base coach goes through the following sequences

1. hand to face—hand to pants—hitch belt—right hand to brim of cap—left hand to letters—right hand to left arm

    sign given was sacrifice bunt sign

2. right hand to pants—hand to brim—hands rubbing each other—left hand to letters—right hand to pants

    sign given was for steal with the hitter having option to hit away

3. hand to brim—left hand to face—right hand to pants—right hand to brim—left hand holding right arm—left hand to letters

    sign given was for steal with the hitter taking

4. right hand to letters—both hands wipe pants—left hand to belt—right hand to face—left hand to letters

   no sign given

The coach and players should adopt a set of hand signals for use with runners. For example, putting both hands up in the air with the palms out can mean stop. Pointing to a base can mean get to that base. One arm moving in a circular direction might mean keep running. As with all other aspects of baseball, a team must practice using and responding to these signals if it hopes to be successful with them in the game situation. Just as important, the coach must be decisive so that the runners will have no doubt as to what his instructions are.

The first-base coach must give all possible aid to a runner rounding first base. He must also help the runner leading off from first by yelling immediately when he thinks the pitcher might be initiating a pick-off toward that base. An experienced first-base coach often has a greater knowledge of a pitcher's move to first than does the base runner. The first-base coach can also be useful whenever the first baseman decides to play behind the runner (in fielding position). The runner should be able to get an extra step or two lead-off in this situation—if the coach does his job. In addition, the first-base coach can tell the runner what to do on fly balls hit to the outfield. If the fly is not hit to a deep part of the outfield, the runner should be advised to go half-way down the baseline until the catch is made. How-

The first-base coach must help the runner determine whether a left-handed pitcher is preparing to throw to first or to home plate.

ever, if the ball is deep, or if the outfielder in question has a weak arm, the first-base coach can tell the runner to tag up and attempt to advance to second base after the catch is made.

The third-base coach also has several functions vis-à-vis runners. He helps runners leading off from second base, for example. Some coaches believe the third-base coach should watch the shortstop and the runner should watch the second baseman in this lead-off situation. We believe that the third-base coach should watch both the shortstop and the second baseman so that the runner can concentrate fully on observing the pitcher. The language that a base coach uses in this situation is very important; it must always be the same so that the runner can learn to react automatically to the coach's words. A standard set of terms should be developed for use by the entire team. It does not make much difference what the terms are as long as they are always the same and everybody knows what they are. The third-base coach must be able to tell the runner to: 1) come farther off the base (more-more); 2) stop where he is (far enough-far enough); 3) move back a little toward the base (back-back); and 4) get back to the base quickly (jump-jump).

The third-base coach must also help the runner who is tagging up at third base in an attempt to score after the catch of a fly ball. To do this, the coach should move down the baseline toward home plate until he is in a position that can be easily seen by the runner crouching at third. The runner should not watch the ball; he should watch only the coach. The coach should put his right arm up in the air for the ready signal. When the ball is obviously caught by the fielder, the coach should bring his arm forcefully downward. This is the runner's signal to break for home plate. The third-base coach should also move down the baseline and make a circling motion with his arms if he wants a base runner approaching third to round the base. By so doing the coach can help the runner to round third base quickly, but he can also be in a position to halt the runner and help him get back to the base safely. If the base coach stands too near third base he cannot tell a runner who has rounded the base to halt and go back because the runner will be past him and on his way to home plate.

The on-deck hitter also serves as a coach to the runners. When a runner is approaching home plate, the on-deck hitter should signal to him whether he should stand up or slide, and—if he should slide—to which side of the plate he should make his slide. This should be standard procedure for all on-deck hitters.

Base coaching is important. The team coach must impress this fact upon his players so they will view the job seriously. The team coach, whether he uses players as coaches or whether he selects nonplayers for the job, should choose carefully, train thoroughly, and allow the team to practice sufficiently with the base coaches. This strategy will pay dividends.

Generally speaking, we believe that a good philosophy of base coaching involves taking greater chances when there are more outs in an inning. With no outs, the team should be guided to play things safely on the bases because an out on the bases could break up a potentially big inning. With one out, the coach can begin to take a few more chances with the base runners. With two outs in an inning, the time has come to take many chances. The importance of developing this philosophy as a team philosophy is that the base runners and coaches then know generally what to expect in any given situation. With two out, a runner will expect to be given the go-ahead to try for an extra base.

10. An important aspect of offensive strategy in baseball is the use of the pinch hitter. This strategy is used less in college baseball than in professional baseball, and even less in high-school baseball. Frequently, the non-professional coach does not recognize the many situations in which a pinch hitter might help his team offensively. Too often, the coach thinks of a pinch hitter only as a substitute hitter—to be used when a base hit is needed or when a team is far behind in the late innings. While these may be the primary uses of pinch hitters, they are not the only ones. A pinch hitter can be used effectively when a capable bunter is needed. Many offensive rallies are initiated or kept alive by successful sacrifice or squeeze bunts, and it is sometimes well worth using a pinch hitter to get a good bunt. Another situation that sometimes warrants the use of a pinch hitter occurs when a team badly needs to avoid a strikeout. With a runner on third base, for example, and only one out in an inning, almost any batted ball is better than a strikeout.

There are several requirements for good pinch hitters. First, they should be capable of hitting the ball most of the time. That is, they should not be strikeout prone. Secondly, they should know the strike zone well and only swing at good pitches. This is important because pinch hitters usually appear in situations where there is a great deal of pressure on the pitcher. At

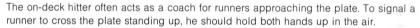
The on-deck hitter often acts as a coach for runners approaching the plate. To signal a runner to cross the plate standing up, he should hold both hands up in the air.

such a time the hitter does not want to help the pitcher by swinging at pitches outside of the strike zone. Perhaps most importantly, the pinch hitter should have poise. The player who gets nervous easily and is upset by tight situations will not be a good pinch hitter.

11. Many base-running situations that occur regularly in games do not fit under any of the categories previously discussed in this chapter. A cursory discussion of a few of them now will allow the reader to see the importance of considering all possible situations *before* they occur and developing strategies for each one.

Whether to tag up or go half-way on a fly ball to the outfield is an important question in baseball strategy. The first thing to consider is how deep the fly ball is hit. If it is a shallow fly, the base runner should move off the base and take a position about one-third of the way toward the next base. If, however, the fly ball is hit fairly deep, the runners could profit by tagging up. We like this strategy because we like to play percentage baseball, and the clear fact is that most fly balls are caught. By tagging up, the runner can start his run to the next base and draw a throw from the outfielder. Anytime the base runner can draw a throw, he has increased the possibility of an error being committed since many more errors are made on throws than on catches of fly balls. Of course, if there is any question as to whether the ball will be caught or not, the runner should move off the base and take his half-way position in the baseline.

The base runner should seldom try to go from second to third on a ball hit to the third-base side of the shortstop's position. With less than two outs in an inning, the runner should make sure that the ball is through the infield before starting toward third base. The ball hit in the "hole" is particularly difficult for the shortstop to handle successfully, and the runner on second base should not help the shortstop by giving him an easy throw to third base for a putout.

With runners on first and third and less than two out, the runner on third base should always try to score on a ground ball. This will eliminate the possibility of the other runners being caught in a double play. Such strategy must be relayed from the third-base coach to the runner on third base *every time* this situation occurs. While the coach can expect that some of his veteran players will learn this strategy, he should not assume that they will always remember to run for the plate automatically when they see a ground ball hit in this situation.

Perhaps the best overall strategy for base-running situations is "don't hesitate." Once a player has committed himself to a certain strategy he should go all out. The player who starts to move in one direction and then changes his mind usually becomes the victim of a putout.

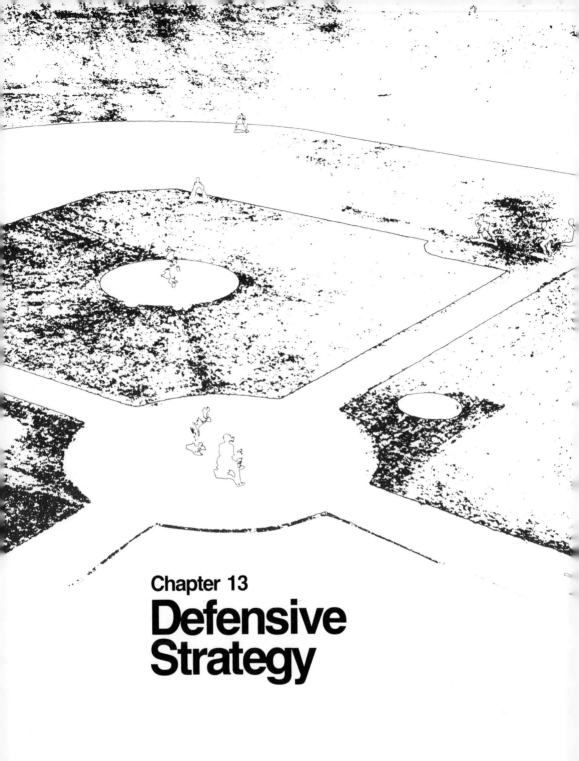

Chapter 13
Defensive Strategy

At the beginning of the previous chapter, we suggested that a baseball coach could have a winning team, even though he used very little offensive strategy, if he had six or seven outstanding hitters on that team. His strategy would simply call for hitting line drives and scoring many runs. The same pattern does not hold true for defensive strategy in baseball. Even with an outstanding defensive player at each position, the coach would need to employ defensive strategy just as diligently as his counterpart who has a poor defensive baseball team. While good hitting can make up for a lack of offensive strategy, good fielding can not completely reduce the need for defensive strategy.

The successful execution of defensive strategy depends upon the coordinated effort of several players. That is, defensive strategy is a matter of team defense rather than individual defense. A full analysis of individual defensive skills can be found in Chapters 6, 7, and 8, and it is recommended that the reader have an understanding of individual defensive play before attempting to master team defensive strategy.

As in Chapter 12, this chapter will suggest areas of concern, rather than list definite principles, for the coach who is interested in developing a successful team defense. Within each area of concern, certain key situations will be discussed. Where alternative methods of defense are available, we will attempt to suggest which method might be the best, and we will defend that choice.

Areas of Defensive Concern

1. Positioning of infielders
2. Positioning of outfielders
3. Cut-offs from the outfield
4. Sacrifice bunts
5. Squeeze bunts
6. Steal situations
7. Hit-and-run situations
8. Pick-off situations
9. Balls hit to the right side
10. Run-down situations
11. Relief pitchers

Discussing the Areas of Concern

1. The positioning of infielders is a matter of primary concern to every baseball coach. By carefully positioning these players, the coach hopes to maximize his defensive potential for any given situation. Decisions about the positioning of infielders depend upon three primary factors: the hitter,

the runners on base, and the game situation in terms of score and innings. The relative importance of each of these factors will change during the course of the game. In the early innings, for example, a right-handed pull-hitter might be played quite far back by the third baseman and shortstop even if there is a runner on third base. In the ninth inning with a runner on third, the same hitter might be played up on the grass. In the latter instance, the game situation is the dominant factor. At other times the hitter will be the determining factor, and at still other times, the runner on base will most significantly affect the coach's thinking about the positioning of his infielders.

Generally speaking, there are three basic ways to position a defensive infield: 1) in a deep position, 2) at double-play depth; and 3) in a short position. In the deep position, all four infielders play near the edge of the outfield grass. At double-play depth, the shortstop and second baseman are in a few steps from the deep position and a step or two closer to second base. The positioning of the third baseman and first baseman is dependent on the position of the runners. The short defensive position finds all four infielders playing toward the home-plate side of imaginary lines between first and second and between second and third bases. This position is used when the goal is to prevent a runner from scoring on a ground ball. Most defensive infield positions are combinations of these basic positions. With runners on first and third, for example, a popular defense consists of having the shortstop and second baseman play at double-play depth with the first

Infield in place to defend against runners at first and third with two out.

baseman and third baseman playing at the short depth. This enables the shortstop and second baseman to initiate a double play if the ball is hit to their positions, and the first and third baseman to throw to the plate if the ball is hit in their direction.

Each basic position or combination of positions will be modified somewhat according to the abilities of the hitter. The modifications will be made on the basis of the hitter's speed and whether or not he is a pull-hitter. With a fast, left-handed hitter at bat, the third baseman must play a short position regardless of how the other infielders play. The pull-hitter must be played more toward the baseline than a straight-away or opposite-field hitter. A strong pull-hitter can affect the entire positioning of the infield. For example, a good right-handed pull-hitter, such as Harmon Killebrew, will often cause the defensive second baseman to move to the third base side of second, thus putting three infielders in the area of his power.

A secondary factor that can affect the defensive position of an infield is the pitch that is being thrown by the pitcher. Many coaches want their infielders to know whether the pitcher is throwing a fast ball or a breaking ball. If the pitcher is throwing a breaking ball, the infielders will take a step toward the foul lines to anticipate the hitter's pulling this slower pitch. In making this type of adjustment, however, infielders must be careful not to tip off the opponents as to what kind of pitch to expect.

Several pictures of defensive infield positions appear in this section. These pictures verify the ideas presented here.

The first and second baseman play toward the right-field line against a left-handed pull-hitter.

2. The outfielders can also be moved around to suit the defensive needs of any given situation. We have previously advocated the defensive strategy of having the center fielder play shallow in most situations. (See Chapter 7, "Coaching the Outfielders.") This is especially useful in high-school and college baseball because there are so few genuine long-ball threats in such competition. The baseball coach must decide which area of the outfield he wants to protect the most, and, conversely, which area he feels can be least protected. For example, against a right-handed pull-hitter, the coach may have his left fielder guard the left-field foul line, his center fielder shift into left-center field, and his right fielder shift into right-center. This leaves the right-field foul line unprotected, but the coach is playing the percentages — that is, he is guessing that the batter will be least likely to hit the ball to that area.

An important factor in the positioning of outfielders is the pitcher. With a fast ball pitcher on the mound, the outfielders should play more of a straight-away position or even shade some of the hitters to their opposite fields. In addition, the inning, the score of the game, the type of field, and the weather conditions must all be considered by the coach when he is making decisions about the positioning of his outfielders.

When an important run is in scoring position in the late innings of a game, the coach will normally pull his outfielders in from their regular depths and have them play more shallow positions. This is done, of course, so that the outfielders can have a better chance to keep the run from scor-

Infielders at double-play depth to defend against a left-handed power hitter.

ing by making a good throw to home plate. The coach thus sacrifices the chance to field the long hit, because he knows that the long hit would score the runner anyway. Outfielders should practice fielding balls, particularly grounders, and throwing to the plate from these shallow positions.

3. An important aspect of overall team defense in baseball is the cut-off play from the outfield. This play is a defensive maneuver that involves virtually every member of the team. A definite system of cut-offs must be developed by each baseball coach. The cut-off play is designed to accomplish two tasks. First, it must provide the best possible opportunity to cut down a runner who is trying to reach a particular base. When there is a man on second, and a base hit is made to center field, the defense must cut the runner down at the plate if he attempts to score on the hit. The second object of the cut-off play is to prevent any other base runners from taking an extra base on the throw to the plate. If, for example, the catcher feels that the throw to the plate cannot beat the runner attempting to score from second base, he will tell the cut-off man to take the throw and prevent the hitter from advancing to second.

Several guidelines can be suggested for developing a cut-off system. First, the cut-off play must be automatic. That is, each player must react to the situation in the correct manner so that the total team defense is effective. If any member of the defense fails to do his job, the entire play is ruined. Second, each player on the team must know where every other player is when the cut-off play is attempted. The only way to fulfill this

Infielders at double-play depth to defend against a fast left-handed hitter.

requirement is to practice the cut-off enough that the players become familiar with the total play. The outfielders, for example, must have a good idea
of the approximate position of the cut-off man in each of the various cut-off
situations. Third, each cut-off throw made from the outfield should be
aimed at the chest of the cut-off man, not at the base for which the ball is
ultimately intended. This is the key to the entire play. If the cut-off man
has himself properly aligned, the throw made to his chest will also be a perfect throw to the intended base — should he decide to let the throw go
through.

The cut-off play normally involves three primary players: the outfielder
making the throw, the cut-off man, and the player covering the base to which
the throw is aimed. When a long base hit falls between two outfielders,
however, another player becomes directly involved in the cut-off chain.
He is the "long relay" man — usually the shortstop or the second baseman,
depending on where the long hit has gone. This man takes the throw from
the outfielder, turns, and throws toward the cut-off man in the infield.

To execute a successful cut-off play, the cut-off man must make himself
as apparent as possible so that the outfielder or relay man can easily see
where the throw is to be made. The cut-off man should spread both his
arms above his head and wave them so that he can catch the attention of
the relevant fielder. This technique will tend to prevent unnecessary confusion in what is always a fast-moving defensive play. In addition, the cut-off

The infield shift against a right-handed power hitter finds three infielders between second
and third.

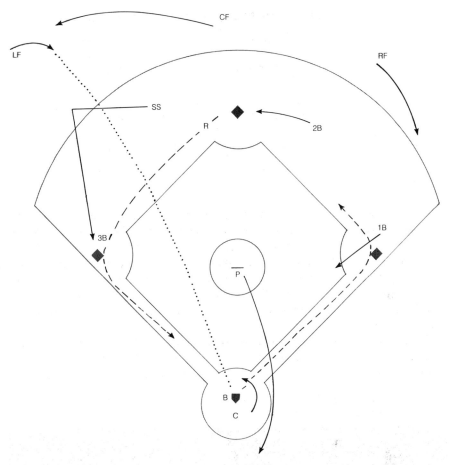

A typical cut-off play on a base hit to left field with a runner on second base.

man should station himself just far enough from the base for which the throw is intended so that a throw aimed at his chest, if allowed to continue, will reach the base on one bounce. This distance will vary according to the abilities of the outfielders and the field conditions. The only way to learn this distance is through practice; thus this play should merit considerable attention in each pre-game session. Players should consult the complete chart of cut-off responsibilities provided below for determination of specific cut-off duties.

4. There are two sacrifice-bunt situations that merit a specific teamwide defensive reaction. With a runner on first base, the following strategy should be adopted. The pitcher should attempt to hold the runner close to first. If there has been some indication that a bunt is planned by the offense, the pitcher should throw fast balls to the upper half of the strike zone. The first baseman should, after holding the runner on the base, break quickly toward home plate. The third baseman should "cheat in" several

RESPONSIBILITIES OF PLAYERS IN CUT-OFF SITUATIONS

	Left Fielder to			Center Fielder to			Right Fielder to		
	2B	3B	Home	2B	3B	Home	2B	3B	Home
Long Relay	—	—	SS	—	—	SS 2B	—	—	2B
Cut-Off	SS	SS	3B	SS	SS	1B 2B	2B	SS	1B
Back-up	1B RF	P	P	P	P	P	3B LF	P	P

steps in anticipation of the bunt. Once the hitter commits himself to bunt, the third baseman should charge quickly. The pitcher should move in a few steps after he delivers the ball. As the bunt is being made, the second baseman should break for first to cover that base in case the first baseman cannot get back there in time. The shortstop should move toward second base to cover for the possible play there. The outfielders should move in to back up the bases in case of an overthrow. In short, all nine players should become involved in this defensive play.

Whenever a sacrifice bunt is laid down, there is a choice as to what base the throw should go to after the bunt is fielded. The correctness of this choice is often crucial to the outcome of a ball game, and the choice is espe-

The cut-off man should spread his arms wide or assume any other stance necessary to provide a clear target for the outfielder.

cially difficult because it must be made instantaneously. The third baseman, pitcher, and first baseman are all charging in from their normal positions; if any one of these players fields the ball, he will not be in a position to see where the play should be made. The only player who has the full play in view is the catcher. Thus, he should make the decision as to where the ball should be thrown. He must do this with confidence and without delay, and he must make his decision known, loudly and clearly, to his teammates. As the fielder picks up the bunt, he must know where he is supposed to throw. The catcher should follow the general guidelines for defensive strategy that have been established by his coach. The coach might want to play safe in the early innings and call for a throw to first base, thus making sure of one out and preventing a big inning. In the later innings, he might want to take a chance on throwing out the lead runner in order to keep him out of scoring position. Whatever his preferences, the coach should discuss them with the catcher and all the other players so that all are aware of the general strategy he wishes to employ.

In all sacrifice situations the pitcher should hold the runner close to his base. This will prevent the runner from getting a big jump on the play and making it easily to the next base no matter how poor the bunt may be. One way to keep runners close is to throw to the base at regular intervals. In addition the pitcher can throw to a base several times in a row. The "move" to the base does not always have to be the pitcher's best move; even a token gesture is often sufficient to keep the runner from taking a long lead.

The second sacrifice-bunt situation that calls for team defense occurs when there are runners on first and second bases and no outs. This is almost always a bunting situation for the offense. The usual method of defending against this situation is as follows: the pitcher should attempt to hold the runner on second close to the base. Sometimes the defensive team will go so far as to station its shortstop near second to prevent the runner from taking too long a lead-off. The first baseman should "cheat in" in anticipation of the bunt and charge very quickly when the hitter commits himself to bunt. The first baseman should not charge straight in, however; rather he should move to a position midway between the baseline and the pitcher's mound. The pitcher must charge off the mound directly toward the third-base line; the third baseman can then stay back to cover third base. In sum, the defense is trying to cover the bunt with two players, the first baseman and the pitcher, thus keeping open the possibility for the force out at third base.

A second method can be used to handle this situation *if* it is anticipated that the offense will try to bunt the ball hard down the third-base line so that the third baseman will have to field the ball, thus eliminating the possibility of the force at third. Use of this method requires that the pitcher hold the runner on *first* close to his base. Also, the third baseman should charge instead of staying back. If the bunt is hard down the third-base line, the third baseman should have a chance to make a double play from third to second to first. The success of this method, however, is completely dependent upon the hitter bunting the ball forcefully toward third base.

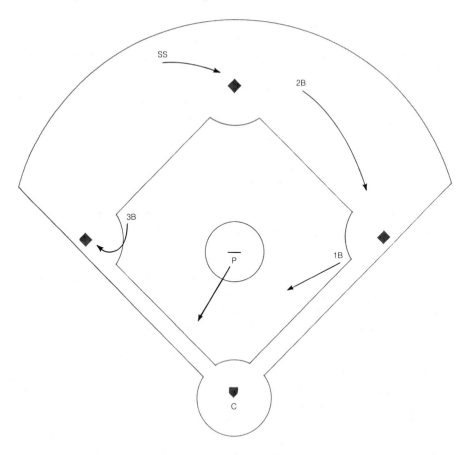

With runners on first and second, the infielders must move quickly to defend against a sacrifice bunt.

It must be emphasized that defending against a sacrifice bunt when there are runners on first and second is a very difficult task. Numerous errors are committed in this situation. To avoid such errors — some of which are costly mental errors that never get into the scorebook — the coach should allow ample time for his team to practice defending against this type of sacrifice bunt. The third baseman, pitcher, first baseman, and catcher all must learn difficult skills if they are to execute a successful team defense in this situation. The third baseman must know when to charge the bunt and when to hold back and cover third base. The pitcher must learn how to move quickly to the third-base line, how to field bunts, and how to throw to third or to first from that position. The first baseman must learn how to run in quickly and maneuver so that he can cover the rather wide area that is assigned to him in this defense. Above all, the catcher must practice making the crucial decision as to where to throw the ball. Each of these skills must first be learned and then put together to make a coordinated and successful team defense.

5. The safety squeeze bunt does not present a difficult defensive play if the defensive team is properly prepared to handle the situation. The pitcher can help to make this play relatively easy by pitching from the stretch position with a runner on third base. If the first and third basemen charge quickly when the hitter shows that he may attempt a safety squeeze bunt, this play should not be too close unless the bunt is perfectly placed, and even then the defense should have better than a 50–50 chance of getting the runner at the plate.

The suicide squeeze bunt is considerably more difficult to defend against because the runner on third base breaks for home plate *before* he sees whether the bunt is safely on the ground. In the suicide squeeze play, virtually any bunt that goes on the ground will score the runner from third base. The best defense in this situation, therefore, is to prevent the hitter from making a successful bunt. To do this, the pitcher must throw a pitch that is almost impossible for the hitter to bunt. That is, the pitcher should throw a high and inside pitch. Most hitters will not even attempt to bunt this type of pitch. Some catchers, however, are quite hesitant to field such a pitch, claiming that it is too difficult to field the ball and still move down to tag the runner. These catchers fear that they will become entangled with the hitter while trying to make the play. A catcher who holds this view usually calls for a low, outside fast ball, virtually a pitchout. This type of pitch, however, is sometimes easier for the hitter to bunt. Regardless of the type of pitch thrown, the key to defending against this offensive play is for the pitcher and catcher to react correctly once they learn that the runner on third has broken for the plate. Then, no matter what pitch had been signalled by the catcher, the pitcher must shift to the pitch that has been decided upon in advance for use in this situation—and the catcher must expect that this predetermined pitch will be thrown. If neither player is fooled by the play, the chance of successfully defending against the suicide squeeze will be enhanced.

6. There are three important guidelines that should be followed in defending against all steal situations. First, the pitcher should hold the runner close to his base. (This aspect of pitching is discussed at length in Chapter 10.) Second, the pitcher should deliver the ball to the plate as quickly as possible once he decides to initiate his motion. These two techniques will prevent runners from "getting the jump on the pitcher." This is important because as many bases are stolen because the pitcher did not do his job as are stolen because the catcher's throw is not in time or not accurate enough. Third, the catcher must get rid of the ball as quickly as possible. Too many young catchers attempt to make a forceful "clothesline" throw to the base—which usually results in the runner's being safe. (For a detailed analysis of catching techniques associated with steal situations the reader should consult Chapter 8.)

Other team members should help the pitcher and catcher in all steal situations. They can do this by yelling when they see a runner take off in an attempted steal. The catcher cannot always see the runner take off, although he should be generally aware of what the runner is doing and he should come up ready to throw after every pitch regardless of whether the runner is moving or not. Still, an early tip-off from a teammate can help the catcher to make his throw without the jerkiness that sometimes occurs when catchers are caught by surprise by an attempted steal.

The pitch-out is another defensive strategy which helps to combat the steal. It should be called primarily when the defensive team feels that the base runner will attempt to steal on the next pitch. The pitch-out is usually a fast ball, letter high, and several feet outside the strike zone. The catcher can catch this pitch easily and make his throw in the quickest possible way because he has received the ball in a position that is advantageous to throwing. It is sometimes good to let the opposition know that the defensive team is not afraid to use the pitch-out. The entire team can help develop a strategic use of the pitch-out by attempting to learn the opponent's steal sign.

The steal situation with runners on first and third bases requires a special team defense. High-school teams will often concede the steal of second

Diagram of the cut-off defense in the steal situation with runners on first and third.

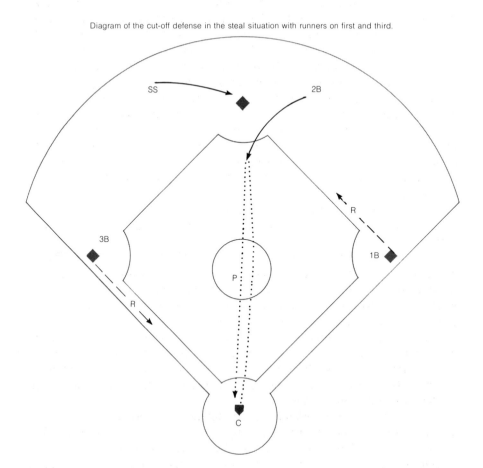

base in order to prevent the runner on third from scoring on a double steal. With proper defensive preparation, however, there is absolutely no need to concede the advancement of the runner on first. In this situation, we prefer to have the shortstop cover second base no matter what side the hitter swings from. In most steal situations, of course, the second baseman will cover his base when there is a right-handed hitter at bat. In the first and third steal situation, however, the shortstop should always cover second base, thus allowing the second baseman to become the cut-off man in this defensive maneuver. The second baseman should move toward the infield grass and position himself fifteen or twenty feet in front of second base in a direct line between home plate and the base. As he runs in to establish this position, he can easily keep the runner on third in clear view. In this manner, the defense can attempt to throw the runner out at second base and also make the adjustment to prevent the runner on third from scoring. To summarize, when the catcher receives the ball and is informed, by whatever signal the team uses, that the runner on first base has broken for second, he should quickly initiate his movements to throw the ball to second base. As he does this, he should glance toward the runner on third; if he has strayed too far off the base, the catcher can merely adjust his movements and throw to third. This short glance toward third is called "looking the runner back to the base," and it is of considerable importance in the total defensive maneuver. If the runner on third has not moved too far toward the plate, the catcher can make his throw to second base. This throw should be low enough so that the second baseman can field it easily as far as twenty to twenty-five feet in front of the base. The second baseman must then make the important defensive decision in this play. If, after the catcher throws toward second, the runner on third breaks for the plate, the second baseman should intercept the ball and throw back to the catcher to prevent the runner from scoring. If the runner on third base holds, the second baseman should allow the throw to continue on to the shortstop who will attempt to put out the runner sliding into second on the steal. Proper execution of this defensive maneuver requires practice; with sufficient practice, however, there is no reason why this cannot become a routine play. At the very least, this defense should prevent the usually unmolested advance to second base by the runner on first.

7. There is no real team defense against the hit-and-run or the run-and-hit situations. The defensive players simply must hold their normal fielding positions as long as possible before breaking for the defensive positions they must assume to prevent the steal. It has already been mentioned that the second baseman usually covers second base on the steal when there is a right-handed hitter at bat. The hit-and-run play is designed to take advantage of this fact. The offense hopes that the second baseman will move to cover second base when he sees the runner on first base break with the pitch. This premature move by the second baseman leaves the entire right side of the infield unprotected, since the first baseman has remained near the baseline to hold the runner on first. The coach should encourage his

second baseman to hold his position as long as possible before starting his move toward second base to cover against the steal. If he holds his position for just an extra fraction of a second, he can determine if the hitter is going to hit the ball toward his position. If so, the second baseman can maintain his fielding position and throw the hitter out at first base. If the hitter lets the ball go or swings and misses, the second baseman must *run* to second base. He will probably arrive at second at about the same moment that the throw does and, hopefully, just ahead of the sliding runner. This play is a difficult one for the second baseman, but with proper practice and instruction he can master the skills and timing.

8. Pick-off situations refer to attempts by the defense to catch a runner too far off his base and put him out as he attempts to return to the base. A pick-off play can help the defense a great deal, but it should be used with caution. Many pitchers and catchers try for pick-offs too often, and the end result is usually an overthrow of the base and an easy advance by the runner. The catcher can attempt a pick-off throw to first any time that he sees the runner move too far from the base with a pitch. The pick-off attempt from the catcher to second base, however, is not usually advisable because it rarely brings results. A bluff throw is usually better in this situation. The pick-off attempt from the catcher to third is risky because an overthrow means a run for the opponents. If this throw is made, it should be made to the inside of the base so that it does not hit the runner. When attempting a pick-off at first, the catcher must also be careful not to hit the batter. If the batter is left-handed, for example, the catcher will have to throw behind him. Often a team has a set pick-off play to use when there are runners on first and second. In this play, the first baseman usually charges hard and quickly toward the plate in an attempt to lure the runner on first off his base. The second baseman, as he normally would in this bunting situation, breaks for first. The pitcher throws a pitch-out, and the catcher throws the ball to the second baseman who has cut in behind the runner to take the throw at first base. This play can be effective but should be used with caution because the runner on second base can easily advance to third if he is alert.

Pick-off attempts by a pitcher fall into two categories. First, there is the throw made by a pitcher who is merely attempting to hold a runner to a base. This play and the techniques involved are covered fully in Chapter 14. The second type of pick-off attempt by a pitcher is the actual pick-off play designed to put out the runner. This play usually comes with a runner on second base, because this runner always takes a longer lead-off than a runner on first. There are two general methods by which this type of pick-off play can be handled: the signal method and the count method. In the former, a predetermined signal—often the "daylight" signal—is used to activate the play. In this case, the shortstop breaks toward second base. If the pitcher sees "daylight" between the runner and the shortstop, he turns and throws in an attempt to pick off the runner. In other cases the pitcher will give the signal. He may do this before he takes his stretch position, or he may do it by some predetermined visual sign.

The "count" method refers to a predetermined play which involves precise timing. Either the pitcher, the shortstop, or the second baseman can initiate this play, depending on who is designated by the coach to give the signal. The signal is usually given before the pitcher gets his sign from the catcher, and the play is normally keyed on the pitcher's stretch move. More often than not, the defensive players begin to "count" when the pitcher comes to his set position. On the second count, the shortstop breaks for second base. On the third or fourth count, the pitcher whirls and throws to second. The advantage of this method is that the pitcher does not have to watch the runner or the shortstop. A variation on the count method which is sometimes used involves bringing the second baseman into the play. In this case, the second baseman will break to second base, causing the runner to move back toward the base. The second baseman will stay at the base momentarily but will then move back to his fielding position. When this occurs, the runner will usually resume his lead-off. It is at this moment that the shortstop must break to second for the pick-off. The signal in this variation of the "count" method is the movement of the second baseman when he returns to his fielding position.

9. The defensive reaction by a team to a ball hit to the right side of the infield should be automatic. The pitcher should run to cover first base on *every* ball hit to the right side. He should run hard until he is waved off the play by the first baseman. This must become a habit for each pitcher; there is absolutely no excuse for the first baseman to find nobody covering first after he has fielded a ground ball on the edge of the outfield grass. The coach should allot ample practice time to perfecting the movements and coordination of this defensive play.

10. The run-down situation occurs when a base runner is trapped between bases. The runner should be a sure out for the defense if the defensive players follow several simple guidelines. First, the runner should always be run back toward the base from which he started. In a run-down between second and third bases, for example, the runner should be run back toward second. When the putout is finally made, it should occur closer to second base than to third base. Second, the fielders involved in the run-down play should always keep the ball in sight. The throws in this situation sometimes have to be very quick and short. To field them, the fielder must be able to see the ball clearly. Third, the defensive players involved in the run-down must move according to some predetermined pattern. Most coaches prefer to use a pattern in which the player throwing the ball will then drop back to become a back-up man. A run-down play usually involves four defensive players. For example if the run-down occurs between second and third bases, the shortstop and third baseman may be the two players originally involved, with the second baseman backing up the shortstop and the pitcher or catcher backing up the third baseman. When the third baseman chases the runner back toward second and throws to the shortstop, he then should drop back to back up the pitcher who should have moved up to take his place in the run-down sequence. If this progression is followed, the defensive players will not become entangled with one another and will maintain proper spacing for the run-down play.

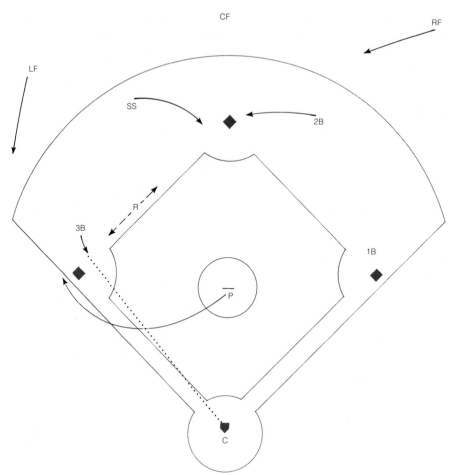

A run-down situation with a runner trapped between second and third. Notice the movement of the four players who will form the basic run-down defense.

On run-downs between first and second, the shortstop, second baseman, first baseman, and pitcher form the four-man run-down defense. Between third base and home plate, the shortstop, third baseman, catcher, and pitcher provide the defense for the run-down play. In each of these situations, the basic principles of run-down defense should be applied. That is, the runner should be run *back* to the base where he started; the ball should always be kept in sight; and the defensive player who throws should then drop back to back up his teammate who must move up in the run-down sequence.

There is no excuse for a runner ever to get out of a run-down situation. If the defensive team has established run-down procedures and has had time to practice them, the job of putting the trapped runner out should be an easy one.

11. Strategy for a relief pitcher to use once he is in the game is discussed in Chapter 14; nothing further will be said about pitching strategy here.

The entire infield sometimes becomes involved in run-down plays, with each defensive man protecting a base, backing up a throw, or attempting to tag the runner.

The question of when to put in a relief pitcher, however, is clearly a matter of defensive strategy and will thus be discussed in this chapter.

Perhaps the most difficult decision that coaches must make during the course of a game is when to bring in a relief pitcher, particularly in relief of a starting pitcher. In professional baseball, relief pitching is a special skill, and there are special players to do this job. Even so, the decision is often a difficult one for the manager. In college and high-school baseball, there are seldom established relief pitchers. In fact, relief pitchers on these levels are usually the ones who are not good enough to become starting pitchers. This makes any decision about taking out a starting pitcher doubly difficult for the high-school or college coach. The biggest factor in making the decision, is how good the relief pitcher is. The more confidence the coach has in his relief pitcher, the easier it is to make the decision to bring him in. The relief pitcher must be able to consistently get the ball over the plate. This is especially important in high-school baseball because starting pitchers at this level are most often taken out of the game because of wildness. To bring in a relief pitcher who is also wild would be suicidal to the chances of the team. Another factor which helps the coach make decisions about relief pitchers is the overall defensive ability of the team. If a coach has a good defensive team, he can be more confident about bringing in a mediocre relief pitcher.

Coaches at all levels might do well to designate and put the responsibility for relief pitching on one of the second-line pitchers on the team. If the player has some poise, he will probably rise to the challenge and do a good job for his team. As the team's number one relief pitcher, he will acquire status in the eyes of his teammates, and this should spur him on to an all-out effort.

Chapter 14
Pitching Strategy

This chapter deals with the techniques and strategies involved in pitching in game competition. The material presented here should be considered along with that in Chapters 1 and 12, which are concerned with the fundamentals of throwing a baseball and the basic coaching techniques for developing good pitchers. Together, these three chapters provide a comprehensive treatment of pitching. Chapter 12 contains a discussion of coaching techniques for building successful pitching performances. That discussion covers such subjects as balance, rhythm, leverage, and imparting spin to the ball. The chapter now under consideration deals with putting these techniques to good use in game situations. It is futile for a coach to teach his pitchers the technique of throwing good fast balls and breaking pitches if he ignores the strategies involved in putting these skills to use in a game. Many a major league pitcher has had his most successful seasons long after he has lost the great fast ball of his earlier years. While commentators often suggest that this late-blooming success is due to the addition of certain breaking pitches to the pitching repertoire, it is much more likely that the success is due to the pitcher's greater knowledge of strategy and his ability to execute that strategy successfully. Such a pitcher has, in fact, "learned his trade." He has become a pitcher in the fullest sense of the word, as opposed to the many young "throwers" who fill the rosters of high-school, college, and even professional teams. The principles listed here can serve as guidelines to help both the coach and the pitcher to develop an adequate knowledge of pitching strategy. In addition to these principles, it is of paramount importance that the pitcher *always* attempt to throw strikes. The first and most crucial task of any young pitcher is to learn how to throw strikes consistently. Learning strategy will be of little use to a pitcher if he has not first mastered this skill. Moreover, the pitcher must have poise. He must not let anything upset him while he is on the mound, regardless of the success of the offensive or defensive play.

Principles of Pitching Strategy

1. The main goal of the pitcher is always to retire the hitter, to get an out.
2. The pitcher must warm up adequately before starting a game.
3. As the pitcher warms up, he should find out what his best pitch is for that day.
4. The pitcher should, for the most part, aim his pitches from the center of the plate outward—according to the number of strikes on the hitter.
5. The pitcher should work to keep most of his pitches low, especially breaking pitches.
6. The pitcher should avoid falling into a pitching pattern.
7. The pitcher should find out if any opposing hitter can be "intimidated" by specific pitches.
8. The pitcher should never waste a pitch.

9. When the pitcher is in a jam he must challenge the hitter, pitting strength against strength if necessary.
10. The pitcher should work toward the goal of being able to throw a breaking pitch in the 2-0 and 3-2 situations.
11. The pitcher should not give unnecessary help to the weak hitter by throwing too many breaking pitches.
12. The change-up pitch is usually more successful against the strong hitter than against the weaker hitter.
13. The high fast ball is the best pitch to throw in the obvious bunting situation.
14. The high-inside fast ball is the best pitch to throw when a squeeze play
• is anticipated.
15. There are at least eight major pitching faults that should be avoided.
16. The pitcher should never "outthink" himself.

Discussing the Principles

1. The main goal of the pitcher is always to retire the hitter, to get an out. While this may seem elementary, our experience in baseball suggests that many pitchers do not recognize the primacy of this goal. Too often, the pitcher, especially if he is young, attempts to strike out almost every batter. He tries to either overpower the hitters with his fast ball or to break-off sharp curves. The problem with this strategy is that the overpowering fast ball of the young pitcher has a tendency to go too high, and his sharply breaking curve ball often either hangs too high or breaks too low. Thus while he may, indeed, record many strikeouts, he will also frequently have to come in with a very good pitch when he is behind the hitter. Such a pitcher would be far more effective if he would recognize that the strikeout is not the only way to retire a batter. Once he realizes that fact, he will see that he can utilize different strategies. He can throw his fast ball for "spots" and hope that the hitter will attempt to hit a pitch that is to the hitter's disadvantage. He can also throw his curve ball in the low-outside quarter of the strike zone, getting the hitter to hit the ball on the ground without a great deal of force. Occasionally, when the situation warrants a full-blown attempt at a strikeout, the pitcher should work toward that goal. But normally, he should take the strikeouts as they come without making any special effort in that direction. His main goal should be to throw pitches that put the hitter at a disadvantage. This type of strategy takes advantage of the probabilities that exist in the pitcher-hitter duel. By throwing to selected "spots," the pitcher can reduce the hitter's batting average by .100 or .150 points, and the odds on his retiring the hitter are overwhelmingly in his favor. It is not unreasonable, then, to suggest that the main goal of the pitcher should always be to retire the hitter by getting the hitter to swing at pitches that put him (the hitter) at a disadvantage.

2. The pitcher must warm up adequately before starting a game. There are two very important reasons for a coach to insist on this. First, there is the matter of the physiological warm-up of the musculature. Pitching involves most of the musculature of the body, and to perform the skill at a high level requires that the musculature be fully warmed up. If the pitcher fails to warm up properly, he will simply not be able to throw his best pitches during the first inning or so of the game. His fast ball will not quite have the speed that it should have, and his curve ball will not break as sharply as he would like it to. The result, of course, may be that the inadequately warmed-up pitcher may have to be taken out of the game early.

3. The second reason for the coach to insist on an adequate warm-up is so the pitcher can find out what his best pitch is for that particular day. Normally, most pitchers have at least two pitches that they depend on a great deal in games. Each pitcher must find out, in the warm-up period, which of his pitches seems to be best that day. On the basis of this information, he can then begin the game relying on his best pitch. Many pitchers, for example, have great difficulty throwing good breaking pitches until they are fully warmed up. This kind of pitcher will not know how well his breaking pitches are breaking unless he warms up adequately during the pre-game period.

There can be no hard and fast rule for the amount of time that a pitcher should take to warm up. This is an individual matter, and the coach must work with each of his pitchers so that they can come to an agreement on the amount of time that should be spent at this task. Some pitchers can be ready after five minutes of throwing, while others need at least twenty minutes. The weather is an important factor in determining the length of the warm-up. On a very warm summer day, the pitcher is greatly aided by the heat during his warm-up period. On a cool, damp day, however, he may need twice as long as he normally would take to warm up. Ultimately, only the pitcher can tell when he feels his pitches are such that he can begin the ball game; but the coach must help the pitcher to understand the importance of an adequate warm-up period.

4. The pitcher should, for the most part, aim his pitches from the center of the plate outward—according to the number of strikes on the hitter. While this strategy might not be precise enough for a major league pitcher, it will generally be fully satisfactory for the college and high-school hurler. This strategy simply suggests that with no strikes on the hitter, the pitcher should use a target that is somewhere near the center of the strike zone. A point just below the center of the strike zone would probably be best in this situation. With one strike on the hitter, the pitcher can afford to be slightly more exact with his pitches. For example, he can aim for the low-outside quarter or the high-inside quarter of the strike zone. With two strikes on the hitter (this assumes of course that the count is not 3–2), the pitcher can go for the corners, attempting perhaps to catch the low-inside corner with a breaking pitch or the high-outside corner with a fast ball. This strategy will help the pitcher to avoid walking hitters.

5. The pitcher should work to keep most of his pitches low, especially

his breaking pitches. In principle 4, it was suggested that the best place for the target when there are no strikes on the hitter is just *below* the center of the strike zone, not the center itself. This is important. Low pitches tend to be hit on the ground, while high pitches tend to be hit in the air. The ball that is hit on the ground is never as potentially dangerous to the pitcher as the one hit in the air. Very few long balls will be hit from low pitches, but the high fast ball and curve ball are often the best pitches for the hitter to swing at. Thus every time a pitcher throws a pitch, he should be concentrating on keeping the ball low. "Pitching strings" can be a tremendous aid in accomplishing this purpose. The pitching strings tell the pitcher exactly where each pitch goes, and a daily record of pitches thrown with strings can be a useful asset to the coach in terms of both learning and motivation. Keeping the pitch low is especially important when throwing breaking pitches. Enough has been said in baseball circles about the "hanging curveball" to impress on the pitcher fully the error of throwing this type of pitch.

6. The pitcher should avoid falling into a pitching pattern, that is, he should not keep repeating the same sequence of pitches. Many young pitchers will throw fast balls until they are ahead of the hitter and then come in with a curve ball, hoping for the strikeout. This is called the F-F-C pattern (Fast ball-Fast ball-Curve). Other pitchers will always throw a breaking pitch when they have an 0-2 count on the hitter. Another pattern that is sometimes seen is the C-F-F-C combination. We do not mean to suggest that any particular sequence of pitches is not good. The sequence may, in fact, be excellent, but when it is repeated over and over again so that it becomes a pattern it loses its effectiveness. The hitter can easily learn to predict what pitch he will face next. Thus, he will have an advantage that he otherwise would not have. Therefore, the pitcher should continually alter his sequence of pitches so as to maintain his edge over the hitter. The best method for insuring that this will be done properly is for the team to keep a pitching chart during each game. The pitcher can then check the chart from time to time to make sure that he is not falling into a pattern. This checking procedure should also be followed by the catcher, especially if calling the pitching signals is primarily his responsibility.

7. The pitcher should find out if any opposing hitter can be "intimidated" by specific pitches. This information should be sought out as early in the game as possible, if it is not already available from previous games with the opponents. It has been suggested earlier (see page 126) that many hitters have a fear of the ball, especially the breaking pitch. While most hitters overcome this fear as they move up the competitive ladder, some retain it. Such a hitter can be "intimidated" by an inside curve ball or an inside fast ball. After having thrown such a pitch, the pitcher usually finds the hitter backing away on succeeding pitches, regardless of where they are thrown. Note that there is *no* suggestion here to throw *at* a hitter. *We do not condone this practice.* On the other hand, no pitcher should be afraid to throw an inside pitch. Most of the rules of baseball favor the hitter. But the pitcher can, at least, use the entire area around the strike zone for throwing his pitches. If a hitter can be intimidated by an inside pitch, he deserves to

have inside pitches thrown to him. The wise pitcher will store up this information and put it to use when the situation calls for a sure out.

8. The pitcher should never waste a pitch. The 0–2 pitch in baseball is often called "waste" pitch. This term is misunderstood. For the successful pitcher, there is no such thing as a waste pitch. Each pitch thrown should have purpose. If the pitch is delivered to the desired spot, then the task has been successfully completed. The desired spot in the 0–2 situation is usually just outside the strike zone and in a location that puts the hitter at a maximum disadvantage. The pitcher who always throws the ball in the dirt or three feet outside the strike zone in the 0–2 situation is truly wasting a pitch. This practice should not be condoned. The coach should work with his pitchers to establish realistic objectives for the 0–2 situation, and then he should make sure that every attempt is made to reach those objectives.

9. When a pitcher is in a jam he must challenge the hitter, pitting strength against strength if necessary. The majority of hitters are most effective when hitting a fast ball. For most pitchers, too, the fast ball is the best pitch. When the pitcher is in a tight situation, he must have enough confidence and courage to challenge the fast ball hitter with his fast ball. Some hitters are low-ball hitters; most pitchers work to keep their pitches low. When the situation gets tense, the low-ball pitcher must challenge this kind of hitter with a low strike. A pitcher must not be afraid to challenge a hitter's strength. Many young pitchers attempt to be "cute" in this situation; they attempt to pitch defensively when they are in a jam. They should, instead, pitch with their strength and challenge the hitter. It is only by following this practice that they can gain the confidence and courage to be aggressive pitchers.

10. The pitcher should work toward the goal of being able to throw a breaking pitch in the 2–0 and 3–2 situations. While this may seem contradictory to the principle stated above, it should not be so construed. We are not suggesting that a fast ball pitcher should *always* throw a breaking ball in a tough 2–0 situation. Rather, we say that he should have a good breaking ball that he can use in this situation occasionally. The purpose, of course, is to avoid falling into a pitching pattern (see principle 6). Most fast ball pitchers will want to throw their fast ball in the majority of 3–2 situations that they will face during a game or season. They should not always do this, however, because it would establish a pattern that the opponents could predict. Most hitters will look for a fast ball in the above situation. A breaking pitch can fool them and immediately create an advantage for the pitcher. To throw good breaking pitches in such a situation requires confidence and practice. The young pitcher usually has difficulty controlling his breaking pitches well enough to use them in the 2–0 or 3–2 situation. Thus, he must practice his breaking pitches and then begin to use them occasionally in these situations.

11. The pitcher should not give unnecessary help to weak hitters by throwing too many breaking pitches. The weak hitter will often look foolish attempting to hit a breaking pitch, but he will also often get a scratch hit from such a pitch. The weak hitter does not react as quickly as a good hit-

ter. He cannot get his bat around quickly enough to connect consistently with the ball. This type of hitter is often helped by a breaking pitch because the breaking pitch is a slow pitch which gives the weak hitter more time to react. If a pitcher has a good fast ball, the coach should encourage him to rely primarily on that pitch when he faces a weak hitter. It is difficult to resist the temptation to throw a breaking pitch to this type of hitter, but the pitcher should do so. He may not get quite as many strikeouts with his fast ball, but he will have the greatest success.

12. The change-up pitch is usually more successful against the strong hitter than against the weak hitter. The change-up is designed to upset the rhythm of the hitter and to disrupt his timing as he attempts to hit the ball. One of the characteristics that contributes to successful hitting is good timing and rhythm. The better the hitter, the better his timing and rhythm. This type of hitter is most prone to the disruption in timing that is caused by the change-up pitch. The weak hitter, on the other hand, may well be a weak hitter precisely because he lacks good timing and rhythm. To throw a change-up to him is often to aid him. In most high-school and college situations, a coach would do well to instruct his pitchers to throw change-up pitches only to the three or four better hitters on the opposing team. In this way, the pitchers will make good use of the pitch. They will not be hurt by having a weak hitter perfectly time a well-thrown change-up.

13. The high fast ball is the best pitch to throw in the obvious bunting situation. When there is a runner on first base, no outs in the inning, and the pitcher at bat, an obvious bunting situation exists. Likewise, with runners on first and second and no one out. When the pitcher has a good indication that the hitter may attempt to sacrifice, he should rely primarily on the high fast ball, because it is the most difficult pitch to bunt. The batter usually has to move his bat up to bunt this pitch, and he is likely to pop the ball up rather than bunt successfully on the ground. The pitch that should be most avoided in these situations is the low curve ball. The low breaking pitch is the easiest pitch to bunt. The hitter has to move down to bunt the ball, and with the ball also moving in a downward direction, he will almost assuredly bunt on the ground. This aspect of strategy should be made clear to both the pitcher and the catcher. Nevertheless, the pitcher should not attempt to throw the ball too high, thus running the risk of walking the hitter. Moreover, the high fast ball is not normally a good pitch for most pitchers to throw because it is too often a "long ball" pitch for the hitter. Therefore, the pitcher should make sure that use of the high fast ball is warranted by the high probability of a bunt.

14. The high-inside fast ball is the best pitch to throw when a squeeze play is anticipated. The high-inside fast ball is not only a very difficult pitch to bunt, but if thrown properly it will force the hitter to back away from the plate. This is an advantage to the catcher because the hitter will in no way impede his getting the ball and putting the tag on the runner coming in from third base. The disadvantage of using this pitch in the squeeze situation is that after catching it the catcher has a long way to move downward to tag the runner at the plate. We feel that this disadvantage is not serious enough

to detract from the advantages offered by the use of this strategy. Many teams employ a pitchout in this situation, particularly if the catcher prefers not to handle the inside pitch at this juncture. The major drawback to the pitchout is that it can often be easily bunted by a hitter reaching across the plate. Since this must be avoided at all costs, the high-inside fast ball is felt to be more advantageous to the defensive team. The high-inside fast ball strategy should be a matter of team policy, so that the catcher and pitcher react to the squeeze play automatically. That is, when a pitcher is in his pitching motion and he hears his teammates signal that a squeeze play is underway, he should automatically throw the high-inside fast ball, and the catcher should expect this pitch. The pitcher must remember, however, that he should only so react when a definite verbal signal from his teammates indicates to him that the runner on third has initiated the squeeze play by breaking for home plate. He should not react to the visual cue of a hitter moving into the bunting stance with a runner on third base. If the pitcher reacts to this, the hitter will merely take the bunting stance and then let the pitch go by for a ball. The important point is that a team policy must be established by the coach, understood by all the players, and practiced enough so that the response is automatic.

15. There are at least eight major pitching faults that should be avoided. These errors are important enough that a coach may attempt to correct them *during* a game situation. Normally, the pitcher should be free to concentrate on his game without having to listen to suggestions from the coach on minute aspects of pitching technique. The eight errors listed here, however, are major enough that the interference of the coach can be justified.

Eight Major Pitching Faults

1. Poor concentration on the target
2. Poor concentration on the pitch
3. Failure to step toward the target
4. Failure to accelerate during the motion
5. Pitching too "close" to the corners
6. Failure to put adequate spin on the ball
7. Failure to forcefully snap the wrist downward
8. Loss of poise during a game

The technique and theory behind each of these errors has already been dealt with in this book. With experience, coaches can come to recognize these errors in their pitchers *as they occur*. Thus, occasionally the coach may want to remind a pitcher to concentrate a bit more on his wrist snap or on exactly where he wants to throw his pitch. Such suggestions are helpful and are not technical enough to impede pitching performance during a game.

16. The pitcher should never "outthink" himself. He must concentrate on the pitch he is throwing and the target that he is aiming at and attempt, for the most part, to drive all else from his center of attention. The pitcher must also avoid being too "cute" with hitters. As has been suggested, he must ultimately test his strength against the strength of the hitters. Some coaches tell their pitchers to "pick up the ball and throw it." Other coaches give their pitchers so many instructions that the pitcher has to mentally fill out a check-list before each pitch. These two extremes should be avoided.

Holding the Runner on First Base

This aspect of total pitching performance is so important that it warrants a special section of its own. Too many coaches are willing to merely instruct their pitchers to "hold the runner close," and offer the pitcher no concrete instruction on how this task can best be accomplished.

Principles of Performance

1. The pitcher should ration his best move and not use it every time he throws to first base.
2. The pitcher should constantly change his pattern of eye focus.
3. The pitcher should vary his count after coming to the set position.
4. Most often, the pitcher should make up his mind where he is going to throw before he comes to the set position.
5. The right-handed pitcher can get a better look at first base by opening his stance.
6. The pitcher can usually stay within the rules by keeping his pick-off move toward first to the first-base side of a line drawn on a 45-degree angle off of the straight line from the mound to first base.
7. Getting the ball to home plate quickly is an important part of holding a base runner close to first base.

Discussing the Principles

1. The pitcher should save his best move and not use it every time he throws to first base. When a pitcher throws to first to hold the base runner close, he should always throw with authority but not necessarily with the purpose of picking the runner off the base. By merely throwing to first base at varied intervals, the pitcher can break the runner's rhythm and get him in the habit of moving back toward first rather than on toward second. This is especially true for a left-handed pitcher. The goal of the pitcher in these

situations is to establish in the runner's mind the clear possibility of a
throw to first base, not necessarily to pick the runner off the base. Occasionally, however, the pitcher should use his best move toward first in an
attempt to pick the runner off. This will force the runner to take precau-
tions against the good move on every pitch.

2. The pitcher should constantly change his pattern of eye focus. Some
pitchers always look at first base when they are going to throw there. Other
pitchers will look, look away, and then throw to first. Sometimes, the pitcher
should initiate his throw to first while he is looking at the target. Other
times, he should throw to home plate while looking toward the runner. The
point is that the pitcher must avoid any pattern that is detectable by the
opponents. Once an opponent detects a pattern, he can predict the pitcher's movements and get a big jump on him. The coach should check his
pitcher during a game situation to see that such patterns are avoided.

3. The pitcher should vary his count after coming to the set position. As
in principle 2, the pitcher must avoid falling into a pattern with the count he
uses before throwing to first base. Some pitchers throw immediately after
coming to the set position. Others always wait two counts and then throw
to either first base or home plate. The smart pitcher will vary this count.
He will work to make his pitching as unpredictable as possible. Occasionally,
he will throw to first immediately after coming to the set position. Other
times, he will wait five or six counts before committing himself. When a
pitcher varies the count, he places the runner at a maximum disadvantage
and, therefore, keeps him close to first base.

4. Most often, the pitcher should make up his mind where he is going to
throw before he comes to the set position. This allows him to concentrate

Getting a jump on a left-handed pitcher is difficult for a base runner because of the
deceptive lift of the pitcher's stride leg.

fully on the execution of either the pitch or the attempted pick-off. If a pitcher waits to make up his mind after he comes to the set position, he will not be able to concentrate fully on the pitch, and he may poorly execute the pitch or the pick-off because he has hesitated momentarily in making the decision. Moreover, the pre-set decision helps the pitcher to throw to first base more often. Too many pitchers throw to first base too seldom. But by deciding to throw before coming to the set position, they tend to think more carefully and remember that the occasional throw to first is a real aid in holding the runner close to the base.

5. The right-handed pitcher can get a better look at first base by opening his stance. The rule book indicates that the shoulders of the pitcher may not move once he is in the set position. Some right-handed pitchers have a difficult time looking back over their left shoulder to see the runner on first base. These pitchers will get a clearer view of the runner if they open their set stance so that the body is angled slightly toward the first-base line. Another advantage of this stance for the right-handed pitcher is that it requires less of a turn to throw the ball to first base, and, therefore, helps the pitcher to throw the ball there in less time. The open stance does not hinder the pitching motion to any appreciable degree, and, therefore, it seems to be good strategy for many right-handed pitchers.

6. The pitcher can usually stay within the rules by keeping his move toward first to the first-base side of a line drawn on a 45-degree angle off of a straight line going from the mound to first base. The rule says that the pitcher must step *directly* toward first base, but actual game interpretation usually views any move to the left of the abovementioned 45-degree line as a legal move. Pitchers can practice making this kind of move by merely drawing a line in the dirt around the pitching rubber and keeping just to the left of that line when moving toward first base. This strategy cuts down on the distance of the move so that it can be completed in less time.

7. Getting the ball to home plate quickly is also an important part of holding a base runner close to first base. Many pitchers ignore this part of pitching strategy. Some hold a runner very close to first base, but take so long to deliver the pitch to the plate that the runner can easily steal second base after the delivery has been initiated. The pitcher who delivers the ball to home plate quickly can have great success in preventing the steal even though his move to first base may not be a very good one.

Chapter 15
How to Teach
Baseball
Skills

A baseball coach may possess a vast amount of knowledge about the skills of baseball, but if he does not know how to teach these skills to his players then the knowledge he possesses will not help his team to win baseball games. While it would be absurd to suggest that there is one best method for teaching baseball skills, it would be equally incorrect to fail to point out what is known about the proper methods for teaching sports skills.

A great deal of research in the area of motor learning has been conducted by numerous investigators in many disciplines. Enough unanimity of opinion exists concerning the results of this research that one can now begin to offer guidelines based primarily on scientific evidence rather than on "cracker-barrel" opinion. It is interesting that several of these guidelines are quite different from the teaching methods used by many coaches. Although it is true that there is no one best method for teaching sports skills, it is just as true that not all methods are of equal value. In this chapter an attempt is made to propose a select, but nevertheless useful, set of principles for the coach to use. These principles deal with factors that can affect the rate at which players learn the skills of the game.

The baseball coach must attempt to see his practice session as a total learning environment. The principles in this chapter deal with that learning environment. These principles may be considered to be substantiated by scientific experimental evidence. Although no research studies are cited, the number of studies supporting each principle could easily run into the hundreds. The chapter concludes with a section dealing with the development of drills.

Principles for Teaching Baseball Skills

1. The learning situation should be precisely defined for the learner.
2. Each skill should be presented to the learner as an understandable whole.
3. The skill should be demonstrated to the learner at somewhere near the speed at which he will have to perform it.
4. The behavior expected should be defined in a general manner, but no precise form should be imposed on the learner.
5. The information feedback to the learner should be maximized.
6. A proper response from the learner should be rewarded.
7. The time lapse between the response and the information feedback and reward is crucial to the learning situation.
8. Only major errors should be corrected during the early stages of learning.
9. Verbal instruction by the coach is of limited usefulness during the early stages of learning and should seldom replace active participation at any level.
10. Live demonstrations by a competent performer appear to be superior to any other method currently used for teaching baseball skills.

11. A motivated learner can learn despite many obstacles.
12. The chances for significant learning are increased when a moderate stress exists in the learning environment.
13. Mental practice between actual practice sessions can aid learning.
14. To correct an error at the higher levels of skill, the player must first be made aware of the error; then the erroneous action must be gradually replaced by the proper behavior.

Discussing the Principles

1. The learning situation should be precisely defined for the learner. When a coach uses a bunting drill he should define exactly the spot to which he wants his players to attempt to bunt the ball. It is not enough to *tell* them that the ball should be bunted down the first- or third-base line. Some method of marking the desirable areas should be used. If the bunter sees a towel, a chalked area, or a different colored area, he will form a precise idea of where the ball is to be bunted. The stimulus situation has become better defined, and this creates a better learning situation. If the coach wants his runners to run to first base as fast as they can, he should always have a stop watch ready when they make this run during practice sessions. If the goal for a certain hitter is 4.2 seconds, the coach has defined the stimulus situation for the player, and the information feedback (his actual time) that the player receives after he runs will take on new meaning and enhance the possibility of learning. If a coach wants his shortstop and second baseman to throw the ball underhand to each other when they are iniating a double play within 15 feet of the base, he should chalk off a semi-circle around second base so that the players may practice this skill with the learning goals precisely defined. The need for such definition of the learning situation cannot be emphasized too much.

2. Each skill should be presented to the learner as an understandable whole. Research indicates that the "whole method" of teaching skills is superior to the part method. A whole should be thought of as an understandable and meaningful unit. The hitting stroke, for example, is a meaningful whole and should not be taught by the part method. Players who possess higher levels of skill can practice parts of a skill to great advantage, but they know that skill well enough so that they actually fill in the rest of the movements of the skill mentally and therefore are really practicing a meaningful whole. We believe that virtually all baseball skills should be taught by the whole method. There are no skills in baseball that are so complex as to require the part method of teaching. Fielding ground balls, fielding fly balls, throwing, hitting, bunting, and pitching can all be taught as complete units.

3. The skill should be demonstrated to the learner at somewhere near the speed at which he will have to perform it. Many coaches feel that beginning learners should practice a skill at a slow speed with an emphasis

on accuracy and correct form. Research evidence does not support this method of teaching. Skills should be practiced near the speed at which they will be used in performance. When a player learns a skill at a much slower pace than he will have to perform it, he is actually learning a different skill. Different muscle fibers become involved and a different pattern of coordination and timing is established. In pitching, for example, many coaches advise young players to throw with a slow motion to establish accuracy or control. What the young pitcher is learning, however, is merely to throw slowly and accurately. The accuracy will not transfer when the pitcher begins to throw harder. If a pitcher wants to learn control, he has to do it while pitching at speeds that are near his game performance speeds. The same is true for other baseball skills.

4. The behavior expected should be defined in a general manner, but no precise form should be imposed on the learner. All the learner needs is an *idea* of what the skill generally looks like. He can get this idea by observing the general appearance of the skill. No young learner should ever have a particular form imposed upon him by a teacher. In hitting, for example, there is nothing more evident that the fact that there is no one correct hitting form. The Berras, Mayses, Clementes, and McAuliffes have shown clearly that the "classic" swing of a Kaline or Killebrew is not the only way to achieve success in hitting. Each young learner has to find out for himself which form will work best for him. The coach should merely give the learner an idea of what he considers to be good form. If the coach insists that young learners hit with a certain precise form, he will inhibit learning considerably and any learning that might occur will take place *in spite of* his coaching rather than *because of* it. The same is true for other baseball skills. For example, not all pitchers will throw overhand like Koufax and McLain. No coach should impose an overhand form on a young pitcher. If he does, he may prevent the development of another Bunning or Chance.

5. The information feedback to the learner should be maximized. Anytime a learner can discover useful information concerning his performance, his learning experience will be enhanced. Precisely defining the learning environment most often increases the amount of information feedback available to the learner (see principle 1). In recent years, researchers have discovered that the quality and quantity of information feedback is a factor of primary importance in the total learning situation. The more information feedback, the faster the rate of learning. There are several methods by which the amount of information feedback available to the learner can be increased. First, the coach can simply talk to the learner about his performance, pointing out any major errors that might have occurred during the learning trials. More information feedback can be gained, however, through the use of visual aids. Players can greatly benefit from seeing themselves in action. Eight-millimeter film is not so expensive that it cannot be used in most school situations. A stop action projecter might also be available. The learner can then watch himself in action and learn from his own performance. The only drawback to this type of film is that the time lag between the performance and the information feedback is long. This time lag can be

eliminated by the use of video tape or a "graph-check" camera. The graph-check camera takes eight sequence pictures on one print. The print can be developed on the spot, making it a tremendously valuable coaching aid. The uses of video tape, of course, are very obvious. Most major league teams have adopted this method and have found it to be very helpful.

6. A proper response from the learner should be rewarded. Rewarding correct responses definitely tends to increase the rate of learning. The coach should define the rewards that can be earned in the practice and game situations. Merely having teammates *know* the results of a player's good performance is a valuable reward. A word of praise from the coach is usually a powerful reward, although it is inefficient because the coach can normally only praise one player at a time. The coach should consider establishing some systematic method of rewarding good performances in practice situations. A point system usually works best. Something simple and inexpensive, such as candy bars, is usually sufficient for the reward. If the coach himself does not have to be the main supplier of rewards (by praising good performance), he can devote most of his time to actually coaching the players.

7. The time lapse between the response by the learner and the information feedback and reward is crucial to the learning situation. Research has shown that delayed information feedback and reward are not nearly as effective as those presented immediately following the player performance. This is why video tape is more effective than film in providing feedback. This is also why point systems and candy bars can be more effective than praise from the coach. The information feedback and the reward are built into the point-system method. With praise, too, the coach should understand that his laudatory words will be more effective if they come immediately after the player performance. A delay of even five minutes can diminish the effectiveness of the praise as a factor in learning.

8. Only major errors should be corrected during the early stages of learning when the learner is attempting to find a successful strategy for performing a particular skill. This search for a successful strategy is largely a trial-and-error process where the learner tries one strategy, judges the results (on the basis of information feedback), and then tries a different strategy. He needs a great deal of freedom to conduct his search so that he may adopt whatever will be the most successful strategy for him. If a coach corrects minor errors during this stage of the learning, he will tend to inhibit the learner. Such correcting literally gives the learner too much to think about. Thus, only major errors should be corrected at this point. A major error in throwing, for example, might consist of a youngster's having the same leg forward as the throwing arm. Another major error might be the complete lack of rotation in the shoulders during the throwing motion. Errors in form, however, are not usually major errors, and these should not be corrected because no particular form should be imposed upon the young learner.

9. Verbal instruction by the coach is of limited usefulness during the early stages of learning and should seldom replace active participation

at any level. Players learn baseball skills by practicing them, not by continually listening to someone else (usually the coach) talk about them. Nevertheless, ororverbalization is a methodological error made by many coaches. Research clearly indicates that telling a player how to perform a skill is an inefficient method of teaching. This is especially true if the player has not had many chances to practice the skill. Once a player has begun to learn the skill, he can then profit from some verbal instruction. Players at higher levels of skill can also profit from verbal instruction because they *know* what is being talked about. They not only have a skill vocabulary, but they have experienced the skill that the coach is talking to them about. At no level, however, should verbal instruction replace actual participation. The coach must carefully examine his teaching method. If, during practice sessions, the players are frequently standing around listening to him talk, he is wasting valuable practice time. More learning would take place if the players were practicing their skills. Verbal instruction, for the most part, is better handled in a classroom before practice.

10. Live demonstrations by a competent performer appear to be superior to any other method currently used for teaching baseball skills. This means that the coach can play a more crucial role by demonstrating the skill than by talking about it. If the coach does not feel he is good enough to give a useful demonstration, he should select his best player to provide the demonstration. Regardless, it is important that the coach recognize the role that demonstration can play in the learning process, and he should provide for almost constant demonstrations, especially during the early stages of learning a skill.

11. A motivated learner can learn despite many obstacles. It is obvious that many currently active major league players learned the skills of baseball without systematic instruction from qualified coaches. They learned strictly through the long process of trial and error, and they improved because they were highly motivated and were willing to devote the long hours necessary to develop their skills to a high level. The baseball coach should never underestimate the role of motivation in the learning situation. Poor facilities, poor equipment, and even poor instruction can all be overcome by the motivated learner. Likewise, a coach can have the best facilities and equipment and offer the best instruction without any noticeable success if his players have insufficient motivation to learn. Thus, the baseball coach must constantly seek ways to increase the motivation of his players to improve their skills.

12. The chances for significant learning are increased when a moderate stress exists in the learning environment. Game conditions produce a natural amount of stress, but for players to improve during practice a certain amount of this stress must be created. The presence of stress does not mean that the possibility of having fun in practice is eliminated. The stress in practice sessions should not be so great that players have a difficult time handling it. If the stress is too great, very little learning will take place. In short, the coach must learn to create a *moderate* amount of stress in his practice sessions. If he can accomplish this task, he will find that his play-

ers will accomplish more and progress more rapidly than they would if no stress were present. The most common method for inserting stress into the practice situation is to make the players clearly understand that what happens in practice is important. For example, the players may be told that who plays first base and who sits on the bench for a specific game will depend on the skills demonstrated in practice sessions. If players feel that their practice performances are important, a natural amount of stress will exist and this will enhance learning.

13. Mental practice between actual practice sessions can aid learning, and it tends to prevent what psychologists call "retroactive inhibition." There is ample research evidence to support this principle. The coach must decide how much he wants to encourage his players to think about the game and their own performances between actual sessions. He may not want to encourage too much of this if he feels it might affect their other school responsibilities, but he certainly will want to urge his players to devote some of their free time to thinking about these matters.

14. To correct an error at the higher levels of skill, the player must first be made aware of the error; then the erroneous action must be gradually replaced by the proper behavior.[1] It is not enough to tell a highly skilled player about an error and expect that he will correct it. Such a skill has actually become an automatic act; that is, the player has literally ceased to think about the skill itself, and the information necessary to execute the skill has been relegated to some subconscious part of his brain. To correct an error in such a highly automatized skill is therefore difficult. The coach must first bring the error to the conscious attention of the player by having the player execute the error while his attention is focused on it. Once the player clearly recognizes the error and has it in his conscious attention, he can correct the problem, replacing the error response with the correct response. The correct response must then be practiced until it becomes fully automatized. This entire process is long and arduous. The coach must constantly check to see that the old error has not crept back into the player's automatized act of performance.

THE DEVELOPMENT AND SELECTION OF DRILLS*

Participating in drills is a fundamental aspect of player participation in any organized sport. Coaches in every sport use drills in their practice sessions. The purpose of drills is to organize the learning environment so that the player has repeated practice of carefully designed aspects of certain sports skills. While drills in baseball do not always play the important role

---

[1] John Lawther of Pennsylvania State University developed this concept.
*Some of the material in this section was originally developed for *The Theory and Science of Basketball* by John M. Cooper and Daryl Siedentop (Philadelphia: Lea & Febiger, 1969).

that they do, for example, in basketball, they are important and useful teaching aids—particularly during the indoor practice season and during the early stages of outdoor practice. The limits of time and space that accompany indoor practice sessions require that the coach plan and conduct his practices with high efficiency. Drills can be especially valuable in this regard.

Certain drills will be suggested in this chapter, but only to illustrate various points concerning the development and selection of drills. Many books and articles have been written concerning baseball drills. (Danny Litwhiler's fine book on drills is perhaps the best basic source of information in this area.) It is not within the scope of this book to attempt to duplicate any of these efforts. The principles suggested in this chapter are designed only to offer guidelines that the coach may use in the development and selection of drills.

Principles for the Development and Selection of Drills

1. The coach should adapt his drills to the needs and goals of his particular situation.
2. Drills should contain elements of the crucial actions found in game situations.
3. Each drill should be fully explained to the players before any attempt is made to practice it.
4. The goal of the drill should be clearly defined.
5. Successful performances in drills should be rewarded.
6. Competition in drills can enhance learning.
7. Drills should be based on a progressive difficulty scale.
8. Proper team reaction to a specific game situation should be emphasized.
9. As many team players as possible should participate in drills as often as possible.
10. Drill practice must be purposeful for improvement to take place.
11. Drills can be used for different purposes with different players or at different times during the baseball season.

Discussing the Principles

1. Drills should be adapted to the needs and goals of the situation. There can be no doubt that the "homemade" drill is the best drill. This does not suggest that the baseball coach can not learn about or pick up drills from other sources. But each drill should be carefully analyzed to make sure that

it meets the needs and goals that the coach has in his particular situation. Slight modifications in established drills can make them much more useful learning tools.

The coach can also develop drills of his own. If he sees a particular aspect of a baseball skill, or of an offensive or defensive situation that he feels his players should practice, he can analyze the performance and develop a drill of his own to meet the needs of the situation. The most imaginative — and successful — drills are often developed in this way.

2. Drills should contain elements of the crucial actions found in game situations. The baseball coach should analyze both the skills of the game and the various offensive or defensive situations which he feels are most important. Once the skills and situations have been selected, the coach should carefully scrutinize them to extract those elements that are the most crucial to successful performance. Drills can then be built upon these important elements. For example, it is important that catchers be able to block the low pitch that is outside of the strike zone. Analysis of this skill will show that the situation has a movement phase, in which the catcher moves to the right or the left, and a blocking phase, in which he blocks the ball so that it stays in front of him. To recreate this situation as closely as possible, and to have the drill reflect the crucial aspects of the skill, the coach should develop a drill in which the catcher must move from his squat stance to block a ball thrown by a teammate. The catcher should not know to which side the ball will be thrown. Further analysis will show that the catcher's hands do not play an important role in *blocking* the pitch. So, the coach can have the catcher put his hands behind his back so that the ball has to be blocked off the chest protector and mask. If the goal is to keep the ball in front of the catcher, the coach will have developed a drill that will help the catcher to learn the proper techniques of the *crucial* aspects of this important game skill.

3. Each drill should be fully explained to the players before any attempt is made to practice it. A misunderstood drill will usually result in the participants' practicing an incorrect technique. The players should *fully* understand what is expected of them. The purpose of the drill and detailed information concerning the methods of participation should be made available to the players *before* they begin to practice. Coaches should never forget that players will be more highly motivated when they know *why* they are doing a certain thing. There is nothing so damaging to team morale than for the players to feel that the practice activities have no purpose.

4. The goal of the drill should be clearly defined. As was mentioned above, the purpose of the drill must be known. Just as important, the goal of the drill must be *physically* defined for the players. This means that the behavior or performance expected of the players must be made as clear as possible. (See principle 1 in the first section of this chapter.) It is not enough, for example, to merely tell players participating in a bunting drill that they should bunt the ball down the first- or third-base lines. The coach should use towels, string, lime or some other material to give the bunters a precise target area to aim for. When they do bunt the ball, then, they can

get immediate information feedback on the results of their efforts. When the coach wants his players to run to first base quickly, he should help them by using a stopwatch to clock each runner. The defined behavior can then be established (4.2 seconds for right-handed hitters, for example). The players can match their time (behavior) against the established time (defined behavior). In this way, much more learning will take place.

5. Successful performances in drills should be rewarded. In many situations the performance itself will be sufficient reward when it is viewed by the entire team. In the above examples, for instance, the player who bunts the ball into the highest-ranking target area will be immediately rewarded by the fact that both he and his teammates know of his performance. The player who runs 4.1 to first base will also be rewarded when the coach or manager informs the group of his time. In other areas of practice, however, the coach may want to explore some form of reward system. In hitting practice, for example, he may want to set up some form of hitting-practice average and post the practice averages from time to time. In infield practice, he may want to establish a point system that takes into account misplayed ground balls and bad throws. Whatever form he chooses, the establishment of a reward system will create a better learning environment for all of his drills.

6. Competition in drills can enhance learning. This is merely an extension of the above principle. Success in competition is one of the most powerful incentives known to man. The baseball coach should put this competitive urge to good use by experimenting with various forms of competition in his drills. He might encourage individual competition or squad competition. He might decide on direct competition, in which players are pitted against other players, or indirect competition, in which a player is pitted against his previous performance or some selected standard of behavior. Players, for example, often compete indirectly to reach the .300 mark in hitting. This is an arbitrarily selected mark that many players feel defines a successful season. The players will indirectly compete *with that mark* as much as they will against other players. The coach might explore the possibility of setting up marks for performances in drill situations and have his players compete to reach these marks.

7. Drills should be based on a progressive difficulty scale. Traditionally, there have been certain problems associated with the use of drills to enhance learning. For example, drills become monotonous. This can be avoided by making the drills progressively more difficult as the players increase in skill. Indeed, drills should have an increasing degree of difficulty built into their design. It is not easy for the players to maintain interest in, and therefore give 100 percent in effort to, a drill that is repetitious and monotonous. In the bunting drill mentioned above, for example, the target areas might be made smaller as the season progresses and as the bunting skill of the players increases. The danger in using a drill which never changes is that it may preclude the possibility of realizing any significant improvement in performance. In this case, it merely wastes time and should be avoided.

8. Certain drills should be developed which emphasize proper team reaction to a specific game situation. Each coach, for example, will have a certain preference for defending against the bunt with runners on first and second bases. He should develop a drill that the entire team may practice so that team behavior in this situation becomes both automatic and satisfactory to him. This situation involves team defense, and the chain of defense will only be as strong as its weakest link. That is, if one player does not perform properly, the entire strategy for team defense is largely negated. The coach must analyze his own view of offensive and defensive baseball and make sure that he is using drills that emphasize his strategic approach to certain game situations.

9. As many team players as possible should participate in drills as often as possible. The more repetition involved in a learning situation (other factors being equal), the more likely that the desired learning changes will be reinforced and become habit. Nothing is more detrimental to both effective learning and team conduct than to have long lines of players waiting to take part in a drill. The coach must design his practice sessions so that there is maximum participation in drills. On a normal-sized baseball field, there is absolutely no reason why there cannot be three or four groups practicing one drill simultaneously. In this way, four times more practice would be going on than with the "one-at-a-time" method. When he considers that this much more learning might take place, the coach should realize that the time spent creating and planning for full participation will be well spent.

10. Drill practice must be purposeful for improvement to take place, or, indeed, for any learning to occur. If a drill is ill-defined, unmotivated, monotonous, or unrewarded, it lacks all sense of purpose. No learning or improvement will take place; the players will merely go through the paces because they have to. Too much hitting practice is not purposeful. The same is true for many other drills. If the coach will adhere to the principles suggested in this chapter, he will find that his drills will be purposeful and that his players will show improvement.

11. Drills can be used for different purposes with different players or at different times during the season. For instance, the "hotbox" drill has been a long-time favorite of baseball coaches. In this drill, a player will roll the ball to one side of another player. The second player fields the ball and tosses it back to the first player. The first player then rolls the ball to the other side of the second player. In this way, the ball goes from one side to the other. When this drill is used with pitchers, it is primarily a conditioning drill. There is a great deal of bending, total body movement, and sustained side-to-side running. When the same drill is used with infielders, it can become primarily a drill for the proper execution of correct technique in fielding a ground ball. Thus, one drill can serve two entirely different purposes. The baseball coach should examine the drills that he uses to determine if he can find new uses for what he considers to be good drills.

Chapter 16
Conducting Indoor Practices

For coaches in areas where the climate precludes constant outdoor practice—at least 60–65 percent of the baseball coaches in this nation—the
topic of indoor practices is crucial. For these coaches, the quality of their
indoor practices goes a long way toward determining the success of their
total baseball program.

The facility, naturally, is the primary factor in determining what type of
indoor baseball practice a coach can conduct. At Western Michigan University, for example, the use of the athletic fieldhouse for indoor baseball
practice is a major factor in the success of the excellent baseball program
at that school. The fieldhouse is large enough to accommodate regular
infield practice, two or three hitting cages, and pitching mounds. Most of
what might be done outside can be done inside there. At Hope College,
however, the facility is an antiquated gymnasium in which there is a
50' x 80' floor. During the spring months this gym must serve the baseball
and track teams, as well as the college intramural program.[1] It is important
to note, however, that many, many things can be done to provide for a
good baseball practice even in such a completely inadequate facility. The
baseball coach cannot afford to use a poor facility at his school as an excuse for not conducting good indoor baseball practices. Below are principles that will help the coach to plan meaningful and useful indoor practices.

Principles for Conducting Indoor Practices

1. The facility is the primary factor in determining the types of activities
   that can be carried out during indoor practices.
2. Indoor practices should be well organized and fully planned in advance.
3. The coach should attempt to keep each player busy during the entire
   practice session.
4. A primary goal of the indoor practice season must be to get the players'
   arms in shape.
5. General conditioning should not occupy too much of the total practice
   time.
6. Pitchers and catchers should report earlier than other players.
7. Pitchers should throw every day at the beginning of the season.
8. Infielders and outfielders should not be allowed to use their gloves for
   the first several days of practice.
9. Coaches can employ "gimmicks" to make up for inadequate facilities
   and to keep each player occupied.
10. No matter what type of facility is available, batting practice can be
    conducted indoors.

---

[1] A new facility is now being planned.

11. The players should be divided into defensive groups for many of the indoor drills.
12. In almost every facility, it is possible to practice live bunting indoors.
13. The short and fast-paced practice is better than the long and slow-paced practice in indoor sessions.

Discussing the Principles

1. The type of facility available is the primary factor in determining the types of activities that can be carried out during indoor practices. The more restricted the indoor facility, the more the coach has to develop imaginative drills and activities to achieve his goals. The main restricting factor is the size of the facility. One simply cannot carry out the same activities in a small facility that he can in a large facility. A second important factor is the type of floor in the facility. A dirt floor is naturally more conducive to baseball practice than a wooden floor. A third important aspect of the facility is the absence or presence of a batting cage. If the coach is fortunate enough to have a batting cage or cages, he can conduct live batting practice for part of his team while the other players are busy with other practice activities. If no cage is available, the coach will have to find some substitute method for conducting hitting practice. A fourth important aspect is the amount of time that the facility can be used for baseball practice. This is often determined by how frequently the facility is used by other spring sports teams such as the track team and the golf team.

If the coach has 1) a large facility, 2) with a dirt or composition floor, 3) several batting cages suspended from the ceiling, and 4) two hours allotted to baseball each day, a first-rate indoor baseball program can easily be developed. If, however, the coach is faced with 1) a small facility, 2) with a wooden floor, 3) no batting cages, and 4) forty-five minutes a day allotted to the baseball program, it will take a great deal of imaginative planning to provide a good indoor baseball program. However, a good indoor practice program can be developed even within these restrictions.

2. Indoor practices should be well organized and fully planned in advance. The baseball coach must pre-plan his indoor practices if he is to accomplish all the goals that he sets for himself and his team. To carry out more than one activity at a time indoors, for example, takes prior planning.

We are definitely in favor of highly organized indoor practices. Many goals can be accomplished in these practice sessions. If, however, there is a lack of organization, the indoor practice may quickly disintegrate into chaos, and the coach will find that his players are not only failing to develop their skills but are also losing interest in playing baseball. At the outset of his indoor practice season, therefore, the coach must establish the attitude that playing baseball under him is a serious matter. This is not to say that practice sessions should not be fun for the players. The players should be able to enjoy playing baseball while at the same time working to improve their baseball skills. If the practice session is highly organized and fully preplanned, the amount of "horsing around" will be held to a minimum.

3. The coach should attempt to keep each player busy during the entire practice session. This is consistent with and a natural extension of principle two. When a player is busy practicing a baseball skill, he has little time to think about other matters. In some indoor baseball practices we have observed, there have been some players who have not participated in twenty minutes of actual activity in an entire hour-and-a-half session. The coach must find ways to keep all his players busy in a meaningful way. To do this he must usually have many things happening at the same time. One way to do this is to set up "stations" where different skills may be practiced. For example, the coach might have an isometric station, a weighted bat station, a sliding station, a batting tee station, and a calesthenic station. The players can move from station to station at specified times or between team activities. What each coach must avoid is having too many players standing around watching one or two of their teammates engaged in the practice of some baseball skill.

4. A primary goal of the indoor practice season must be to get the players' arms in shape. There is nothing more detrimental to early season performance than sore arms or arms that are not fully in shape. Once the baseball team moves to outdoor practices, the players must be ready to throw hard and long. To do this they must have had adequate preparation indoors. Most of the errors committed during the early parts of the spring season are throwing errors; this is primarily due to the fact that players have not had adequate opportunities to get their arms in shape. Time is the crucial variable. Many coaches allow for only ten minutes of indoor throwing at the outset of each practice, and this is simply not enough time to fully prepare an arm for hard throwing at long distances. The coach must convince himself that time spent indoors throwing is not wasted time.

5. General conditioning should not occupy too much of the total practice time. Some coaches seem willing to take twenty minutes each day (almost one-fourth of an hour-and-a-half practice session) to have the entire squad go through conditioning drills. We believe that this time could be better spent practicing baseball skills. Coaches should expect their players to report in some sort of reasonably good physical condition. Each coach should call his squad together during the winter months and explain this to them. At this session he can hand out some suggestions for conditioning. He may give them a list and description of various exercises, or he may simply pass out a written statement on the types of exercise that will help them prepare for spring baseball. Regardless, the point should be emphatically made that he *expects* the players to be in at least fair physical condition when they report in the spring. Then he will need to use only five minutes or so of his practice session for conditioning, or he may want to have "excercise stations" that the players can visit individually sometime during the practice session. Either way, he will not have to take up large amounts of practice time to get his squad in shape.

6. Pitchers and catchers should report earlier in the spring than other players. As soon as there is facility time available and the conference rules permit, these players should report — even as early as January. The more throwing time that a pitcher can get in during the winter months, the stronger and more ready his arm will be in April and May when the bulk of the high-school and college games are played. The pitcher needs a long time to get ready to throw a seven or nine inning game. Pitchers who are told to report the first of March should not be expected to be ready to throw a full game by the first of April.

Another good reason to have the pitchers and the catchers report early is that when the entire team reports the facility problem may be acute. If the pitchers and catchers can occasionally have the facility to themselves, they can get in a good practice session. If, however, they have to share the facility with the rest of the team, they may not get the time they need to loosen up, throw hard, and loosen down. In addition, the coach can spend full practice sessions with the pitchers and catchers. In that way, he can watch each pitcher over a period of time and fully learn what each man's strengths and weaknesses are. This can be done best in the very early practice sessions when only the pitchers and catchers are present.

7. Pitchers should throw every day at the beginning of the season to get their arms in shape. This is a major reason to have the pitchers and catchers report at a different time each day than the remainder of the squad. With a large indoor facility, the entire squad can practice at the same time during the pre-season, but with most high-school and college facilities the available practice time must be divided up. The coach may have his pitchers and catchers throw from 4:00 – 4:40 P.M. and the rest of his team practice from 4:40 – 5:45 P.M. Once the pitcher begins to throw hard every day for a period of time, the coach can move to a situation where the pitchers throw every other day, and finally he can allow them to throw hard only every third or fourth day. Since most coaches agree that pitching is the most important part of baseball, they must organize and conduct their indoor practice sessions to reflect that belief.

During these early practice sessions for pitchers, "pitching strings" should always be used. The cost should be no more than the price of some strong string at a neighborhood hardware store. The string can be stretched across the entire width of a gymnasium, and target areas can be set up every fifteen to twenty feet. Pitching strings are of immense value to the pitcher, be he young or experienced. The physical marking off of the strike zone becomes a visual stimulus by which the pitcher can actually learn the strike zone. The information feedback is maximized, and it is also instantaneous. After the first week of throwing, the pitchers can begin to chart their pitching performance each day. This is an added incentive to throw the ball in the strike zone. We cannot overemphasize the basic importance of pitching strings to a pitcher who is attempting to improve his skills.

8. Infielders and outfielders should not be allowed to use their gloves for the first several days of practice. If the coach has done a good job of building a baseball program, he will find that his players are tremendously eager

to begin baseball each spring. The first few days of practice will be full of enthusiasm and great desire. A problem arises, however, when this enthusiasm causes players to attempt to do too much too early in the season, to try to throw too hard and too long during the first few days of practice. The result is almost always a sore arm that prevents the player from getting his arm in good shape for the outdoor season. This problem can be avoided if the coach will not allow the players to bring their gloves to the first few practice sessions. Without gloves, the players cannot throw the ball harder than they should throw early in the season because they will just be playing catch with one another. Second, the players must, in the absence of a glove, catch the ball with both hands. This helps them to develop good catching habits. Once these goals are accomplished, the coach can have the players begin to bring their gloves. They will then be ready to catch the ball correctly and to throw harder and longer without running the risk of getting a sore arm.

9. Coaches can employ "gimmicks" to make up for inadequate facilities and to keep each player occupied during the indoor practice sessions. Generally speaking, we are not particularly in favor of using gimmicks in sports training. If the actual skill can be practiced, then it should be practiced. The best way to become a good pitcher is to practice pitching, and the best way to become a good hitter is to practice hitting. If the facility does not permit actual practice of skills, however, and if the coach is attempting to find meaningful ways to keep his players occupied during the practice sessions, he should explore the possibility of using some practice gimmicks. He can use weighted bats, batting tees, balls on strings, mirrors, sawed off bats, or many of the other gimmicks that are suggested in numerous coaching journals and coaching books. Eventually, the coach may want to develop his own gimmicks to fit his particular goals and situation. These gimmicks can be valuable substitutes for skills practice when the latter is not possible. They can also prove beneficial as supplements to the actual practice of skills.

10. No matter what type of facility is available, batting practice can be conducted indoors. The ideal situation, of course, is to have several batting cages available so that pitchers can practice throwing to hitters and hitters can practice batting against front-line pitching. The absence of batting cages, however, should not render batting practice impossible. If the facility has no windows or lights that are easily breakable, the coach can conduct hitting practice with soft rubber baseballs. These balls approximate very closely the actual weight, size, and feel of a regulation baseball. The major disadvantage to this type of practice is that it is doubtful if pitchers should throw these balls. Thus, either a pitching machine or another player should do the batting practice pitching. If this kind of ball cannot be used, then the coach may have to use a ball that will not travel far when hit. While this ball is difficult to throw, it can be hit without danger of breaking a light or a window. Another possibility is to use a "whiffle" ball. These plastic balls have holes in one side. They do not go far when hit, and the possibility of breakage is very low. They are difficult to throw with any control, how-

ever. The holes in the side cause the ball to break in many different directions; thus it does approximate the type of break that a regulation baseball has. Such balls are, however, good for helping hitters learn to follow the ball better, and can be used in any type of facility. It is important that hitters practice during indoor practice sessions. With some imagination and investigation the coach can find what type of ball can best be used in his facility, and he can then schedule adequate hitting practice.

11. The players should be divided into defensive groups for many of the indoor drills. Group work is a practice concept that has been in use in football for many years. The concept is a valuable one for baseball also. The coach should divide his players into catcher, infielder, and outfielder groups for all of his drills that have to do with the defensive skills of baseball. Each drill can then be slightly modified for each group so that the drills will closely approximate the defensive skills the players must perform in game situations. The use of the group-work concept will also allow the coach to develop specialized drills for each group.

12. In almost every facility, it is possible to practice live bunting indoors. Bunting is an important baseball skill (see Chapter 4), but it never seems to be allotted adequate practice time, particularly after coaches move their teams outdoors. Bunting can be practiced indoors. This allows the coach to concentrate fully on this important skill and to give each player enough trials to begin to improve his ability in some significant way. With a minimum of planning and precaution, the coach can have his team practice live bunting indoors without the use of a hitting cage. Thus, he can impress upon his players the importance of this skill and allow enough time for them to develop their abilities in sacrifice bunting and in bunting for the base hit.

13. The short and fast-paced practice is better than the long and slow-paced practice in indoor sessions. Enthusiasm and desire is usually high when baseball practice begins each spring. The coach should seek to maintain this enthusiasm during the entire season. One of the biggest hurdles he will face in this regard is to get through the indoor season without having his players lose their desire. Baseball, after all, is an outdoor sport, and unless one has an "astrodome" to practice in, the indoor practice is not as inherently interesting to the player as the outdoor practice. The principles suggested in this chapter can guide the coach in developing interesting and meaningful indoor baseball practices. The final suggestion is to have the practices reasonably short and very fast-paced. An hour and three-quarters is most often sufficient time for indoor baseball practice. If this time is well planned, the players will move through the practice session with eagerness and desire and will still accomplish a great deal.

Chapter 17
Conducting Outdoor Practices

Outdoor baseball practices at many schools tend to be less organized and less efficient than practice sessions for any other organized, interschool sport. Outdoor baseball practices are usually centered around hitting practice in which each player gets a certain number of swings. The coach or another player will sometimes also hit fungos to a few of the players. The other players stand around watching the hitter and fielding the balls that are occasionally hit toward their positions. There is no reason why outdoor practices should be so dull and inefficient; many coaches have proven that they can be lively, imaginative, efficient, and useful for improving baseball skills. The purpose of this chapter is to offer suggestions and guidelines that will help the baseball coach plan and organize outdoor practices to make the best possible use of time and facilities.

Several principles that were suggested in Chapter Sixteen also pertain to conducting outdoor practices. For example, every player should be kept busy during the entire session; many different activities must be going on simultaneously. This suggests that the coach must very carefully organize and supervise each practice session so that each player is engaged in some purposeful practice for the bulk of the time. Like indoor practices, the outdoor practice session will generate more enthusiasm among the players if it is reasonably short and fast-paced. The long, drawn out practice session does little to create or maintain enthusiasm among the players. In addition to these axioms, the following principles should prove helpful to the coach in his attempts to conduct successful outdoor practices.

Principles for Conducting Outdoor Practices

1. The facility is the primary factor in determining what activities can be practiced during outdoor sessions.
2. Players must be given adequate time to carefully warm up their arms.
3. Because a hitter needs constant practice to maintain and improve his abilities, the baseball coach must consider adequate hitting practice as the most important activity in the outdoor practice session.
4. Maximum efficiency will be achieved if the hitting area is adjacent to the regular playing field.
5. The coach should have protective screens built if he has to conduct hitting practice on the same field where the rest of the practice activity is going on.
6. Hitting practice must be purposeful.
7. The coach must make sure that his pitchers have sufficient time and adequate facilities to practice their skills.
8. The coach should make good use of his managers and other squad members if no assistant coaches are available.
9. Scrimmages can be effective as a practice technique.

10. The activities of practice sessions should differ according to the stage of the season.

11. The coach should develop a checklist to make sure that his players are always working on the important baseball skills.

Discussing the Principles

1. The type of facility available is the primary factor in determining what activities can be practiced during sessions. Is there just one baseball field, or is there an adjacent field on which certain activities might be conducted simultaneously with those on the regular field? Are there outdoor hitting cages, such as those developed by Danny Litwhiler when he was coaching at Florida State University? Are there adequate practice pitching mounds? Is there a sliding pit? The answers to these and other questions will determine the range of possibilities that are open to the baseball coach for conducting outdoor practices. Most coaches at the high-school and college level will have the use of only one baseball field for their practices. This means that many activities must be going on simultaneously on the *same* field. Obviously, then, organization, preplanning, and imagination can spell the difference between a lively, successful practice session and a sluggish, unsuccessful one. The coach should attempt to get the best facility possible for his practice sessions, and he should constantly work with the athletic administrators to improve that facility. He should also see what adjacent space might be available to accommodate his baseball needs. He should not, however, use a less than adequate facility as an excuse for not conducting the best possible practice sessions.

2. Players must be given adequate time to warm up their arms carefully. It is difficult for any baseball player to handle his responsibilities with a sore throwing arm. An adequate warm-up before each practice session is the best single preventative measure for avoiding sore arms. Players are often overanxious to get involved in a hitting practice or a scrimmage. They will throw for three or four minutes and then charge eagerly onto the field. The coach must help them understand that a forceful throwing motion places a great deal of stress and strain on the arm, particularly on the elbow joint and the shoulder joint. If the muscular groups around these joints have not been adequately warmed up, the throwing arm is extremely vulnerable to injury. An injury to a muscle or tendon is not only painful, but it usually takes a long time to heal fully. There is also the danger of developing tendonitis or calcium deposits near the joints. By making sure that players have adequate time to warm up their arms each day before practice, the coach can in large part avoid these problems.

3. To be a successful hitter, a baseball player has to practice constantly. There is no substitute for long hours of hard work in the batting cage. The coach, therefore, must see that his hitters get enough practice time. In

short, he must consider hitting practice as the most important activity of his outdoor practice sessions. At many schools hitting practice involves only the regular players, especially if the entire practice must be conducted on one baseball field. The coach should try to avoid this situation, however, by organizing his practice sessions so that the rest of the squad, as well as all of his regulars, have adequate hitting practice. Moreover, one bunt and five swings per practice session is simply not enough to help a hitter maintain a sharp hitting eye, let alone bring about improvement in his batting. The greater the efficiency of the practice session, the more swings each hitter will get each day, and the better the team will perform.

4. Maximum efficiency will be achieved if the hitting area is adjacent to the regular playing field. All that is really needed for hitting practice is a pitching mound, a home plate, and a backstop. If a spot adjacent to the regular field can be developed for use in hitting practice, the coach can then use his regular field for working with infielders and outfielders, or for working on special offensive and defensive plays. In short, with two fields activity can go on simultaneously, and more can be accomplished. When the baseball coach has no assistant coaches to help him, he will have to find other methods to supervise the two practice areas adequately.

5. The coach should have protective screens built if he has to conduct hitting practice on the same field where the rest of the practice activity is going on. A low screen (approximately waist high) should be placed in front of the pitching mound. This screen will protect the batting practice pitcher from all ground balls and low line drives. A high screen (approximately seven feet high) should be placed in the baseline, six to ten feet in front of first base. This screen will protect the first baseman from all batted balls while he takes throws at first from other infielders. With screens in these two places, ground balls can be hit to infielders who in turn can throw to first base — while hitting practice is being conducted on the same diamond. The screens should be constructed from steel pipe and covered by strong outdoor netting. Frequently, the school's maintenance department or the shop can be of help in getting such screens made with only a small outlay of cash.

6. Hitting practice must be purposeful. While this seems obvious, it is amazing how many hitting practices are conducted with no real purpose in mind other than "to get in a few swings." Concentration is absolutely essential to success in hitting, and the best way to get hitters to concentrate is to have some definite purpose for each series of swings. If a hitter is going to practice bunting, he should bunt to a definite spot in the infield. The coach can mark the target spot with a towel or a line. If a hitter is going to take five swings, he should have some definite purpose in mind with each swing. Sometimes the coach may want the hitter to attempt to hit every pitch back at the pitcher. Other times, he may want the hitter to hit to the opposite field or to pull the ball. The point is that hitters should seldom swing away for any extended period of time without a definite goal. If the coach wants his hitters to swing away, he should attempt to make the hitting practice as much like the game situation as possible. He should call

balls and strikes and have the hitter run out his hits. Practice itself is no guarantee of improvement; improvement comes with purposeful practice. To give his players incentive, a coach can allow each hitter to hit again for every time he gets on base.

Part of the problem in making hitting practice meaningful and purposeful is that it is difficult to have pitching that reasonably approximates what the hitters will see in games. Once a season begins, it is doubtful if front-line pitchers should pitch hitting practice. This, however, leaves the coach with a problem. He can of course, use his second-line pitchers. This is a good solution, but often there are not enough of them. Most coaches therefore, have to enlist the aid of infielders and outfielders to throw hitting practice. The coach should carefully scrutinize his players to find which ones might be best for this task. Needless to say, absolutely no real practice occurs when a player merely throws slow, straight pitches to the hitters. Thus, the coach should attempt to find players who can throw the baseball hard and can break off a reasonably good curve ball. While the fast balls and curve balls thrown during practice need not be as fast or break as sharply as pitches in game situations, they should approximate game pitches.

7. The coach must make sure that his pitchers have sufficient time and adequate facilities to practice their skills. Pitchers have to throw between their pitching assignments, but most coaches prefer that they not pitch hitting practice. This means that the pitchers usually end up throwing on the sidelines or in some area adjacent to the field. The coach should have practice mounds for this purpose. He should never ask his front-line pitchers to throw from a flat surface; that is too unlike the game experience. Building practice mounds near the baseball field does not require a great deal of expense, and it will pay good dividends in the pitchers' performances. Between game appearances, pitchers should throw daily, and the coach should make sure that this part of the practice session is approached with a great deal of seriousness. The pitchers should throw from regulation pitching mounds that are equipped with pitching rubbers; they should throw to regulation home plates. Moreover, they should probably throw to strings. The strings can be easily mounted on temporary or permanent poles, depending on where the practice pitching area is. We believe that throwing to strings is excellent practice because it provides the precise information feedback that the pitcher needs in order to constantly improve.

8. The coach should make good use of his managers and other squad members if no assistant coaches are available. This is especially true if the outdoor practice facility consists of a field plus an adjacent hitting area and an adjacent pitching area. In this case, the coach would have to be in three places at once to supervise his program effectively. Since this is not possible, he should choose from among his players and managers the most responsible persons and have them act as supervisors. The team captain can usually fill the role of the primary assistant coach. The senior member of the pitching staff is often able to perform a similar duty with the pitchers. We are firmly convinced that head coaches who invest certain responsibilities in their players will usually reap excellent results from this practice.

When only one field is available, the coach must still have some help in supervising the practice. One player, for example, might be put in charge of seeing that the hitting practice is moving along smoothly. Other players can hit fungos to infielders and outfielders (it is often practical to use pitchers in this role). If these supervisory roles are filled, then the coach will be free to actually coach; that is, to provide instruction to his players. He can move around to the various activities and offer advice and encouragement to his players.

9. Scrimmages can be effective as a practice technique. These may take two forms. The first and most obvious is the full-scale intrasquad game. This insures a lively practice and enables all players to have a chance to show their abilities under game conditions. For most practices, however, the intrasquad game is inefficient and does not allow the coach to work on those aspects of the game that he feels the team needs most to improve on. A second method of scrimmaging in baseball can be borrowed from basketball and football practice techniques. In this type of scrimmage, one team remains on offense or defense for a long period of time. Thus, unlike with the intrasquad game, time is not wasted by the teams' changing sides. In this type of scrimmage, the coach can have his first team be on offense for an entire practice session with the second team playing in the field. In this way, the coach can work on particular situations, and each regular can have six to twelve times at bat in one afternoon. The next day the coach may want to switch and have his regulars in the field while his second-line players are on offense. There is less time wasted and more actual baseball played with this method than with the intrasquad scrimmage.

10. The activities of each practice session should differ according to the stage of the season. In the early season, practices can be long because enthusiasm is high and many skills need to be worked on at some length. As the actual schedule begins, the coach will want to develop a shorter practice routine that is primarily designed to keep his team at a high pitch for the scheduled games. Toward the end of the season, the practices can be shortened even more. The coach is concerned with three primary factors in his practice sessions. He wants his players to improve their skills, and this will occur in practices that are primarily learning sessions. He also wants his players to be enthusiastic about their sport; this is primarily a motivational problem. Moreover, the coach wants to get his team in top mental and physical condition to play. Thus, he will want to emphasize different factors during different parts of the season, although it is good to work toward all of these factors in each practice session.

11. The coach should develop a checklist to make sure that his players are always working on the important baseball skills and on the crucial offensive and defensive strategies that he will expect them to use in games. The checklist enables the coach to remind himself to review various skills and strategies at different times during the season. He may want to teach the skills and strategies early in the season, review them toward the middle of the season, and, toward the end of the season, work individually with those who are having difficulty mastering them.

Chapter 18
Training for Baseball

Baseball is not normally considered a sport for which a great deal of training is required, and it is true that a baseball player does not have to train as rigorously as, for example, a miler in track. This, however, does not mean that a player can attain success in baseball without training. Generally speaking, two types of training are important in baseball. First, there is the conditioning that allows a player to function adequately when playing a doubleheader on a hot afternoon. This conditioning builds adequate strength and endurance to withstand the rigors of a baseball schedule. A second type of conditioning aims primarily at the development of higher levels of skill. Players may train so they can swing a bat with more force, throw a ball with more speed, or run faster from home plate to first base. Both types of conditioning are important—to the coach as well as to the players. This chapter contains general principles to help the coach better understand what is involved in these types of training. No specific system of training is advocated because we feel that each coach must develop his own system to meet the particular needs of his coaching situation. What is hoped is that the coach will be better able to develop his own system as a result of reading this chapter. He should have a clearer idea of what goals to work toward, what methods to use to reach those goals, and what methods to avoid.

Principles of Training

1. There is no substitute for an athlete's maintaining a year-round high level of conditioning.
2. All conditioning activity should be preceded by a warm-up period.
3. Muscular strength and endurance should be developed in accordance with the requirements for specific skills.
4. Isometric exercises tend to develop less bulk in the muscle than isotonic exercises, but the former are functional only for the limb angle at which they are practiced. Isotonic exercises, in the long run, tend to produce more favorable results than isometrics.
5. To increase its strength, a muscle must be overloaded; that is, it must be exercised against increasing resistance.
6. Conditioning for baseball should focus more on the development of speed than on the development of endurance.
7. Practice in starting is perhaps the single best running exercise for baseball players.
8. It is questionable whether pitchers should be allowed to use the overload principle with their pitching arms.
9. The coach should be prepared to suggest a program of functional exercises for each player.
10. The pre-season and off-season conditioning programs must be quite different from the in-season conditioning program.
11. Precaution should always be taken to prevent injuries.

Discussing the Principles

1. There is no substitute for an athlete's maintaining a year-round high level of conditioning. For the athlete who really cares about his sports performance, there is no off-season; the good athlete keeps himself in reasonable condition throughout the year. The athlete who trains only during the season usually takes half of the season to get into top shape, and the more years that he follows this pattern, the longer it takes him to get back into shape each season. The coach who has convinced his players that they should maintain a high level of conditioning will never need to institute "crash" conditioning programs during the period immediately preceding his season. His players will report in shape because they have never really been out of shape. The coach should suggest total-body activities for his players to participate in during the off-season. Handball, basketball, squash, volleyball, or badminton are useful in this regard. The coach should also emphasize to his players that there is no substitute for running. If his players prefer weight training during the off-season, the coach should prescribe a suitable program. The important point is that year-round activity is the most important ingredient in a truly adequate conditioning program for any athlete.

2. *All* conditioning activity should be preceded by a warm-up period. Otherwise, the athlete runs the risk of injury. The muscular system is very prone to injury when it has not been given adequate warm-up preparation. The coach must constantly stress this point to his players. Too often they will want to move immediately into the conditioning activity, but they must be convinced that the warm-up period is for their benefit.

3. Muscular strength and endurance should be developed in accordance with the requirements for specific skills. A general strength-development program will be of only limited use to a player in actually improving specific baseball skills. Strength and endurance both tend to be somewhat specific to a given activity. The baseball coach wants his players to be able to swing a bat more quickly and to throw a ball faster. He should then develop a program that allows for the build-up of strength and endurance in these specific skills. The use of weighted bats will do more to develop the kind of strength needed in baseball than will a general program of weight lifting.

4. Isometric exercises[1] tend to develop less bulk in the muscle than the use of isotonic exercises, but isometrics are functional only for the limb angle at which they are practiced. Isotonic exercises, in the long run, tend to produce more favorable results than isometrics. Despite the recent

---

[1]An isometric contraction is one in which no movement takes place; that is, it is a static contraction in which the muscle does not shorten. An isotonic contraction is one in which both shortening and lengthening of the muscle takes place.

isometrics fad, it is generally believed that isotonic exercises are more beneficial to the development of muscular strength and endurance over the long run. There are several reasons for this. First, isometrics appear to contribute very little toward the development of circulo-respiratory fitness. Second, isometrics do not develop as much strength in the muscle as isotonics. Third, isometrics tend to be useful only for the specific angle at which the exercise occurs, while isotonics tend to develop strength across the full range of motion. For these reasons, we recommend weight training programs that are primarily isotonic in nature. Many coaches, however, have had great success using a combination of the two exercise programs.

5. To increase its strength, a muscle must be overloaded; that is, it must be exercised against increasing resistance. If a coach wants to develop more force in his players' hitting strokes he can do so by using weighted bats. Starting with a bat that weighs just slightly more than normal, he can work up to bats that weigh much more than the norm. Players working gradually through the entire series of weighted bats will develop more and more strength in their hitting strokes because each bat provides more resistance that must be overcome by the muscular contractions involved in hitting. This overload principle should be observed in all training that aims at the development of strength. If a coach merely wishes to develop speed of contraction in a muscle, however, this is best accomplished by practice against light resistance.

6. Conditioning for baseball should focus more on the development of speed than on the development of endurance. While running two miles each day may be an excellent habit from a health standpoint, it probably will not help a player to play baseball any better. A baseball player needs to be able to run relatively short distances very fast. To help his players accomplish this, the coach should primarily focus on developing speed. This means repeated short sprints with the emphasis on correct sprinting form. The coach should also require the players to run in a path similar to that used in running bases. It does little good for a baseball player to be a 9.5 sprinter if he cannot also run around the bases with ease. His great speed will be lost in making the turns. Thus, the coach must find ways to have his players maintain speed at these points. (See Chapter 5.)

7. Practice in starting is perhaps the best single running exercise for baseball players. This is true for two important reasons. First, most baseball players, whether starting from home plate or from a base, do not start correctly. The player should lean forward, paying particular attention to the first step, which should be as long and as low to the ground as possible. The player should also use his arms to aid in the acceleration phase of the start. Once the acceleration phase is completed (usually within the first 45 feet), the player should come up to an upright running position. The second reason for practicing starts is that they require a great deal of work, thus contributing to the specific conditioning of the players. A great deal of energy must be expended to overcome inertia, i.e., to get started. Practicing the start is a strenuous exercise and therefore beneficial to the player.

8. It is questionable that a pitcher should be allowed to use the overload

principle with his pitching arm. Several experiments have been conducted using various methods of overload to improve pitching performance. The experiments usually involve a weighted ball or an exercise system which puts progressively heavier resistance against the throwing motion. Most experimenters have found that this type of training does enable a pitcher to throw faster, but they have also found that it tends to make him less accurate in his throwing. Therefore, it is doubtful, on the basis of the experimental evidence, that a coach should use weighted balls or other progressive-resistance exercises with his pitchers.

9. The coach should be prepared to suggest a program of functional exercises for each player. The coach must be knowledgeable enough to determine the individual exercise needs of his players and to prescribe activities that will yield the desired results. He can do this by first obtaining a knowledge of exercises, with special reference to muscle physiology. He can then use his imagination to suggest useful exercises.

10. The pre-season and off-season conditioning programs must be quite different from the in-season conditioning program. Weight training and

Soaking the pitching arm in ice water after a hard game helps the pitcher avoid injury to his muscles, tendons, and ligaments.

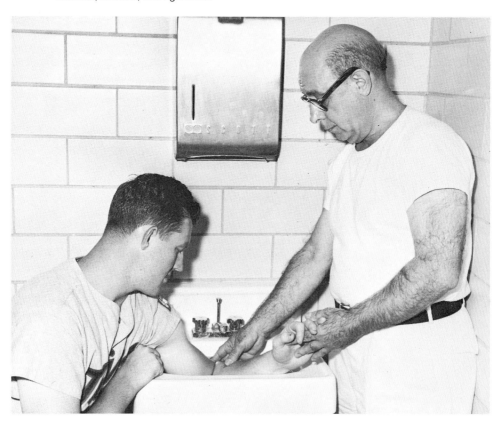

other functionally specific training programs should be conducted during the pre-season and off-season periods. The baseball season is no time to *develop* strength. It should be developed prior to the season and *maintained* during the season. The coach should see that each player gets enough training during the season to maintain his conditioning so that he can perform at maximum levels during the games.

11. Precaution should always be taken to prevent injuries. Two such injuries are of special interest to the baseball coach. They are the sore arm and the blister. The sore arm can be prevented by proper care of the arm before and after throwing. Before throwing hard a player should take an adequate warm-up period in which he gradually throws harder and harder. After throwing hard, a player (particularly a pitcher) should take care of his arm by soaking it in ice water for ten minutes. The ice will prevent the arm from hemorrhaging too much. A pitcher's arm, after he throws hard, reacts as if he had sprained it. Blood vessels break from the strain of the hard throwing and cause hemorrhaging in the arm, especially at the elbow joint which receives a great deal of stress during the throwing motion. Blisters can be prevented by spreading petroleum jelly on areas of the foot prone to blisters and covering the areas with bandages. This practice will prove particularly beneficial during the early stages of the season when blisters are more likely to occur.

Chapter 19
The Purchase
and Care
of Equipment

The purchase and care of equipment is an important phase of coaching responsibility in any sport.* In baseball, the quality and condition of the equipment can have a significant effect on both the physical and psychological aspects of performance. Inferior bats will definitely affect the ability of a hitter to perform successfully, and ragged uniforms can have a major psychological effect on a team's performance. In certain situations, the baseball coach will play a minimal role in this aspect of coaching. The athletic director may do the purchasing and also handle the equipment inventory. In this case, the coach will probably have an advisory role, suggesting needed items to the athletic director who will then handle the details of the transactions. In most situations, however, the coach will play a major role in the planning, selection, purchase, and care of equipment. Then he must take an active interest in seeing that this phase of the program is administered as professionally and competently as the actual playing phase of the game. To that end, this chapter contains principles to guide the administration of a good equipment program and help build the foundation for a long-range plan for the purchase and care of equipment.

Principles for Equipment Administration

1. Full equipment should be purchased for each participant.
2. Equipment to be purchased should conform to specifications.
3. Economy should be the goal of equipment purchasing; large quantities should be purchased when feasible.
4. Equipment purchases should be planned and made early.
5. Reputable firms and salesmen should be patronized.
6. An accurate inventory of all equipment should be available at all times and should guide buying.
7. Coaches should keep abreast of the latest equipment innovations.
8. Records of all equipment issues should be kept on hand.
9. Rules concerning equipment and the administration of the equipment room should be made known to all players.
10. Uniforms and certain other items of equipment should be exchanged regularly.
11. A full inventory should be taken at the end of each season.

Discussion of the Principles

1. Full equipment should be purchased for each participant. Each coach should make it his goal to provide a complete set of equipment for *each player on his team*. This means that the school should provide baseball shoes, warm-up jackets, hats, and other items that are often not considered

*Some of the material in this chapter was originally developed for *The Theory and Science of Basketball* by John M. Cooper and Daryl Siedentop (Philadelphia: Lea & Febiger, 1969).

"essentials." The only exception to this is the player's glove. Very few schools can afford the capital outlay for 20–25 baseball gloves, and since a glove is so personalized once it is used, schools may rightfully expect each player to be responsible for the purchase of this item. This full-equipment principle should apply to each participant, regardless of his status on the team. Reserve players may be issued older equipment, but they should not have to use different equipment that is inferior to that used by first-string players. Nothing is psychologically more devastating to a player, for example, than to have to wear a uniform that differs from that of other members of a team. If a coach is going to have an eighteen-man squad, he should make sure that he has eighteen uniforms and eighteen sets of equipment to issue to these players.

2. Equipment to be purchased should conform to specifications. Specifications should be set up carefully and after considerable planning, and equipment which falls below or even above those specifications should not be accepted. The specifications used may have to be a combination of those established by a national agency (such as the NCAA or the NAIA), an athletic conference, and the individual school. If, for example, a conference has decided to use a certain grade of baseball, the individual school should conform to this practice and not purchase game balls that are either below or above the quality suggested in the specifications. When specifications are created, those making the final decisions concerning them should attempt to allow for alternative selections. The rules of the National Collegiate Athletic Association (rule 2, section 1, article 1), for example, require that all collegiate games shall be played with one of the following baseballs: DeBeer–100, MacGregor–97, Rawlings–RO, Spalding–1, Wilson–A1010, or Worth–912C. This practice establishes specific guidelines, but allows the individual school a degree of flexibility within those guidelines.

3. Economy should be the goal of equipment purchasing. This does not mean that the cheapest items available should be the ones purchased. Rather, the school should attempt to "get the most for its money." This, more often than not, is accomplished by purchasing equipment of a reasonably high quality. When the cost is calculated over a five- or ten-year period, purchasing quality equipment is almost always the most economical practice. Only the highest quality bats, for example, should be purchased. A cheaper bat not only is more prone to deterioration, but it also is considerably less efficient than a high-quality bat. Uniforms vary greatly in original expense, but the inferior uniform wears out more quickly and is more costly to repair. This is not to suggest that each school must purchase a major league quality uniform. That, obviously, is impossible. A school should, however, attempt to purchase uniforms of sufficient quality that they can be used for several years. Durability of equipment should be one of the primary factors that a coach considers in his purchasing choices. In addition, the purchase of large quantities of equipment is usually recommended. The larger the quantity, the cheaper the individual item will tend to be. Also purchases should be made on an annual or biannual basis in order to

secure legitimate discounts from retail and wholesale dealers. However, since styles of equipment tend to become outmoded, care should be exercised so that equipment will not have to be discarded before it has been used for a reasonable length of time. Some types of equipment are made from materials, such as rubber, that tend to deteriorate on the shelf. The coach should avoid purchasing large quantities of equipment made from such nondurable materials. It must be noted, too, that the purchase of large quantities of equipment means that the storage of items not in current use becomes an important facet of the administration of the equipment room.

4. Equipment purchases should be planned and made early. In baseball, this should be done in the fall months just after school begins. In this manner, the coach can insure that the equipment will arrive well in advance of the time when it is needed. It is frustrating to begin spring practice without enough bats, or to have new uniforms arrive after the first few games have been played. During the late winter months, manufacturers of baseball equipment become flooded with orders. Thus, the baseball coach would do well to consult his local agent or the manufacturer to determine what deadline date would have to be met to insure delivery of goods before they are needed.

5. Reputable firms and salesmen should be patronized. Established companies will repair or replace faulty equipment and are usually more dependable on delivery dates. The coach should make sure that the salesman that he is dealing with has an adequate knowledge of the equipment he is attempting to sell. Salesmen who represent established firms or dealers usually have this knowledge. Firms that are not well known to the coach should be investigated. Generally speaking, prices of sports equipment tend to be fairly standard. An article that appears to be equal to other standard brands in quality but is priced way below the going market price should be scrutinized carefully before being purchased. The coach should adopt an attitude of skepticism toward the "good buy" or the "quick deal."

6. An accurate inventory of all equipment should be available at all times and should guide buying. A good inventory allows the coach to keep track of the various stages of wear of each item of equipment (see the sample inventory record at the end of this chapter). Thus, he can order the correct number of new items each year. In other words, his orders for replacement equipment can be kept to a minimum because he knows exactly what he needs. This is important for items such as supporters, sweat socks, sanitary socks, and undershirts.

7. The baseball coach should keep abreast of the latest equipment innovations. If he does this, he will not make the mistake of ordering old, outmoded equipment after new and better things have been put on the market. This is especially true for items such as catcher's equipment, sanitary socks, and undershirts. New materials are constantly being developed by industry, and the manufacturers of sports equipment are continually adopting these materials for use in baseball equipment. This principle also applies to coaching aids. Each year new coaching aids find their way to the market. The coach must evaluate each one to see if it can help him develop

better players. The coach is the "expert," and he must exercise his professional judgment in the choice of equipment and aids.

8. Records of all equipment issues should be kept on hand. Whenever an item of equipment is issued, it should be carefully noted in detail on an equipment record form. (A sample form is supplied at the end of this chapter.) The equipment manager or the team manager should be in charge of all equipment issues. By consulting the inventory records and the equipment issue records, the coach can determine at any time the exact number and location of each item of equipment. The record forms should be kept in a file in the equipment room or in the office of the equipment manager. No athlete should be able to obtain an item of equipment without going through the equipment manager, the team manager, or the coach. Each of these persons should make sure that the issue is written down on the proper form at the time of the issue. In this way, no item of equipment will ever be "lost"–so that the coach and equipment manager do not know where it is.

9. Rules concerning equipment and the administration of the equipment room should be made known to all players. The coaching staff, the athletic director, and the equipment manager must determine what the rules should be, but once the rules are decided upon, they should be made clear to the players. There are two good methods of preventing any mix-up on matters of equipment. At the outset of the season, each player should be handed a mimeographed sheet containing the rules on equipment. The coach should go over these rules with his team so that there is no misunderstanding. In addition, the basic and most important rules should be listed in a conspicuous place near the equipment room so that they are in clear view of the players as they exchange equipment or are issued new equipment.

The rules concerning equipment vary from school to school. Some coaches like to set prices for the replacement of lost equipment. This means that a schedule of prices is established so that each player knows how much he will have to pay if he *loses* an item of equipment. This is usually the best method for discouraging the pilfering of equipment. Equipment that is damaged during use or wears out, of course, does not fall under this rule. Some coaches prefer to keep players out of the equipment room altogether. This is generally a good policy to follow. In this way, the equipment manager or the team manager do all the issuing of equipment and are the only ones allowed inside the equipment room. The baseball coach should make sure that clear rules on this subject are established.

10. The baseball coach should insist that uniforms and certain other items of equipment be exchanged regularly. This is to insure clean equipment and help maintain the health of the players. The ideal situation, of course, is to change such equipment as socks, supporter, shorts, undershirt, sweatshirt, and towel every day. Most schools, however, cannot handle the cost or the administrative problems connected with daily equipment changes. Nevertheless, equipment should be changed twice weekly at a minimum. To accomplish this goal, the coach will have to develop a feasible plan for exchanging dirty equipment for clean. If two sets of practice

gear are available for each player, the equipment can be exchanged before or after a practice session. If, however, only one set of practice gear is available for each player, the gear will have to be turned in after each practice and returned to the players before the next practice. This means that the laundering of the equipment will have to be done efficiently and on schedule.

11. A full inventory should be taken at the end of each season. This should become a standard practice for the coach and his equipment manager. After all players have turned in their equipment, it should be laundered or dry-cleaned. Then the coach and equipment manager should go over the entire inventory and determine the state of wear of each item. This information should be marked in detail on the inventory record. Adherence to this principle will allow the coach to check his records in the fall and to place his orders for the next season on the basis of recent, detailed information.

INVENTORY RECORD OF EQUIPMENT

Date of inventory: _____ Sport: _____

Person in charge of inventory: _____ Head coach: _____

Item of equipment	Number of items accounted for at last inventory	Number of items purchased since last inventory	Total number of items now available	Number of items in good condition	Number of items in fair condition	Number of unusable items	Number of items needed for next season

RECORD OF EQUIPMENT ISSUED

Name: _____

Campus phone: _____

Campus address: _____

Locker number: _____ Combination: _____

Article of equipment	Number	Date issued	Condition	Date returned	Condition
1. practice sweat pants					
2. practice shirt					
3. warm-up jacket					
4. practice hat					
5. practice shorts					
6. sliding pads					
7. basic set (socks, supporter, shirt, towel)					
8.					
9.					
10.					
11.					
12.					

Appendix
Important Baseball Rules

   While a complete knowledge of the rules of the game of baseball is essential for coaches and players, there are some rules that are more important than others because they are called into play often and sometimes require interpretation. A summary of the important rules is presented below. The numbers in the parentheses following each rule refer to the rule, section, and article of the Official National Collegiate Athletic Association Rules.* Thus, (4–1–1) refers to Rule 4, Section 1, Article 1 of the NCAA Rules.

1. The head umpire is the only judge of whether the baseball is fit to continue in play. (2–1–2)
2. Each member of the team must have a uniform of the same color and style. (2–4)
3. The coach of the home team decides whether or not a game shall be started when weather conditions are questionable. This, however, does not apply to the second game of a doubleheader. (4–2–1)
4. Once a single game (or the first game of a doubleheader) has started, the head umpire shall be the sole judge of continuing play. (4–2–2) (4–2–3)
5. If the field has a temporary fence (such as the snow fence commonly used) and the fielder catches a batted ball and continues through or over the fence, still retaining possession of the ball, the batter is out and the ball is called dead, with runners advancing one base. If the ball is dropped, it is a home run. (4–4–2)
6. When two or more substitutes enter the game simultaneously, the coach must designate to the head umpire the position of each player in the batting order. (4–6–4)
7. Each conference shall make its own rules governing protest procedures, but no protest shall be permitted which questions a judgment decision by the umpire. (5–7–9)
8. If a thrown ball strikes a coach or umpire, it remains in play. (6–2)
9. In the wind-up position, any natural movement associated with the pitcher's delivery commits him to pitch to the batter. (7–1–1)
10. The pivot foot must remain in contact with the rubber. Picking up the pivot foot and taking a slight forward step with it is known as running into the pitch and is illegal. (7–1–1, note)
11. In the set position, the pitcher must come to a complete stop with his hands

---

*The 1970 Official National Collegiate Athletic Association Baseball Guide (Phoenix, Arizona: College Athletics Publishing Service, 1970) pp. 67-94.

together in front of his body. (7 – 1 – 2) The instantaneous stop is interpreted as a complete change in direction.

12. After assuming the set position, any motion naturally associated with his delivery commits the pitcher to throw to the batter. (7 – 1 – 2)
13. Until his natural motion commits him to throw to the batter, the pitcher may throw to any base provided he steps directly toward the base before throwing. (7 – 1 – 3)
14. When the pitcher removes his pivot foot from the rubber by stepping backward, he becomes an infielder. (7 – 1 – 5)
15. The pitcher must take his sign while on the pitching rubber, and he must deliver the ball to the batter from the position he has taken (set or wind-up). (7 – 1 – 6)
16. A balk may be committed in any of the following ways:
    a. by feinting a movement without completing the throw (7 – 3 – 1)
    b. by throwing to a base without stepping directly toward it (7 – 3 – 2)
    c. by making an illegal pitch (7 – 3 – 3)
    d. by unnecessarily delaying the game (7 – 3 – 4)
    e. by assuming a pitching position on, near, or astride the rubber without having the ball (7 – 3 – 5)
    f. by not throwing to the batter after making a movement that is part of the natural motion (7 – 3 – 6)
    g. by taking either hand off the ball after taking a stretch (7 – 3 – 7)
    h. by pitching when the catcher is not in his box (7 – 3 – 8)
    i. by pitching without coming to a stop in the set position (7 – 3 – 9)
    j. by throwing a quick pitch (7 – 3 – 10)
    k. by pumping more than twice (7 – 3 – 11)
    l. by throwing to first base after having broken the plane of the front edge of the rubber with a backward movement of the stride foot. (7 – 3 – 12)
17. The batter is out if he interferes with the catcher's fielding or throwing from home plate. (8 – 10 – 7)
18. The infield fly is a fair fly which could be caught with an ordinary effort by an infielder, provided there are less than two out and runners on first and second or on first, second, and third. (8 – 10 – 11)
19. Obstruction is considered to be physical contact with a base runner by a fielder who neither has the ball in his possession nor is in the process of fielding it. (9 – 3 – 4)
20. There is no infraction if a fielder is trying to field a batted ball in a base runner's path. (9 – 4 – 1)
21. An appeal is made by returning a live ball to the base before the next pitch is made. A ball is considered live after a pitcher receives it from an umpire, toes the rubber, or the umpire calls "play ball." (9 – 4 – 7, note)
22. A base runner is out if he is hit by a batted fair ball before it touches or passes a fielder other than the pitcher. (9 – 4 – 9)

Speed-Up Rules

While speed-up rules may vary from conference to conference, the essence of the rules remains fairly constant and the primary purpose is always to decrease the amount of time necessary to play the game without actually detracting from it.

The factors around which speed-up rules are usually formulated are listed below.
1. Courtesy runners for the pitcher and catcher so they can prepare for the next inning.
2. A limited length of time to change sides.
3. No throwing the ball around the infield after a putout.
4. Intentionally walking a batter by merely telling the umpire.
5. Continuing to wear the protective helmet on basepaths to avoid the time-lag necessary to return it to next hitter or send it back to bench.
6. A limited number of pitches between innings or for relief pitchers.
7. Enforcement of a time limit between pitches to any batter.

The Scoremaster*

One of the least understood elements of baseball is the scoring of the game. Presented here is an explanation, with examples, of the *Scoremaster* system. This system of scoring takes the "mystery" out of baseball and soft ball scoring, and furnishes a sheet whereby the scorer, or his reader, can accurately "read" the game after it is finished. The author realizes that most scorers have their own private system, and this method "simplifies" any system, so that he may have a complete record of every player in every inning, and the final result.

The typical scoring system is, of course, for the scorer to follow the player around the diamond on the scoring form, starting at the home plate, on the lower part of the diamond, going thence to first base, second base, third base, and then to home plate again. When a runner reaches a base, draw a line to that base, and indicate, by the insignia on the right side of the batter's box, how he reached the base. (Every way of getting to base, except on a fielder's choice is represented by an insignia). Then continue the line to each base which he thereafter reaches. A completed line around the diamond represents a score, and the uncompleted diamond shows that the runner has been left on base, and indicates the base he reached before the end of the inning.

Players are numbered as to positions (see numbers on small diamond within batter's box) as follows: Pitcher (1); catcher (2); first baseman (3); second baseman (4); third baseman (5); shortstop (6); left fielder (7); center fielder (8); right fielder (9).

Insignias at right side of each player's box represent the method of reaching the base, thus; "HR"—home run; "3B"—three-base hit; "2B"—two-base hit; "1B"—a single; "SAC"—a sacrifice hit; "HP"—hit by pitcher; "BB"—base on balls. A mark or line through the insignia, or any mark the scorer may desire, shows how the batter reached the base. A single line from the home plate through the diamond may be drawn to show the direction in which the hit was made. A base on balls, hit by pitched ball, or a sacrifice hit, does not count as a "time at bat."

Batter's OUTS are marked within each box by using the number of each player handling the ball, and the number of total outs in each inning, for scorer's convenience, may be indicated by a circle within the box, with the number of the out within the circle, thus ③ would indicate the third and final out of the inning.

If the batter hits a ground ball to the third baseman and is thrown out at first, the figures "5-3" would appear within the batter's box; if a runner is forced out at second, by a fielder's choice, or otherwise, by a ball that is hit to any fielder, the figure in the

---

*This *Scoremaster* and rules reprinted by permission of Scoremaster Company, Hollywood, California.

batter's box would appear as "5-4f", using the proper numbers of the fielders handling the ball. A fly-out is shown by the insignia "F" and the number of the player making the catch, thus: "F9" would indicate that the catch was made by the right fielder. Whether the fly ball is a pop-up or a long fly ball may be indicated by an appropriate "arc" over the "F9". A line drive fly ball would be indicated as "F4." Should a ball be taken by the first baseman on the ground, or other baseman, who steps on a base, and makes the out unassisted, the play would be indicated as "3U"

ERRORS are shown as follows: Fumble by the shortstop: "E6F"; an error on throw by the shortstop: "E6Th"; an error on a dropped throw by the first baseman: "E3D (A4)", the (A4) indicating an assist by the second baseman, who is credited with an assist whether the out is made or not. Overthrows are indicated by "OT"; wild pitch: "WP"; pass balls: "PB"; strike out: "K"; third strike called: "Kc"; balk: "Bk"; bunt: "Bt"; fielder's choice: "FC"; foul to catcher: "f2"; stolen base: "S" placed at the corner of the base stolen. Runs batted in are indicated by writing in each box, at the home plate, the number of the player who hit the ball scoring the run. Double plays are indicated by connecting players' boxes with a small bracket and the sign "DP." The small squares in the lower right-hand corner of the players' boxes are for recording balls and strikes.

FIRST INNING

Storm (7), left fielder and lead-off man, hits a home run to left center. A line is drawn from home to first, first to second, second to third and third to home. The marked square indicates a run scored. The line drawn from home to left center shows the direction of the hit. As Storm hits the first pitch, it is so designated. Also credit Storm with an RBI (run batted in).

Peterson (4), second baseman and second batter, walked, so a line is drawn from home to first. How he got on base is designated by a smaller line through "BB." While Morrison (6), the third hitter, was at bat, Peterson stole second base. You record that by marking S-6 at second base in Peterson's square.

Morrison (6), the shortstop and third batter, grounded out, third base to first base with Peterson holding second. Record a 5-3 in the center of Morrison's square showing how he went out, third to first, and below that a circled 1 as the first out of the inning. Also credit the third baseman (5) of the opposing team with an assist (A) and the first baseman (3) with a putout (PO).

Cockroft (8), center fielder and fourth batter, doubled to left. Record his double by drawing a line from home to first and first to second. Show the direction of the hit by drawing a line from home to left field and record the hit as a double by drawing a small line through 2B at the side. As Peterson (4) scored on Cockroft's double, put an 8 (Cockroft's Position Number) at home plate in Peterson's square, drawing a line from second to third and third to home to indicate a run. (Give Cockroft credit for an RBI.)

Clements (3), first baseman and fifth batter, grounded out, short to first. Record that by inserting a 6-3 in Clements' square. As his was the second out, circle a 2 at the bottom of the square. Credit the shortshop (6) of the opposing team with an assist (A) and the first baseman (3) with a putout (PO).

Rosuck (2), catcher and sixth batter, flied to center field ending the inning. Record his out with an F8 and a small circled 3 to designate the third out. Credit the center fielder (8) of the opposing team with a putout (PO).

Don't forget to close out your inning by drawing a line diagonally through the

PLAYERS	Pos.	1	2	3	4	5	6
STORM	7	hit first pitch	K ②				
Sub.							
Peterson	4	5-6 / 8	5-3 ③				
Sub.							
Morrison	6	5-3 ①					
Sub.							
Cockroft	8						
Waller Sub. in 4th	8						
Clements	3	6-3 ②					
Sub.							
Rosuck	2	F-8 ③					
Gazella Sub. in 5th	2						
Lambert	9	5					
Sub.							
Mastro	5						
Kazie Sub. in 8th	5						
Chandler	1		F-7 ①				
Scott Sub. in 8th	1						
Sub.							
SUMMARY		2 / 2	1 / 1				

WINNING PITCHER __Chandler__ LOSING PITCHER _ _ _ _ _ _ _ _ _ INNINGS

AT BAT OFF __Chandler__ 28 _ OFF __Scott__ 6 _ _ _ _ _ _ _ _ HITS OF

RUNS OFF __Chandler__ 4 _ _ _ _ OFF __Scott__ 1 _ _ _ _ _ _ _ _ BASE ON

STRUCK OUT BY __Chandler__ 8 _ _ _ BY __Scott__ 2 _ _ _ _ _ _ _ _ HIT BY

DOUBLE PLAY __Peterson to Morrison to Clements__ _ _ _ _ _ _

PASSED BALLS __NONE__ _ _ _ _ _ _ _ _ _ _ LEFT ON BASE _ _ _ _ _ _ _ _ vacant square below Rosuck. The summary: 2 runs, 2 hits, no errors and one man left on base — Cockroft.

SECOND INNING

Lambert (9), right fielder and seventh batter, walked, so a line is drawn from home to first. How he got on base is designated by a smaller line through "BB." While Mastro (5) the eighth batter was at bat, Lambert stole second base. You record that by marking S-5 at second base in Lambert's square.

Mastro (5), third baseman and eighth batter, singled to left. Record his single by drawing a line from home to first. Show the direction of the hit by drawing a line from home to left field and record the hit as a single by drawing a small line through 1B at the side. As Lambert (9) scored on Mastro's single, put a 5 (Mastro's position number) at home plate in Lambert's square, drawing a line from second to third and third to home to indicate a run. (Give Mastro credit for a RBI.)

Chandler (1), pitcher and ninth batter, flied out to left field. Record his out with an F7 and a small circled 1 to designate the first out. Give the opposing left fielder (7) credit for a putout (PO).

Storm (7), left fielder and lead-off man batting for the second time, strikes out. Record that by placing the letter K in the batter's box, the letter K being the symbol for a strike out. Circle a 2 at the bottom of the square for the second out. Give the opposing pitcher credit for a strikeout and the catcher credit for a putout (PO).

Peterson (4), second baseman, grounded out, third to first. Record that by inserting a 5-3 in Peterson's square. Circle a 3 at the bottom of the square to designate the third out. Give the opposing third baseman (5) credit for an assist (A) and the first baseman (3) with a putout (PO).

The summary: 1 run, 1 hit, no errors and one man left on base — Mastro.

Glossary of Baseball Terms

Alley: the area between outfielders.

Assist: a fielding credit for a player who is involved in a defensive play which results in a putout.

Backing-up a play: a defensive maneuver in which a player takes a position behind the base for which a throw is intended.

Backstop: 1) the screen behind home plate; 2) the catcher.

Balk: an illegal maneuver by a pitcher.

Banjo hitter: the type of hitter who swings only hard enough to hit the ball over the infield.

Battery: the pitcher and the catcher.

Bean ball: a high, inside fast ball which causes a hitter to move quickly to avoid being hit by the pitch.

Blooper: a short fly ball in the area just between the infield and outfield positions; also called a Texas-leaguer.

Bobble: an error.

Boner: a mental mistake by a player.

Boot: an error.

Bull-pen: the area of the field used by relief pitchers to warm up.

Bush: originally a reference to the lower minor leagues, but now more commonly used to refer to behavior which is below standard.

Can of corn: an easy fly ball.

Change-up: any off-speed pitch which is designed to throw the batter off his timing.

Choke: 1) to grip the bat away from the knob; 2) to perform badly under pressure.

Count: the number of balls and strikes on a hitter.

Cripple: refers to a fast ball over the center of the plate; usually occurs on 2–0, 3–0, or 3–1 count when the pitcher is forced to throw a strike.

Cross-fire: a sidearm delivery by the pitcher, especially when the pitcher steps more to the side with his stride foot.

Cut-off: a defensive maneuver in which an infielder positions himself in the line of a throw from an outfielder to a base.

Diamond: the baseball field, which is diamond shaped when viewed from behind home plate.

Double-play combination: the shortstop and the second baseman.

Double-steal: when two runners advance on the same play.

Duster: same as the bean ball; its name comes from the fact that the player has to dust off his uniform after scrambling to avoid being hit by the pitch.

Fat pitch: a pitch that is over the center of the strike zone.

Force-out: putting a runner out by touching the base to which he has been forced to advance.

Foot in the bucket: refers to a batting technique in which the batter pulls his stride foot away from the plate; especially applies to occasions when this is done as a reaction to an oncoming curve ball.

Fungo: 1) in practice, throwing a ball up in the air and hitting it to a fielder; 2) a long, thin bat used to hit practice balls to fielders.

Gopher ball: a pitch that is hit for a home run.

Grapefruit league: the name given to the major league teams when they are playing in citrus growing areas such as Florida and Arizona.

High sky: a cloudless sky, usually with a bright sun.

Hit and run: an offensive maneuver which occurs when a runner breaks with the pitch and the batter attempts to hit the ball through the position vacated by the infielder who has moved to cover the base to which the runner is going.

Hitch: extraneous movement in the hitting style just prior to the initiation of the actual hitting stroke.

Hop: 1) the movement of an overhand fast ball; 2) the bounce of a ground ball.

Hole: the area between two infielders.

Infield fly: a fair fly ball which can be fielded normally by an infielder and results in the batter being automatically called out. The infield fly rule is invoked when there are runners on first and second bases or when the bases are loaded with less than two outs in an inning.

Intentional pass: purposely walking a batter by throwing pitches far outside the strike zone; under speed-up rules, this is accomplished by informing the umpire that such a maneuver is desired.

Key: a signal to inform a player that the next signal will be the one which will call the play.

Lead-off: the distance between a runner and the base before the pitch is delivered.

Lead-off hitter: 1) the first hitter in the line-up; 2) the first hitter in any inning.

Line-up: the placement of players in the order in which they will bat.

Live: 1) a fast ball that moves; 2) a signal that follows a key.

Mask: the protective device that covers the catcher's face.

Move: the movement of a pitcher in an attempt to pick a runner off first base from the set position.

On-deck hitter: the hitter scheduled to follow the batter who is at the plate.

Pass: a base on balls.

Passed ball: occurs when a runner advances on a pitched ball that should have, in the opinion of the official scorer, been fielded by the catcher.

Pepper: a practice game in which several players form a semi-circle and throw balls to another player who hits easy ground balls back to them.

Pinch hitter: a substitute batter.

Pull the string: throw a change-up pitch.

Pull hitter: the type of hitter who seldom hits to the opposite field; usually a power hitter.

Rabbit ears: a player who is easily upset by banter from an opposing team.

Receiver: the catcher.

Relay position: the position that an infielder takes to receive a throw from an outfielder after a long hit.

Retire: to put out a hitter or a runner.

Rookie: a first-year player

Run-down: a defensive play that occurs when a runner is trapped between bases.

Sacrifice bunt: a bunt which enables a runner to advance.

Sacrifice fly: a fly ball which enables a runner to score after it is caught.

Sail: the movement of a fast ball.

Set: the position the pitcher assumes when there are men on base.

Shake-off: the movement by the pitcher of his head or arms to notify the catcher that he does not want to throw the pitch that the catcher has called for.

Sinker: a fast ball that moves downward.

Slider: a fast breaking pitch that usually has a flat, late break.

Slurve: a combination of a slider and a curve.

Slump: a period during which a hitter does not hit up to his usual average.

Spray hitter: a hitter who hits to all fields.

Squeeze play: an offensive maneuver in which the runner on third base attempts to score on a bunt by the batter.

Switch-hitter: a hitter who bats left-handed against right-handed pitchers and right-handed against left-handed pitchers.

Stuff: refers to a pitcher who throws balls that move a great deal.

Tag-up: the position that a base runner assumes when he is going to attempt to advance on a fly ball with less than two outs in an inning.

Take: when a hitter purposely does not swing at a pitch regardless of how good it may be.

Take up to one: an offensive strategy which has the hitter taking all pitches until the first strike is thrown by the pitcher.

Texas-leaguer: a blooper.

Thrower: a pitcher who uses little strategy, but instead merely attempts to throw fast balls past the hitters.

Toss: an underhand throw.

Trapped ball: a line drive that is caught just after it has hit the ground.

Waste pitch: a pitch that is purposely thrown outside of the strike zone when the pitcher has a favorable count on the hitter.

Wild pitch: a type of "error" on the pitcher called when a runner advances on a poorly pitched ball that the catcher is unable to field.

Index